What Your Colleagues Are Saying .

"This book brings together the best of Visible Learning and the teaching of mathematics. The chapters on learning intentions, success criteria, misconceptions, formative evaluation, and knowing thy impact are stunning. Rich in exemplars, grounded in research about practice, and with the right balance about the surface and deep learning in math, it's a great go-to book for all who teach mathematics."

—John Hattie, **Laureate Professor,**
Deputy Dean of MGSE, Director of the Melbourne Education Research Institute,
Melbourne Graduate School of Education

"This handbook supports teachers in moving from pacing to planning instruction by providing the tools needed to ensure that mathematics lessons work for every student. More important, it will engage teachers in the critical process of continual improvement. It is a must-have for teachers, leaders, and mathematics educators alike!"

—Matt Larson, **Past President,**
National Council of Teachers of Mathematics

"Often teachers entering the classroom have had little opportunity for extensive lesson planning in their preparation programs. Throughout the book, definitions and explanations are clear so that readers share a common understanding of the language. As a teacher reads, the vignettes encourage the reader to reflect on similar situations in their own classrooms. The well-written questions included in the text will help guide teachers to personal insights that ultimately lead to increased student learning."

—Connie S. Schrock, **Emporia State University,**
National Council of Supervisors of Mathematics President, 2017–2019

"We all know that good instruction is well-planned instruction. We also know that effective lesson planning is a complicated decision-making process. This incredibly practical book—filled with delightful vignettes and clarifying examples—provides powerful ideas and structures for simplifying the complexities of planning great 6–8 mathematics lessons. This book is a wonderful resource for teachers, coaches, administrators, and teacher educators."

—Steve Leinwand,
American Institutes for Research

"Finally! *The Mathematics Lesson-Planning Handbook* provides that necessary blueprint for serious analysis of the planning process. Planning to teach mathematics is serious business, and this book goes way beyond thinking about the mathematics standard/objective for the next day's lesson, or jotting notes for a planning book. The handbook will truly engage teachers and communities of learning in a carefully choreographed grade-level designated thread of mathematics tasks, which will serve as anchors for developing understanding and use of each aspect of the planning process. This book is a treasure, and will be read, reread, and referenced daily!"

—Francis (Skip) Fennell, **Professor of Education,**
McDaniel College and Past President of the National Council of
Teachers of Mathematics (NCTM) and the Association of Mathematics Teacher Educators (AMTE)

"*The Mathematics Lesson-Planning Handbook* is a comprehensive and practical guide for coaches and teachers of mathematics in Grades 6–8. It provides the background that teachers need before they even begin to write a lesson plan! It then incorporates the research on what teachers need to think about as they begin to lay out a plan for instruction that will meet the needs of all 6–8 students and moves on to effective facilitation. This book is a must for every 6–8 teacher, coach, or school's professional library!"

—Linda M. Gojak, **Past President,**
National Council of Teachers of Mathematics

"One of the hallmarks of accomplished 6–8 teachers of mathematics is the guidance they provide to help students own how to learn. In *The Mathematics Lesson-Planning Handbook, Grades 6–8: Your Blueprint for Building Cohesive Lessons*, authors Williams, Kobett, and Harbin Miles provide a clear, engaging, and masterful roadmap for helping each and every teacher own the lessons they design and use each and every day. The authors reveal the purposes, the success criteria, and the nature of the mathematical tasks and materials to be chosen. They describe in detail the student engagement necessary to design daily mathematics lessons that will significantly impact student learning. Reading, listening to, and using their wisdom and advice will result in an empowering impact on each and every teacher and teacher leader of middle school mathematics."

—Timothy Kanold, **Educator and Author**

"Planning is so much more than identifying materials, making copies, or filling out a form. Many of us were not trained to identify purpose, think about our students, look for quality instructional tasks, consider representations, or anticipate what our students will do. Finally, this handbook is here! We have our blueprint. This tool is a must-have for anyone new to teaching mathematics or anyone else who supports those who teach mathematics."

—John SanGiovanni, **Coordinator, Mathematics,**
Howard County Public School System, MD

"At a time when open educational resources are flooding our classrooms, *The Mathematics Lesson-Planning Handbook* helps bring focus and intentionality as to why we should choose one task over another. It thoughtfully lays out the smaller nuances that are most commonly overlooked and it helps bring clarity to the art of building coherence."

—Graham Fletcher, **Math Specialist, Atlanta, GA**

"Planning is one of the most important instructional activities that teachers undertake. But how many teachers know how to plan lessons that are purposeful, coherent, and rigorous that also take into account the rich perspectives of a diverse classroom of students? This teacher resource makes explicit what it takes to plan lessons that truly support student learning while also speaking to principals, coaches, and preservice educators who support teacher learning. I will certainly be using this valuable resource in my own work with teachers."

—Linda Ruiz Davenport, **Director of K–12 Mathematics,**
Office of Instructional Research and Development, Boston Public Schools

"This book is a step-by-step guide for building a cohesive lesson. It is research based and relevant to what teachers are being asked to do."

—Ann Thomas Lewis, **Content Coach,**
Stafford County Public Schools, Fredericksburg, VA

"Williams, Kobett, and Harbin Miles's book, *The Mathematics Lesson-Planning Handbook, Grades 6–8: Your Blueprint for Building Cohesive Lessons*, begins by sharing the importance of building relationships with students to the mathematical process standards and everything in between! The cohesive research-based book should be the pillar for teachers aspiring to be math teachers and for every teacher that is currently teaching mathematics. The mathematical architecture behind this well-designed book is truly a blueprint for teacher and student success. The information in this book will support me in guiding teachers on what it takes to create high-quality and effective math lessons."

—Sharon Shrum, **Director of Mathematics,**
Frederick County Schools, Winchester, VA

The Mathematics Lesson-Planning Handbook, Grades 6–8
at a Glance

A step-by-step guide to walk you through every facet of planning cohesive, standards-based mathematics lessons, including

CHAPTER 2

YOUR 6–8 BLUEPRINT
Planning Mathematics Lessons for Coherence, Rigor, and Purpose

I was working as a long-term substitute in a sixth-grade mathematics class. During my first day, the class was very unruly. The plans I was given said to teach area, perimeter, volume, and surface area and to use certain pages in the text. With these instructions, I assumed I should go to the text and give the students the exercises on those pages. Needless to say, my lesson flopped and the students were more unruly than before. I knew I had to do something different. I was going to be there for a few weeks. That night, I went online and found a video of a teacher who had the students explore volume by giving them graph paper to fold up into a rectangular prism. The teacher in the video used centimeter cubes to fill the prism and asked questions such as, "How many cubes fill the prism?" and "How does the number of cubes that cover the base of the prism compare to the number of boxes on the graph paper?" I was so excited about this video that I set out to write a lesson for the next day that used the ideas from this video. I intentionally let the ...... work in pairs, each

When Diane took charge as the architect of her instruction, she experienced how designing your blueprint is perhaps one of the most important jobs you can do. Throughout this book, you will have the opportunity to build grade-level mathematics lessons for your students by following the many examples presented. Together, we will explore the answers to questions such as these:

- What is coherence?
- What is rigor?
- What is the purpose of a lesson?
- How can you ensure that you plan lessons for coherence, rigor, and purpose?

Using your curriculum to think about all of your lessons as a cohesive progression across units, throughout the year

Asking yourself essential questions about your standards-based learning intentions, lesson purpose, tasks, materials, lesson format, and how to anticipate and assess student thinking

CHAPTER 3

LAYING YOUR FOUNDATION
It Starts With Big Ideas, Essential Questions, and Standards

As the science and mathematics teacher on my team, I am responsible for practical math, prealgebra, and Algebra I along with my science classes. At lunch the other day, I was sitting with my math and science colleagues. I mentioned to Mo, another science teacher, that I had just come up with a great essential question for our unit on matter. "How about the question, 'Does matter behave predictably?'" Mo responded that she liked it. Then Jamel, a fellow prealgebra teacher, piped in, "I didn't know you had essential questions in science, too!"

"What ...... I exclaim ...

"We s ...... classes ...

This c ...... essent ...... scienc ...... that w ...... are do ...

questions in mathematics, it would sure help me tie the lessons together. I am going to try this!

Kim McCormick
Middle School Mathematics and Science Teacher
New Hampshire

Many teachers think about mathematics as skills, like

CHAPTER 6

CHOOSING TASKS
The Heart of a Lesson

As a beginning sixth-grade mathematics teacher, I remember that my main concern was always behavior. After that, my next recollection is teaching numerous lessons on ratios, proportion, and percents. Much emphasis, back then, was placed on mentally calculating percent of a number using 10%, 25%, and 50% as anchors. For example, a typical question would be, "What is 30% of 35?" Students who were able to do this mentally would respond, "I know that 10% of 35 is 3.5 so I multiplied 3.5 three times and got 10.5."

I realize now I was on the right track by helping my students understand how percents related to one another. Unfortunately, my method of helping the students who struggled was to generate more drill problems for them to practice. When I reflect back on these lessons, I realize my lessons must have been tedious for many of my students. We practiced percent examples day after day until I thought every student had mastered the skill. Not only was this boring for

could work, that is, with multiple entry points. As a beginning teacher, where could I find these types of problems?

Karen Dorgan
Retired Math Instructor
Alabama

Karen has many good questions. What she is searching for are worthwhile tasks. A worthwhile task is the heart of a lesson. In fact, selecting the task is the most important decision teachers make that affects instruction (Lappan & Briars, 1995; Smith & Stein, 2011).

This chapter will address the following questions:
- Why are tasks important?
- What is a worthwhile task?

CHAPTER 5

DECIDING ON PURPOSE
Why Are You Building This Lesson?

I was very specific about the purpose of a lesson I taught recently. This is a heterogeneous, 50-minute, seventh-grade mathematics class, and the topic was generating linear equations from tables. In the past, creating a table and then using the data in the table to create an equation was difficult for the students. This year, I was very deliberate in giving students a model of a function machine to simulate the input and output data to place in the table. I used a shoebox that was lying around in my classroom. We put in a number and the "machine" shot a number out. For example, when we put in a 12, out came a 24. When we input a 9, the output was 18. When we put in an x, the output was 2x. The students understood exactly what to do, and they were able to determine what was happening "inside the function machine" in order to generate equations. I intentionally took the lesson slow, step by step, and was rewarded with the students understanding the process. When a few were struggling, the others took it upon themselves to help. As an added reason for wanting to learn this material, I told the students that they would be responsible for teaching this material to the pre ...... dent. Chris, who was absent that d ...

Writing a series of learning intentions and success criteria from your standards is only the beginning of lesson planning. Your learning intentions inform the *purpose* of each lesson. As mentioned in Chapter 2, there are three types of mathematics lessons organized by purpose: conceptual understanding lessons, lessons that bring about procedural fluency, and transfer lessons. Think of each of these as a room in the house you are building. Just as each room in a house has a different purpose (e.g., a kitchen is built for food preparation), each lesson should have a purpose (e.g., a transfer lesson is designed to let students pull together and apply the previous learning).

This chapter will focus on answers to the following questions:

- What is the role of a conceptual understanding lesson?
- What is procedural fluency, and how does it build from a conceptual understanding lesson?

Determining whether you're designing a lesson to focus on conceptual understanding, procedural fluency, or transfer of knowledge

CHAPTER 9

FRAMING THE LESSON
Formats

As a middle school teacher of Family and Consumer Sciences, my seventh-grade class was involved in a lesson on baking. I asked the question, "What amounts of each of the ingredients do we need so that we can double this cookie recipe?" Who would have thought that this simple question would lead to two full math lessons?

As I asked this question, I saw expressions of "I think I know this" to "I haven't a clue!" The only definitive answer everyone could give me was "Two eggs, not one!" So taking out all the measuring cups (both dry and wet), we went to work. Using flour and water, the cups became manipulatives that transformed multiplying and dividing fractions into something they could understand and apply.

I thought it was a simple question that would take five or ten minutes to answer and then we would bake the cookies. Well, that simple question led to two full lessons on fractions before the actual baking took place! In the end, the students all enjoyed the cookies and came to the conclusion that we do use math in our everyday lives.

Thinking back on this lesson, I wonder, "Why couldn't the stud ...... make the connection between baking a ...

Lessons need structure. Lesson formats give you that structure and refer to how you organize your class for instruction. Some lessons work better when students are in collaborative groups, and some are more effective when students move around to different centers. In middle school, the master schedule is a critical factor because it determines how much time is allotted for instruction, thus becoming a factor in selecting your lesson format. For instance, some middle schools schedule mathematics classes for 45 to 50 minutes daily while others use a 90-minute block. Lesson format can and should vary depending on your purpose, with consideration for how much time you have to implement a lesson. Mathematics labs and project-based learning are easier to execute in a longer block of time. Sometimes partnering with other disciplines can be an efficient use of instructional time, as Sue suggested in her reflection. This chapter will address the following questions:

Choosing how to launch, facilitate, and close your lesson

CHAPTER 11

PLANNING TO
LAUNCH THE LESSON

I love thinking about my lesson launches. I have come to find them as important as the task/lesson itself. I see the launching of a task/lesson similar to a movie. If the opening of a movie is very uninteresting, typically the audience will become distracted and disengage. This will then lead them to missing out on much of the movie until something captures their attention. In the process, they are overlooking details that could bring more meaning to the movie. Similarly, in teaching, if I do not captivate the students in the first five to ten minutes, they are less likely to fully engage in the task/lesson. Students may then miss the opportunity to recognize details, notice patterns, and ask important questions.

On the other hand, if an audience is attracted to the story within the first few minutes, it will anticipate the next twist and turn in the story. I have noticed that if my launch is intriguing, the students will begin to notice, wonder, and predict independently, which, in turn, cultivates an environment of enthusiasm for learning mathematics, making connections, and learning.

Something I have been doing lately is storytelling. Just last week I started a lesson on systems of equations by telling the students the old tortoise and the hare story. I used this story

the dog runs 5 feet per second. The students started calling out questions:

- Who wins the race?
- Who runs the furthest?
- Who is the fastest?
- Can we create an equation to represent the tiger and the dog?

I was thrilled with their questions and knew that they were now ready! I said, "Let's graph the race to represent what is happening in the story." The students excitedly went to work!

Zac Stavish
Middle School Teacher
Maryland

This chapter explores ways to begin your lesson. We will explore the following questions:

- What is a lesson launch?
- How can you ...

CHAPTER 12

PLANNING TO
FACILITATE THE LESSON

I think there is always a fine line between being well planned and recognizing when it is important, even crucial, to veer from the plan. When my students are working together on an investigation or problem, I attend to what my students are doing, saying, and representing. Some of my very best lessons have been when I have acknowledged and highlighted students' mathematical noticings and questions to make meaningful mathematical connections. I most often recognize these moments when students are engaged in discourse with each other but also when they say really powerful and interesting questions.

Recently, I was teaching a lesson where students were investigating patterns. I asked them to represent a visual pattern of $5x + 3$ in multiple ways. In my mind, I was thinking about using 5 as the starting point in the equation. I wanted them to see the slope and y-intercept in all of the representations. As the students were working, they began finding equations that looked very different from what other students had found. At first, there was a buzz in the room as students began questioning one another. I observed this taking place and waited to see what they would say and do. Finally, a student asked, "Should our answers be the same? ... our solutions supposed to be the same or different?

promote student discourse and facilitate healthy, productive struggle, then I must allow students to investigate their mathematical questions. My role is to validate those questions and support these mathematical discoveries. After all, who wants to turn down an opportunity to witness middle school students exclaim in wonder about how cool mathematics is?

Jennifer Outzs
Middle School Teacher
Maryland

Capturing those moments when students are engaged productively in mathematical thinking, reasoning, and communication is so exciting to see. Sometimes they just happen, but most likely they happen when all of your hard work in planning comes together. Planning to facilitate a lesson incorporates the selection of effective instructional activities and strategically planning how you will support and facilitate student learning during the instructional activities. Good tasks, problems, games, and ...

CHAPTER 13

PLANNING TO
CLOSE THE LESSON

I am a bell-to-bell teacher and always want to use every minute possible for instructional time. It is really hard to not run out of time when my students are so excited about what they are learning. I often set a timer as I know closing a lesson is a critical component of good lesson planning and instruction. It is very important for my students to summarize, review, and reflect upon what has been taught during the lesson.

Mary Buck
Mathematics Coach
Montana

Almost every day, I tend to run out of time. I am getting better, but last week my class reminded me it was time to stop. My goal for this year is to improve closure at the end of our math class. I'm trying new things like exit slips and math journals. When I read what students write, I find out what they did not understand and that helps me prepare for the lesson the next day. I definitely want to know what else besides exit slips and journals can be used as closure activities.

Kathleen Londeree
Mathematics Specialist

If you have ever looked at the classroom clock and realized you lack time for closure and have also run overtime, you are not alone. Mary and Kathleen have been using closure for many years and still work hard to fit it in to the end of a math period. Planning for closure is the first step in using it in your classroom. This chapter will discuss closure and several different formats while answering the following questions:

- Why do you need closure in a lesson?
- What are some different closure activities?
- What is an extended closure?

Illustrative vignettes at the start of each chapter focus on a specific part of the lesson-planning process

In every chapter you will find

Standards
Li and SC
Purpose
Tasks
Materials
Student Thinking
Lesson Structures
Form. Assess.
Lesson Launch
Lesson Facilitation
Closure

Figure 6.3 (Continued)

Characteristic	1 (Highest Rating)	2	3 (Lowest Rating)	Notes
Problem solving in nature				
Authentic/ interesting				
Equitable				
Active				
Connects to Standards for Mathematical Practice or Process Standards				

online resources → Download the Determining a Worthwhile Task Rubric from resources.corwin.com/mathlessonplanning/6-8

Thinking about Jose and Carin and their tasks, rate the tasks using the checklist in Figure 6.3. Discuss your results with a colleague. Whose example is a worthwhile task and why? Note your thoughts below.

_____

_____

_____

HOW DO YOU ADAPT TASKS?

You may have experienced a time when you encountered a textbook or school district task that did not match the multiple needs of your learners. Many teachers choose to adapt tasks to increase the cognitive demand (Smith & Stein, 2011) and to provide more entry points for students to reason mathematically. Here are a few examples.

Example: **Michael**

Michael, a sixth-grade teacher, found the task in Figure 6.4 in his textbook and adapted it to incorporate process standards.

Chapter 6 ▪ Choosing Tasks **71**

Opportunities to stop and reflect on your own instruction

Examples of each lesson feature from classrooms in Grades 6–8

WHAT IS THE ROLE OF REPRESENTATIONS IN MATHEMATICS LESSONS?

The Annenberg Learner Foundation (2003) offers this definition:

"Mathematical representation" refers to the wide variety of ways to capture an abstract mathematical concept or relationship. A mathematical representation may be visible, such as a number sentence, a display of manipulative materials, or a graph, but it may also be an internal way of seeing and thinking about a mathematical idea. Regardless of their form, representations can enhance students' communication, reasoning, and problem-solving abilities; help them make connections among ideas; and aid them in learning new concepts and procedures. (para. 2)

Mathematical concepts are abstract and can be difficult to get across to students. Representations of these concepts can be helpful. Representations can be thought of as a broad category of models. According to Van de Walle, Karp, and Bay-Williams (2016), there are seven ways to represent or model mathematical concepts:

1. Manipulatives
2. Pictures or drawings
3. Symbols
4. Language (written or spoken)
5. Real-world situations
6. Graphs
7. Tables

Selecting a representation is a vital part of your decision making while lesson planning. You must decide, "What representations will help me achieve the learning intentions of today's lesson?" Here is an example of a teacher using a representation to help students make sense of absolute value.

Example: **Alfonso**

Alfonso, a sixth-grade teacher, showed his students this number line to teach that **absolute value** is the distance from zero on the number line.

Alfonso asks his students to work with a partner to answer the following questions using the number line:

What is the opposite of a?

What is the opposite of f?

What is the opposite of h?

What is the opposite of c?

After the students share and discuss their responses, Alfonso asks this follow-up question: What do you notice about the relationship of your pairs of opposites to the number line? During the class discussion of this question, Alfonso guides his students to discover the concept that each number in a given pair of opposites is the same distance from zero on the number line. Once students have this understanding, Alfonso introduces the symbol | | for absolute value using the letters along with the vocabulary term *absolute value*. For example, he shows that |a| = 2 and |e| = 2. He then replaces the letters on the number line with integers and encourages the students to use the absolute value symbol with the integers such as |−6| = 6, |9| = 9, |5| = 5.

In this example, Alfonso used a number line with letters as a representation for students to discover the concept of absolute value.

Building Unit Coherence

Connecting lesson purposes across a unit develops coherence because you are strategically linking conceptual understanding, procedural fluency, and transfer lessons to build comprehensive understanding of the unit standards. As you develop a lesson, consider the purposes of the lessons that come before and after the lesson you are constructing. Over the course of one unit, you should develop and facilitate lessons with all three purposes, bearing in mind how and when the lesson purposes should be positioned within the unit. Some teachers map out their unit with lesson purposes in mind to ensure that they are developing coherence within lesson purpose (Figure 5.8).

How features of a lesson are interrelated to build cohesiveness across a unit

---

Figure 5.8

Unit:

Day 1	Day 2	Day 3	Day 4	Day 5
Conceptual	Conceptual	Conceptual	Procedural fluency	Procedural fluency

Day 6	Day 7	Day 8	Day 9	Day 10
Conceptual	Conceptual	Conceptual	Procedural fluency	Transfer

Now that you have been introduced to the three lesson purposes, reflect on the lessons in your curriculum guide, textbook, or supplemental materials. Can you categorize the lessons into these three categories? Do you notice one type being more prevalent than the others? Note any thoughts or concerns here.

_____
_____
_____
_____
_____
_____
_____
_____
_____
_____

Appendix D

Glossary

absolute value. Distance a number is from zero on the number line.

academic language. The vocabulary used in schools, textbooks, and other school resources.

access to high-quality mathematics instruction. Phrase refers to the National Council of Teachers of Mathematics (NCTM) position statement on equal opportunity to a quality K–12 education for all students. Related to the NCTM position on equitable learning opportunities.

agency. The power to act. Students exercise agency in mathematics when they initiate discussions and actively engage in high-level thinking tasks. When students exercise agency, they reason, critique the reasoning of others, and engage in productive struggle.

algorithm. In mathematics, it is a series of steps or procedures that, when followed accurately, will produce a correct answer.

allocated time. Total amount of time for teacher instruction and student learning.

big ideas. Statements that encompass main concepts in mathematics that cross grade levels, such as place value.

classroom discourse. Conversation that occurs in a classroom. Can be teacher to student(s), student(s) to teacher, or student(s) to student(s).

close-ended questions. Questions with only one correct answer.

closure. The final activity in a lesson with two purposes (1) helps the teacher determine what students have learned and gives direction to next steps and (2) provides students the opportunity to reorganize and summarize the information from a lesson in a meaningful way.

coherence. Logical sequencing of mathematical ideas. Can be vertical, as in across the grades (e.g., 6–8), or can be horizontal, as in across a grade level (e.g., sixth-grade lessons from September through December).

common errors. Mistakes made by students that occur frequently; usually these mistakes are anticipated by the teacher due to their frequency.

conceptual understanding. Comprehension of mathematical concepts, operations, and relationships.

content standards. See *standards*.

discourse. See *classroom discourse*.

distributed practice. See *spaced practice*.

district-wide curriculum. A K–12 document outlining the curriculum for a school system.

drill. Repetitive exercises on a specific math skill or procedure.

English Language Learner (ELL). A person whose first language is not English but who is learning to speak English.

essential question. A question that unifies all of the lessons on a given topic to bring the coherence and purpose to a unit. [...] purposefully linked to the big idea to frame student inquiry, promote critical thinking, and assist in [...]

[...] at the end of a lesson or group of lessons that provides a sampling of student performance. An exit task is [...] *exit slip*.

[...] form of lesson closure where students answer a question about or reflect on the main idea of the lesson [...] chers collect these slips of paper.

Bolded key terms that are defined in a glossary in Appendix D

HOW DO IDENTITY AND AGENCY INFLUENCE LESSON PLANNING?

Identity and **agency** are two concepts that help teachers understand the dynamics that take place in a classroom, which, in turn, helps teachers better understand their students and how best to meet their needs. Identity is how individuals know and see themselves (i.e., student, teacher, good at sports, like math, etc.) and how others know and see us (i.e., short, smart, African American, etc.). When defined broadly, identity is a concept that brings together all the interrelated elements that teachers and students bring to the classroom, including beliefs, attitudes, emotions, and cognitive capacity (Grootenboer, 2000).

Agency is the power to act. Students develop their agency when they actively engage in the learning process (Wenmoth, 2014). Since student learning is greatest in classrooms where students are engaged in high-level thinking and reasoning (Boaler & Staples, 2008), teachers need to ensure that tasks they choose promote this engagement on a regular basis.

The types of lessons teachers design, the approach they take to teaching, the tasks they select, the types of questions they ask, the classroom climate, and social norms of the classroom all affect student engagement and are influenced by the teachers' identity. For example, in a classroom where the teacher sees his or her identity as the giver of knowledge, students are passive recipients of knowledge, working individually at their desks on assignments designed by the teacher. In this approach, there is no opportunity for students to exercise agency. In addition, student identities are lost as they are treated as a group with all the same learning needs rather than as individuals with unique learning needs.

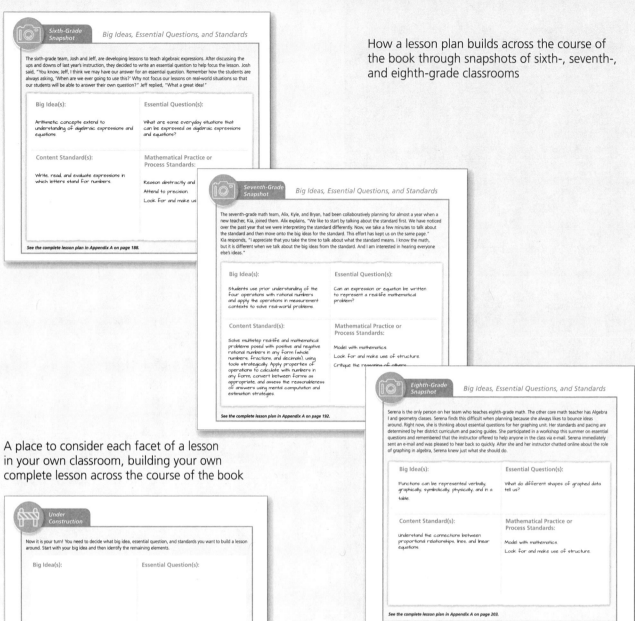

Sixth-Grade Snapshot — Big Ideas, Essential Questions, and Standards

The sixth-grade team, Josh and Jeff, are developing lessons to teach algebraic expressions. After discussing the ups and downs of last year's instruction, they decided to write an essential question to help focus the lesson. Josh said, "You know, Jeff, I think we may have our answer for an essential question. Remember how the students are always asking, 'When are we ever going to use this?' Why not focus our lessons on real-world situations so that our students will be able to answer their own question?" Jeff replied, "What a great idea!"

Big Idea(s):

Arithmetic concepts extend to understanding of algebraic expressions and equations.

Essential Question(s):

What are some everyday situations that can be expressed as algebraic expressions and equations?

Content Standard(s):

Write, read, and evaluate expressions in which letters stand for numbers.

Mathematical Practice or Process Standards:

Reason abstractly and ...
Attend to precision.
Look for and make us...

See the complete lesson plan in Appendix A on page 188.

How a lesson plan builds across the course of the book through snapshots of sixth-, seventh-, and eighth-grade classrooms

Seventh-Grade Snapshot — Big Ideas, Essential Questions, and Standards

The seventh-grade math team, Alix, Kyle, and Bryan, had been collaboratively planning for almost a year when a new teacher, Kia, joined them. Alix explains, "We like to start by talking about the standard first. We have noticed over the past year that we were interpreting the standard differently. Now, we take a few minutes to talk about the standard and then move onto the big ideas for the standard. This effort has kept us on the same page." Kia responds, "I appreciate that you take the time to talk about what the standard means. I know the math, but it is different when we talk about the big ideas from the standard. And I am interested in hearing everyone else's ideas."

Big Idea(s):

Students use prior understanding of the four operations with rational numbers and apply the operations in measurement contexts to solve real-world problems.

Essential Question(s):

Can an expression or equation be written to represent a real-life mathematical problem?

Content Standard(s):

Solve multistep real-life and mathematical problems posed with positive and negative rational numbers in any form (whole numbers, fractions, and decimals), using tools strategically. Apply properties of operations to calculate with numbers in any form, convert between forms as appropriate, and assess the reasonableness of answers using mental computation and estimation strategies.

Mathematical Practice or Process Standards:

Model with mathematics.
Look for and make use of structure.
Critique the reasoning of others.

See the complete lesson plan in Appendix A on page 192.

Eighth-Grade Snapshot — Big Ideas, Essential Questions, and Standards

Serena is the only person on her team who teaches eighth-grade math. The other core math teacher has Algebra I and geometry classes. Serena finds this difficult when planning because she always likes to bounce ideas around. Right now, she is thinking about essential questions for her graphing unit. Her standards and pacing are determined by her district curriculum and pacing guides. She participated in a workshop this summer on essential questions and remembered that the instructor offered to help anyone in the class via e-mail. Serena immediately sent an e-mail and was pleased to hear back so quickly. After she and her instructor chatted online about the role of graphing in algebra, Serena knew just what she should do.

Big Idea(s):

Functions can be represented verbally, graphically, symbolically, physically, and in a table.

Essential Question(s):

What do different shapes of graphed data tell us?

Content Standard(s):

Understand the connections between proportional relationships, lines, and linear equations.

Mathematical Practice or Process Standards:

Model with mathematics.
Look for and make use of structure.

See the complete lesson plan in Appendix A on page 203.

A place to consider each facet of a lesson in your own classroom, building your own complete lesson across the course of the book

Under Construction

Now it is your turn! You need to decide what big idea, essential question, and standards you want to build a lesson around. Start with your big idea and then identify the remaining elements.

Big Idea(s):

Essential Question(s):

Content Standard(s):

Mathematical Practice or Process Standards:

Download the full Lesson-Planning Template from resources.corwin.com/mathlessonplanning/6-8
Remember that you can use the online version of the lesson plan template to begin compiling each section into the full template as your lesson plan grows.

Appendix A shows how the complete lesson plan has come together for each grade

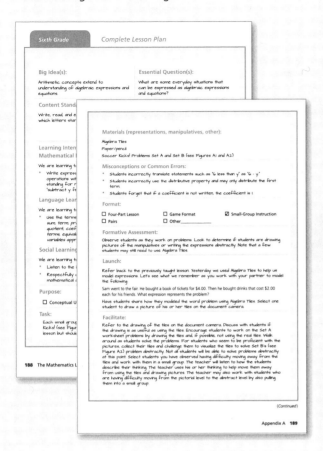

Appendix B includes a blank lesson-planning template for your ongoing use (also available for download at resources.corwin.com/mathlessonplanning/6-8)

Appendix C includes additional key reading and online resources

The Mathematics Lesson-Planning Handbook

Grades 6–8

Your Blueprint for Building Cohesive Lessons

Lois A. Williams

Beth McCord Kobett

Ruth Harbin Miles

Name: _____

Department: _____

Learning Team: _____

A JOINT PUBLICATION

 CORWIN Mathematics NCTM® NATIONAL COUNCIL OF TEACHERS OF MATHEMATICS AMLE

FOR INFORMATION:

Corwin

A SAGE Company

2455 Teller Road

Thousand Oaks, California 91320

(800) 233–9936

www.corwin.com

SAGE Publications Ltd.

1 Oliver's Yard

55 City Road

London EC1Y 1SP

United Kingdom

SAGE Publications India Pvt. Ltd.

B 1/I 1 Mohan Cooperative Industrial Area

Mathura Road, New Delhi 110 044

India

SAGE Publications Asia-Pacific Pte. Ltd.

18 Cross Street #10-10/11/12

China Square Central

Singapore 048423

Executive Editor, Mathematics: Erin Null

Developmental Editor: Renee Nicholls

Editorial Development Manager: Julie Nemer

Senior Editorial Assistant: Jessica Vidal

Production Editor: Melanie Birdsall

Copy Editor: Gillian Dickens

Typesetter: Integra

Proofreader: Susan Schon

Indexer: Molly Hall

Cover Designer: Rose Storey

Interior Designer: Scott Van Atta

Marketing Manager: Margaret O'Connor

Copyright © 2019 by Corwin

Library of Congress Cataloging-in-Publication Data

Names: Williams, Lois A., author. | Kobett, Beth McCord, author. | Miles, Ruth Harbin, author.

Title: The mathematics lesson-planning handbook, grades 6-8: your blueprint for building cohesive lessons / Lois A. Williams, Beth McCord Kobett, Ruth Harbin Miles.

Description: Thousand Oaks, California : Corwin, [2019] | Includes bibliographical references and index.

Identifiers: LCCN 2018035545 | ISBN 9781506387918 (spiral: alk. paper)

Subjects: LCSH: Mathematics—Study and teaching (Elementary) | Mathematics—Study and teaching (Middle school) | Curriculum planning.

Classification: LCC QA11.2 .M5525 2019 | DDC 372.7/044—dc23

LC record available at https://lccn.loc.gov/2018035545

Printed in the United States of America

This book is printed on acid-free paper.

19 20 21 22 23 10 9 8 7 6 5 4 3 2 1

Contents

Visit the companion website at
resources.corwin.com/mathlessonplanning/6-8
for downloadable resources.

Acknowledgments

Thank you to all of the middle school teachers who were willing to share reflections on their practice in the opening vignettes in this book. It is often difficult to expose our intimate, professional thoughts. These teachers are my heroes for sharing their reflections on a world stage, so that all of us can take inspiration and support, as well as feel the comradery that middle school mathematics teachers share with their stories and intimate reflections.

And to my husband, Mike, for always upholding his promise to stand by me.

—Lois A. Williams

To Tim, Hannah, and Jenna for their continuing love, support, and patience. Thank you, Kitty, for always listening. To my mother for thinking I can do anything! Thank you to Skip and Jon for your warm friendship and our productive collaboration. I am also grateful to my Stevenson University family, David and Debby, for supporting my ideas and to my students (past and present) for inspiring me with your passion and commitment to teaching. Thank you to the Elementary Mathematics Specialist Project Coaches for your ongoing support and feedback. Of course a big thank you to my writing partners, Lois and Ruth, on this three-book series—what a ride! A special thank you to Erin Null, our amazing editor whisperer, who has believed in and supported this journey from the beginning. Also thank you to the Corwin crew—Melanie Birdsall, Jessica Vidal, and countless others who make magic happen to plain ole words on a page.

—Beth McCord Kobett

Special thanks is due to the very best teacher I have ever known, my incredible father, Dr. Calvin E. Harbin, who taught me to value my education and at the age of 102 is still modeling lifelong learning. Acknowledgment and thanks must also be given to my extraordinary mentors, Dr. Ramona Anshutz and Dr. Shirley A. Hill, who both inspired me to become a mathematics education leader. Their influence and guidance completely changed my life's work. Words could never express the thanks and credit I owe to my incredible writing partners, Dr. Ted H. Hull, Dr. Don S. Balka, Linda Gojak, Dr. Lois A. Williams, Dr. Beth Kobett, Dr. Jean Morrow, and Dr. Sandi Cooper, who over the years helped me coauthor 37 published books. Most important, I thank my loving husband, Sam Miles, for *always* supporting me.

—Ruth Harbin Miles

We would also like to thank Erin Null for her enduring support for our work on this book, incredible creativity, and commitment to this project. Her insightful perspective, vision for the project, and ability to ask just the right question at just the right time are appreciated and valued.

—Lois, Beth, and Ruth

Publisher's Acknowledgments

Corwin gratefully acknowledges the contributions of the following reviewer:

Deborah Kiger Bliss
Virginia Department of Education, Retired
Onley, VA

Letter to 6–8 Teachers

Dear Grades 6–8 Teachers,

As a teacher, you make hundreds of decisions every day! Many of these decisions fall into the categories of classroom management or paperwork, such as deciding which student should sit next to which student or determining if you need to call that parent tonight or tomorrow. Some decisions are crucial to the classroom climate and environment and set the stage for how students learn. Among the hundreds of decisions you make, the most important are those that influence student learning. Designing, planning, and facilitating lessons reflect critical teacher decision-making opportunities that affect student learning. Oftentimes, these decisions get relegated to a few moments of planning time.

In this book, *The Mathematics Lesson-Planning Handbook, Grades 6–8: Your Blueprint for Building Cohesive Lessons*, you will experience the decision-making processes that are involved in planning lessons, and you will get to build a lesson of your own using a specially designed format just for you. Your decisions will revolve around creating mathematics lessons with purpose, rigor, and coherence. In addition, we will help you address the decisions involved in selecting your resources (e.g., "How do I make the best use of my textbook or state/district instructional materials?"), your classroom structure (e.g., "Is planning different in a block schedule vs. a 45-minute per day schedule?"), your worthwhile tasks (e.g., "How do I know one when I see it?"), your learning intentions (e.g., "What are my objectives?"), and your success criteria (e.g., "How will I know my students have learned?"). We will show you the importance of identifying big ideas, anticipating student misconceptions, implementing formative assessment, facilitating a lesson with questioning, and closing a lesson with reflection techniques.

Each chapter includes a reflection by a middle school teacher, examples for each grade level (6–8), an opportunity to reflect on the ideas presented, suggestions for building a unit from your lesson, and an Under Construction section to help you build a lesson on the content of your choice. A glossary in Appendix D provides definitions for words highlighted in each chapter.

Keep in mind that the goal of teaching is student learning. The best lessons that students can experience always begin with a prepared teacher.

Sincerely,

Lois A. Williams
Beth McCord Kobett
Ruth Harbin Miles

Letter to Middle School Principals

Dear Middle School Principals,

Some teachers *implement lesson plans* written by textbook publishers or by other professional curriculum writers. We argue that this is not enough. To positively affect the learning of their students, teachers need professional decision-making opportunities.

In this book, *The Mathematics Lesson-Planning Handbook, Grades 6–8: Your Blueprint for Building Cohesive Lessons,* your mathematics teachers will experience the decision-making processes that are involved in planning lessons for purpose, rigor, and coherence, and they will build a lesson of their own using a format created for them. In addition, we will help them address the decisions involved in selecting resources (e.g., "How can teachers make the best use of their textbook or state/district instructional materials?"), classroom structure (e.g., "Is lesson structure different in a block schedule than a more traditional middle school schedule?"), worthwhile tasks (e.g., "How do they recognize them?"), lesson intentions (e.g., "What are the objectives?"), and success criteria (e.g., "How will the teachers know their students have learned?"). We will help them examine the importance of identifying big ideas, anticipating student misconceptions, implementing formative assessment, facilitating a lesson with questioning, and closing a lesson with reflection techniques.

Each teacher on your mathematics faculty has a different level of mathematics expertise, but all bring knowledge, unique skills, and distinct ideas to the lesson-planning process. As a leader, you may want to capitalize on these varying skills by supplying every mathematics teacher with a personal copy of this book for use as a department-wide book study. Providing the opportunity for teachers to engage and use the book in planning with colleagues will allow teachers to dig deeply into their standards and collaborate to leverage each other's knowledge and experience. After all, your best-prepared teachers are the most effective players on your team!

Sincerely,

Lois A. Williams
Beth McCord Kobett
Ruth Harbin Miles

Letter to Mathematics Coaches

Dear Mathematics Coaches,

Your work with teachers must, undoubtedly, encompass a great deal of time and effort planning mathematics lessons. This guide is designed to unpack the lesson-planning process to help teachers understand the importance of teacher decision making as they plan effective mathematics lessons to support student growth. Currently, some teachers simply *implement lesson plans* written by textbook publishers or by other professional curriculum writers. We argue that this is not enough. To positively affect the learning of their students, teachers need professional decision-making opportunities.

As you know, collaborative planning can be particularly powerful for teams of teachers. You may find that a three-step process, incorporating a planning, trying, and reflective cycle, will be most helpful for your teachers. Consider beginning small, tackling the content by chapter, to increase successful implementation.

In this book, *The Mathematics Lesson-Planning Handbook, Grades 6–8: Your Blueprint for Building Cohesive Lessons*, your middle school teachers will experience the decision-making processes that are involved in planning lessons for purpose, rigor, and coherence, and they will build a lesson of their own using our format. In addition, we will help them address the decisions involved in selecting resources (e.g., "How can teachers make the best use of their textbook or state/district instructional materials?"), classroom structure (e.g., "Is lesson structure different in a block schedule than a more traditional middle school schedule?"), worthwhile tasks (e.g., "How do they recognize them?"), lesson intentions (e.g., "What are the objectives?"), and success criteria (e.g., "How will the teachers know their students have learned?"). We look at the importance of identifying big ideas, anticipating student misconceptions, implementing formative assessment, facilitating a lesson with questioning, and closing a lesson with reflection techniques.

Your middle school mathematics teachers have varying levels of mathematics expertise, but all bring knowledge, skills, and distinct ideas to the lesson-planning process. Providing the opportunity for teachers to engage and use the book in planning with colleagues will allow teachers to dig deeply into their standards and collaborate to leverage each other's knowledge and experience. Be sure to invite teachers to bring this resource to all planning and professional development sessions. After all, your best-prepared teachers are the most effective players on your team!

Sincerely,

Lois A. Williams
Beth McCord Kobett
Ruth Harbin Miles

Letter to Preservice College and University Instructors

Dear Preservice College and University Instructors,

Preservice teachers for Grades 6–8 must learn how to develop lesson plans to professionally prepare for teaching their students. One of the critical goals of a methods class is to guide preservice teachers and help them learn to create effective, well-crafted, and engaging mathematics lesson plans.

A recent study published in the *American Educational Research Journal* states that preservice teachers remember and use what they learned in teacher-prep programs about writing lesson plans for mathematics (Morris & Hiebert, 2017). You have a major role to play, and this book can help you unpack the lesson-planning process.

The Mathematics Lesson-Planning Handbook, Grades 6–8: Your Blueprint for Building Cohesive Lessons, helps your preservice teachers experience the decision-making processes involved in planning lessons for purpose, rigor, and coherence, and it guides them through the steps of building a lesson of their own using a format created for them. In addition, we help them address the decisions involved in selecting resources (e.g., "How can teachers make the best use of their textbook or state/district instructional materials?"), classroom structure (e.g., "Is instruction different in a block schedule vs. a more traditional middle school schedule?"), worthwhile tasks (e.g., "How do they recognize them?"), lesson intentions (e.g., "What are the objectives?"), and success criteria (e.g., "How will the teachers know their students have learned?"). We look at the importance of identifying big ideas, anticipating student misconceptions, implementing formative assessment, facilitating a lesson with questioning, and closing a lesson with reflection techniques.

The handbook includes 14 chapters that may easily be incorporated into a 14-, 15-, or 16-week methods course. The resource provides the opportunity for preservice teachers to engage and study the content chapter by chapter. As a result of their learning, this book will influence professional practice in lesson planning. After all, the preservice teachers' knowledge influences how they plan for instruction throughout their careers.

Sincerely,

Lois A. Williams
Beth McCord Kobett
Ruth Harbin Miles

How to Use This Book

In the words of Benjamin Franklin, "Failing to plan is planning to fail." The best lessons students can experience always begin with a prepared teacher who considers student learning the primary goal of instruction.

Searching the Internet for lessons plans to use or adapt may seem to be an efficient way to plan. However, you will likely spend hours searching for the perfect lesson only to find that what you needed/wanted was not quite what you found. In contrast, planning your own lessons is a special skill that has invaluable rewards both for you and for your students. This guide will help you plan lessons that are strategically designed with YOUR students in mind.

When you are able to build your own mathematics lessons, you have the power to make decisions about all aspects of your students' learning, including how to make the content meet your students' individual needs. This approach may seem overwhelming in the beginning, because creating an effective lesson plan requires thinking and practice to consider all the factors you need. The good news is that after a bit of practice, it will become second nature.

Start slowly and take each chapter one at a time. We find that teachers who follow this process gain new insight into the mathematics they are teaching, which, in turn, helps them to better facilitate their students' learning.

Part I of this book begins with the premise that good instruction should be planned with purpose, coherence, and rigor in mind. It includes a chapter emphasizing that middle school children have specific needs and that, as a teacher, you need to plan lessons in accordance with those needs. At the beginning of Part II, you will find the lesson-planning template that reflects all of the decisions a teacher makes when planning and facilitating a lesson. It may seem overwhelming at first glance. However, with practice, you will find that these decisions become second nature to your planning process.

Part II comprises a series of chapters for each component of the template. Each chapter includes the following:

- A reflection by a 6–8 teacher wrestling with the decision-making part of the component
- Ideas and information to help with your decision-making process
- Snapshots that model the gradual construction of a sixth-, seventh-, and eighth-grade lesson plan chapter by chapter
- A section highlighting the importance of coherence for future lessons in a unit
- Questions for reflection
- An Under Construction section for you to begin planning your own lesson

Part III helps you put it all together with suggestions for planning to launch, facilitate, and close your lesson. Appendix A will show you the complete lesson plan for each grade (6–8) so that you can see how it has come together in the end. A blank template can be found in Appendix B and is available to download online at resources.corwin.com/mathlessonplanning/6-8.

Additional readings and resources are available in Appendix C. Throughout the book, you will find words that appear in bold type. You can find their meanings in the glossary in Appendix D.

You may wish to begin the planning process by tackling one chapter at a time. You can read about an approach, try it out, and then, after completing the next chapter, integrate additional new concepts into your planning process. Take it slow, reflect along the way, and, before you know it, you will be planning robust mathematics lessons! Let's begin!

PART I

YOU ARE THE ARCHITECT OF YOUR CLASSROOM

CHAPTER 1

SURVEYING YOUR SITE
Knowing Your Students

My students are incredibly diverse in ethnicity, culture, learning needs, and prior experiences. I find that while they are very diverse, they share an innate curiosity about learning. They may not always want to show this to me, but I have my ways of capitalizing on their inquisitive nature! First, I provide a safe space for them to ask questions and explore their ideas. Second, they really, really like to talk. I prefer that they talk about math, so I must give them many opportunities to talk to each other about the math they are learning. I have found that if I use a "thought-provoking" question, image, or task that connects to them or their interests, I can ignite this curiosity. When I am designing these provocations, I think about them—their developmental needs, interests, and even quirks. Just last week, I was looking at the standard for converting measurements and thought about how I could get them interested—worksheets on conversions were not going to do it for them! I know that they need to see why and how this is important to them and that they need to see, feel, and touch the math as much as possible. I decided to set up stations with different types of volume, length, and area measures. As soon as they walked in the room, they started asking questions:

> "What are we doing, Ms. Weyforth?"
>
> "Oooh, there is different stuff at each station. Can we do them all?"
>
> "Is this about measurement?"
>
> "When can we start?"
>
> "Can I start with the measuring cups? I love to help my grandmother cook!"

I looked around the room to see hands busily measuring and comparing while diverse voices created a pleasant buzz of discourse. "This is gold," I thought.

Alix Weyforth
Middle School Teacher
Maryland

How would you describe your students? Every classroom is distinctive. The students you teach are uniquely yours, and they enter your classroom with a vast array of learning needs, interests, hopes, and even dreams about how they will spend their time with you. The focus of this chapter is to encourage you to think about the many needs of your learners and connect it to your preparation for planning. We will explore the following questions:

- Why is it so important to know your students?
- What do access and equity really mean?
- How do identity and agency influence lesson planning?
- What is prior knowledge in mathematics?
- What do culturally and linguistically diverse students need?
- What do students living in poverty need?
- What are learning needs?
- What are the common themes?

WHY IS IT SO IMPORTANT TO KNOW YOUR STUDENTS?

As a teacher, you surely appreciate the value of knowing the learners in your classroom because you recognize how this intricately connects your teaching to your students' learning. Consider a time when you looked at a lesson plan constructed by someone else and thought, "This will never work with my kids." You know your students, and you were able to imagine how they would respond to the particular activities, content, or facilitation in the lesson plan.

As Bransford, Brown, and Cocking (2000) note, your knowledge of students is critical because students "come to formal education with a range of prior knowledge, skills, beliefs, and concepts that significantly influence what they notice about the environment and how they organize and interpret it. This, in turn, affects their abilities to remember, reason, solve problems, and acquire new knowledge" (p. 10). While it is vitally important to understand the mathematics content you teach, it is equally important to know and understand everything you can about the students you teach.

The students in your classroom have unique backgrounds that influence the ways in which they respond to you. At the same time, the ways you respond to your students may be influenced by your own cultural and language preferences and beliefs. All this information can help you plan lessons and design learning activities that both capitalize on students' cognitive, behavioral, and social-emotional strengths and **scaffold** their learning challenges.

As you work your way through this book, you will be constructing a mathematics lesson on the topic of your choice for your grade level and content area. While this book is about lesson planning, it is essential for you to begin the lesson-planning process with a focus on your own learners' needs. As you read the brief discussion about different learning needs, consider how the descriptions apply to your own group of students.

> **Think about a situation when knowing about a student's needs in your class helped you plan an instructional activity that supported mathematical learning. Briefly describe the details here.**
>
> _____
>
> _____
>
> _____
>
> _____
>
> _____

WHAT IS PRIOR KNOWLEDGE IN MATHEMATICS?

As a teacher of middle school students, you know firsthand that students walk into your classroom with a wide array of backgrounds and experiences. **Prior knowledge** refers to the mathematics knowledge or content that students know as they enter your classroom. If you do not help students engage their prior knowledge, they may not be able to integrate new knowledge meaningfully. Accessing and connecting prior knowledge to new learning can affect students' motivation to learn and how much they will learn (Dolezal, Welsh, Pressley, & Vincent, 2003).

How students experience mathematics at home is one influence on their mathematics learning in the classroom. For example, if your students talk with their parents about mathematics and shop with their parents at the grocery store, you can connect these experiences to your instructional activities. If students do not regularly have access to these kinds of opportunities, you will need to create instructional activities that help your students construct foundational knowledge for standards you will be teaching in the future. One way you can do this is by integrating number routines into your overall instructional plan.

Example: Amelia

Amelia, a sixth-grade teacher, conducts a **number routine** at least twice a week. These number routines help students think about numbers and computation in flexible ways, provide an entry point for every student, and offer Amelia opportunities to use students' ideas to facilitate mathematical discussions. At the beginning of the year, she asks students to represent numbers in multiple ways using multiple representations and operations (Figure 1.1).

Figure 1.1

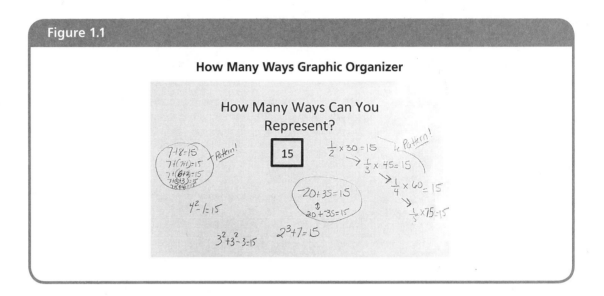

Amelia organizes the students to work with a partner to encourage inquiry and flexibility in thinking about number and operations. This simple number routine prompts students to demonstrate their understanding of numbers and operations and provides Amelia with information about how students make connections and apply the mathematics they have already learned. While all students may not need more opportunities to develop foundational knowledge before moving to grade-level lessons, Amelia knows that all students will benefit from the exploration and conversation that this number routine elicits.

Amelia also uses a rotating bulletin board display to ensure that every student has work represented in the classroom and highlight student strategies for particular lessons that she is going to teach. For example, when she introduced the ratio and proportion unit, she took pictures of the students' models for ratio stories and asked the students to discuss what all the representations had in common.

What do you know about your students' prior knowledge? Make a list and share it with another teacher who knows your students.

_____

_____

_____

_____

_____

_____

WHAT DO ACCESS AND EQUITY REALLY MEAN?

Knowing your students is the first step in providing equitable learning opportunities and **access to high-quality mathematics instruction.** The National Council of Teachers of Mathematics' (2014a) Access and Equity Position Statement states the following:

> Creating, supporting, and sustaining a culture of access and equity require being responsive to students' backgrounds, experiences, cultural perspectives, traditions, and knowledge when designing and implementing a mathematics program and assessing its effectiveness. Acknowledging and addressing factors that contribute to differential outcomes among groups of students are critical to ensuring that all students routinely have opportunities to experience high-quality mathematics instruction, learn challenging mathematics content, and receive the support necessary to be successful. Addressing equity and access includes both ensuring that all students attain mathematics proficiency and increasing the numbers of students from all racial, ethnic, linguistic, gender, and socioeconomic groups who attain the highest levels of mathematics achievement. (www.nctm.org/Standards-and-Positions/Position-Statements/Access-and-Equity-in-Mathematics-Education)

Without equal access, students' opportunities to learn are reduced. Students' knowledge gaps are often the result of instructional gaps, which happen when students are not appropriately challenged because beliefs about what they learn and how they can learn are reflected in the types of instruction they receive. Equitable instruction is a key factor in supporting students' opportunities for access to high-quality mathematics instruction. Knowledge of your students should inform and support high expectations and beliefs about what your students can learn and do in your mathematics classroom. Later in this book, you will have an opportunity to apply what you know about your students to your own lesson-planning process.

> **How do you ensure that *all* your students have access to high-quality mathematics instruction? Record your response here.**
>
> _____
>
> _____
>
> _____
>
> _____

HOW DO IDENTITY AND AGENCY INFLUENCE LESSON PLANNING?

Identity and **agency** are two concepts that help teachers understand the dynamics that take place in a classroom, which, in turn, helps teachers better understand their students and how best to meet their needs. Identity is how individuals know and see themselves (i.e., student, teacher, good at sports, like math, etc.) and how others know and see us (i.e., short, smart, African American, etc.). When defined broadly, identity is a concept that brings together all the interrelated elements that teachers and students bring to the classroom, including beliefs, attitudes, emotions, and cognitive capacity (Grootenboer, 2000).

Agency is the power to act. Students develop their agency when they actively engage in the learning process (Wenmoth, 2014). Since student learning is greatest in classrooms where students are engaged in high-level thinking and reasoning (Boaler & Staples, 2008), teachers need to ensure that tasks they choose promote this engagement on a regular basis.

The types of lessons teachers design, the approach they take to teaching, the tasks they select, the types of questions they ask, the classroom climate, and social norms of the classroom all affect student engagement and are influenced by the teachers' identity. For example, in a classroom where the teacher sees his or her identity as the giver of knowledge, students are passive recipients of knowledge, working individually at their desks on assignments designed by the teacher. In this approach, there is no opportunity for students to exercise agency. In addition, student identities are lost as they are treated as a group with all the same learning needs rather than as individuals with unique learning needs.

If teachers think about teaching and learning as social activities (Vygotsky, 1964, 1978), then they must take the initiative to put structures into place in the classroom that support the social nature of learning. These include creating a classroom climate in which students feel safe to test hypotheses and ask questions. In this environment, teachers present tasks that afford students the opportunity to act, to explore, to move, and to exercise some choice. They set social norms in the classroom that encourage students to work together on challenging tasks and engage in productive struggle. They not only encourage student-to-student discourse but also intentionally plan for it. Students hypothesize, listen to one another, critique ideas, and formulate questions. They exercise their agency. In this student-centered approach, students become "authors" of mathematical ideas and texts and not "overhearers" (Larson, 2002).

Let's look at an example in which students from racial groups often challenged to find voice and agency in classrooms were engaged in a task that allowed them to exercise their agency. Arthur Powell (2004), a researcher from Rutgers University, captured African American and Latinx students exercising their agency during a study under a grant from the National Science Foundation (REC-0309062). In this study, Powell describes how students who had never before used Cuisenaire Rods were given a set to help them investigate fractions. Cuisenaire Rods are proportional rods of ten different colors, with each color corresponding to a different length, as pictured in Figure 1.2.

Figure 1.2

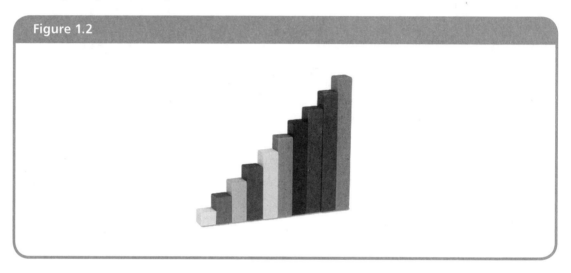

Powell (2004) describes,

> Students were invited to work on the question, "If the blue rod is 1, what is yellow?" Many students manipulated the rods to observe how many white rods they needed to place end-to-end to construct a length equivalent to the blue rod. Malika lists how many white rods make up each of the other rods. She calls the yellow rod 5, and later she and Lorrin say that yellow is five-ninths. Building a model of a blue rod alongside a train of one yellow and four white rods, with a purple rod beneath the white rods, Lorrin and Malika show that the purple rod is four ninths. The students at their table determine number names for all the rods, except that they are uncertain about what to call the orange rod. Eventually, this group of students resolves what number name to give to the orange rod. One student remarks that ten-ninths is an improper fraction. A male colleague [student] … says assertively, "It's still ten-ninths. That ain't gonna change it because it's an improper fraction. That makes it even more right." (p. 46)

In this example, the teacher did not overtly give students a set procedure to follow to work out the name for the yellow rod. The teacher did, however, establish the social norms of the classroom so that students knew what was expected of them. Malika manipulated the materials to name all of the rods. Student-to-student discussion provided the opportunity to use reasoning to name the orange rod, a question that was not asked by the investigator. Students were posing their own questions at this point in the investigation. Powell reports that the students held a misconception about fractions when the investigation began—the numerator cannot be larger than the denominator—but, through their own exploration, had convinced themselves by the end of the session that the belief was incorrect. The students had agency in this example because of the task they engaged in and the social norms in place to help them. The teacher expected students to move around, manipulate objects, engage in the task by talking with one another, and challenge each other's ideas.

In this book, you will read more about tasks, misconceptions, and discourse to support students in exercising their agency.

WHAT DO CULTURALLY AND LINGUISTICALLY DIVERSE STUDENTS NEED?

If you are lucky enough to teach culturally and linguistically diverse students, then you know of the rich experiences these students bring to your classroom. An **English Language Learner (ELL)** is defined as "an active learner of the English language who may benefit from various types of language support programs" (National Council of Teachers of English, 2008, p. 2). While these students may share some common needs because they are learning English and mathematics as well as other subjects, they also can, and often do, have very different learning needs. You can gather information about these students by asking them to show you what they know, observing them as they interact with other students, speaking to them often, using visual cues to communicate, and encouraging them to draw representations. The National Council of Supervisors of Mathematics' (2009) position paper, titled "Improving Student Achievement in Mathematics by Addressing the Needs of English Language Learners," recommends that mathematics educators do the following:

- Realize that mathematics is neither value free nor culture free but instead is a product of human activity. Thus, race, class, culture, and language play key roles in its teaching and learning.

- Understand that language is not only a tool for communicating but also a tool for thinking. Every mathematics teacher is a language teacher—particularly the **academic language** used to formulate and communicate mathematics learning (Lager, 2006).

- Realize that regular and active classroom participation—in the form of discussing, explaining, writing, and presenting—is crucial to ELLs' success in mathematics and that ELLs can produce explanations, participate in presentations, and engage in discussions as they are learning English.

- Recognize that ELLs, like English-speaking students, require consistent access to high-cognitive-demand tasks in mathematics.

- Learn to see the evidence of ELLs' mathematical thinking, hear how ELLs use language to communicate about mathematics, understand the competence that ELLs bring, build on this competence, and provide access to opportunities for advancing their learning.

- Value the home language of each ELL student and find ways to promote its use whenever possible.

- Provide and participate in ongoing professional development to help mathematics teachers shape instructional practices to foster success of ELLs in mathematics, including the development of language-rich classrooms for the benefit of all students.

- Establish district- and schoolwide structures that promote collaboration among teachers of mathematics, specialists in English as a second language, bilingual teachers, and language arts teachers to meld skills and knowledge in the service of ELLs' learning of mathematics.

Culturally and linguistically diverse students also benefit from particular strategies that invite them to regularly engage in mathematical discourse (Banse, Palacios, Merritt, & Rimm-Kaufman, 2016). This discourse is critical because the ELL students need to have opportunities to talk as well as to listen. Banse et al. (2016) recommend that ELL teachers should proceed as follows:

1. Ask **open-ended** questions that invite student thinking and explanation and support students' development of conceptual understanding (Figure 1.3).

Figure 1.3

Example	Nonexample
What do you notice about this ratio table?	Find the value for the missing number.

Number of Items	1	5	25	?
Total Cost	$2.50	$12.50	$62.50	$1,562.50

---

2. As needed, follow open-ended questions with **close-ended questions** that are scaffolded to help the ELLs focus on one or two options (Figure 1.4).

Figure 1.4

Example	Nonexample
Make a prediction and then fold these two nets to find out if they form a cube.	Fold this net to see how it makes a cube.

3. Scaffold students' responses by repeating, extending, and rephrasing so ELLs can benefit from having additional conversations about their explanations and solutions, which can be extended by peers and/or the teacher (Figure 1.5).

Figure 1.5

Example	Nonexample
You looked at the scatterplot of dog breed heights and weights to see if you could find relationships between the data. You noticed that as the height of the dog increased, the weight also increased. I noticed that you kept tracing your pencil on the line you drew. This is called the best-fit line (pointing to the data).	Let me show you how to find the best-fit line.

4. Model mathematical vocabulary in context, always using correct vocabulary and applying it in context so that ELLs can make connections about meaning (Figure 1.6).

Figure 1.6

Example	Nonexample
The absolute value is the distance from 0.	The absolute value is a positive version of the number presented.

5. Strive to include ELLs in mathematical discourse each day; ideally, both teachers and students should engage in mathematical discourse with ELL students (Figure 1.7).

Figure 1.7

Example	Nonexample
ELL students and non-ELL students work in pairs and participate in flexible grouping.	ELL students are isolated in their own group.

Review the five recommendations for teachers of ELL students. Which ones do you already use in your planning? Which ones would you like to integrate more? How might you do that? Briefly list the details here.

_____

_____

_____

_____

WHAT DO STUDENTS LIVING IN POVERTY NEED?

About 21% of the children living in the United States live below the poverty threshold. Another 22% live in low-income homes, comprising 43%, or 30.6 million, of all the children in the United States (National Center for Children in Poverty, 2017). Given this statistic, it is quite likely that you are teaching at least one child living in poverty.

While it is important to not overgeneralize or make assumptions about children living in poverty, research suggests that some children in this situation may experience prolonged stress that may influence the ways in which they respond to the classroom environment and that may negatively affect school performance (Harvard Center for the Developing Child, 2007). Students may have difficulty concentrating or attending to tasks (Erickson, Drevets, & Schulkin, 2003), reduced ability to navigate in social situations (National Institute of Child Health and Human Development Early Child Care Research Network, 2005), and impaired memory, critical thinking, and creativity (Farah et al., 2006; Lupien, King, Meaney, & McEwen, 2001). While many strategies can support your students who are living in poverty, the following three strategies may support your instructional decision making about lesson planning.

1. **Build upon the students' strengths.** Students in poverty need educators to recognize the strengths that they bring to school. Ensure that you are focusing on and building students' specific strengths by first determining those strengths and then highlighting them during lessons.

2. **Consistently work toward building relationships with your students.** Intentionally pursue relationships with your students. Ensure that you use their names in positive ways, and provide opportunities for students to build relationships with each other. Consider using the students' names and interests in word problems and contexts for lessons.

3. **Seek to understand your students' responses to stressful situations.** Consider why students might be responding to classroom situations in particular ways by observing and noting potential triggers. As you plan your lessons, partner students to increase access to problems. Think about how your problem contexts might engage or alienate students who are living in poverty. For example, problems that focus on acquisition or buying items may create unintentional consequences.

Example: Timmy

Raymond, an eighth-grade teacher, used all three of these strategies to attend to one of his eighth grader's needs. He had noticed that Timmy usually entered the classroom in the morning very agitated and had trouble settling into the routine. The student had developed a pattern of entering the room, slamming his books down, and then engaging in conflict with another student. To counteract this pattern, Raymond decided to greet Timmy at the classroom door to have a positive conversation about how he was doing. Raymond enlisted Timmy's help by asking him to help take photographs for a lesson launch. After about a week of making this effort, Raymond noticed that Timmy was much calmer, focused, and ready to learn at the start of each day. He seemed to look forward to their daily chats and was often ready to tell him a story.

How do you use students' strengths to design instructional activities? Briefly note the details here.

_____

_____

_____

_____

_____

_____

_____

_____

WHAT ARE LEARNING NEEDS?

Every student you teach is distinct, possessing specific learning strengths and learning challenges. Students with explicit learning disabilities typically possess a significant learning challenge in one or more of the following areas: memory, self-regulation, visual processing, language processing (separate from ELL), academic skills, and motor skills. The Individuals With Disabilities Education Act (IDEA) requires public schools to provide the least restrictive environment to students with identified disabilities. Students' **Individualized Education Plan (IEP)** must reflect the individual needs of the students.

As you consider the learning needs of your students, you will need to study their IEPs carefully to determine how you can meet their needs in your instructional planning. You may want to develop learning profiles of your students' mathematics strengths and needs to inform your **instructional decision** making. You might complete a learning profile, along with a special educator or coteacher, for each student with the IEP accommodations at the beginning of the year and then add to it as you learn new information throughout the year.

Example: Rhonda

Figure 1.8 shows a completed learning profile that Aimee created after getting to know Rhonda, a student in her class. In the form, she noted Rhonda's strengths in self-regulating her behavior and her advanced critical thinking skills. After just one day, Aimee was beginning to gather some excellent evidence about Rhonda's strengths.

Figure 1.8

Learner Profile for Mathematics Teaching and Learning

Name: Rhonda

Memory and Retention	Self-Regulation	Visual Processing	Language Processing	Academic Skills	Motor Skills
Strengths	Strengths Monitors behavior and expresses her needs with maturity	Strengths	Strengths	Strengths Demonstrates advanced critical thinking skills.	Strengths
Challenges Basic fact retention	Challenges	Challenges	Challenges	Challenges	Challenges Writing explanations

IEP Accommodations:

Provide extra time to write problem-solving explanations.

Extra time to complete assignments. Recorder for some assignments.

 Download the Learner Profile from resources.corwin.com/mathlessonplanning/6-8

By providing students with opportunities to see and use multiple representations in learning activities, from concrete to abstract, you can support their mathematical understanding. This concrete-to-abstract sequence is described in two ways—Concrete-Representation-Abstract (CRA) and Concrete–Semi-Concrete–Abstract (CSA)—and it supports students with disabilities' conceptual understanding (Sealander, Johnson, Lockwood, & Medina, 2012). This teaching sequence is very familiar to educators because it begins with concrete experiences using manipulatives, moves to a representational stage where students draw pictures and use visuals to show their thinking, and then provides opportunities for students to apply their learning using abstract symbols. As you make instructional decisions for your students with learning needs, you will want to consider giving ample time for students to use manipulatives (even in middle school!) before moving to the representation stage. They may also need opportunities to move back and forth between the stages of the CRA/CSA sequence to continue to build fluency (Van de Walle, Karp, & Bay-Williams, 2013). For instance, Figure 1.9 shows the concrete to abstract continuum for addition of negative numbers.

Figure 1.9

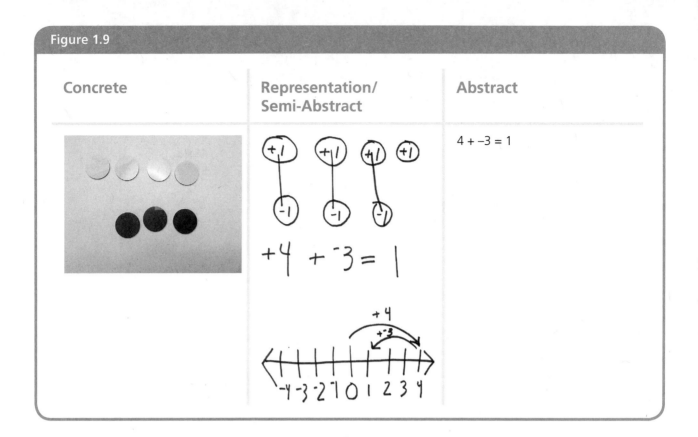

Concrete	Representation/ Semi-Abstract	Abstract
		$4 + -3 = 1$

<hr>

How do you integrate your students' learning needs into your instructional planning? Briefly note the details here.

_____

_____

_____

_____

_____

_____

_____

WHAT ARE THE UNIQUE NEEDS OF THE ADOLESCENT?

As a middle school teacher, you know that early adolescence is a special time between the elementary and middle school years when your students experience swift intellectual and social-emotional developmental changes. In fact, the middle school was founded on the idea that young adolescents' developmental needs should be at the forefront of the middle school educational experience. Middle school educators championed the opportunity to make decisions about curricular design, pedagogical strategies, and assessment practices (Eichhorn, 1966). The Association for Middle Level Education (AMLE, 2010) report, *This We Believe: Keys to Educating*

Adolescents, highlights four essential attributes that middle schools must have to best address the unique needs of adolescents:

Developmentally responsive—Using the distinctive nature of young adolescents as the foundation upon which all decisions about school organization, policies, curriculum, instruction, and assessment are made

Challenging—Ensuring that every student learns and every member of the learning community is held to high expectations

Empowering—Providing all students with the knowledge and skills they need to take responsibility for their lives, to address life's challenges, to function successfully at all levels of society, and to be creators of knowledge

Equitable—Advocating for and ensuring every student's right to learn and providing appropriately challenging and relevant learning opportunities for every student

In addition to the four essential attributes, the AMLE highlights five evidence-based practices of effective middle-level education:

- Educators value young adolescents and are prepared to teach them.
- Students and teachers are engaged in active, purposeful learning.
- Curriculum is challenging, exploratory, integrative, and relevant.
- Educators use multiple learning and teaching approaches.
- Varied and ongoing assessments advance learning as well as measure it.

The AMLE essential attributes, coupled with the evidence-based practices, emphasize the importance for teachers to understand the unique developmental needs of their students and plan for and facilitate instruction that incorporates and responds to those needs. As you most assuredly have noticed, middle school students' physical, intellectual, social, and emotional development is unique during this stage of their lives (Scales, 2010). These developmental characteristics interconnect with one another and can be influenced by race, ethnicity, gender, culture, environment, and family (Caskey & Anfara, 2014).

Physical Development: A quick visual survey of your own classroom may demonstrate the vast array of middle school physical development. In fact, early adolescents experience an accelerated period of physical growth, second only to the birth to two years old range! Contrary to the infant growth period, the adolescent development is fraught with extreme, rapid, and uneven development (Kellough & Kellough, 2008). Adolescents need to alternately move their bodies and rest, and they need many opportunities and structure to pace their ever-abounding energy!

Intellectual Development: As Alix described in the opening reflection, adolescents are innately curious, enjoy active learning experiences, and prefer social learning over passive learning activities (Kellough & Kellough, 2008). They are moving from concrete to more abstract thinking processes (Piaget, 1964), although their cognitive function varies wildly within the span of the middle school years. Your teaching practices and the students' learning opportunities strengthen connections in the brain, which heavily influences future learning (Wilson & Horch, 2002). In short, your decisions have long-lasting impact! They also enjoy humor, but sarcasm should be used with caution. They are keenly interested in authentic problems and need to see how academic exercises can be applied to their lives (Kellough & Kellough, 2008).

Social and Emotional Development: Once again, a simple trip through the halls of a middle school provides evidence of the adolescents' burgeoning social and emotional development. Peer influence is at the forefront of this development. Although the family is very important to the middle school student, adolescents have a strong desire to associate with their friends. They are often conflicted in their desire to be independent and develop a personal identity while at the same time adhere to the peer groups' social norms (Brighton, 2007). They want to belong and need many opportunities in the classroom to develop healthy and positive relationships with one another (Scales, 2010). You can design collaborative activities that focus on rich problem-solving experiences to support productive social and emotional development for your students.

WHAT ARE THE COMMON THEMES?

As you were reading this chapter, you may have thought that many of the suggested strategies could be applied to all of your learners. Instructional decision making begins with building relationships with students by getting to know them. This newfound knowledge helps you to create positive connections and build a learning community that fosters a rich learning environment. When you know your students, you can make the very best instructional decisions that will best meet their academic and social-emotional needs. Knowledge and awareness of your students' learning needs makes for purposeful lesson planning.

> Consider all of the learning needs discussed in this chapter. Make a list of your own students' learning needs using the categories listed in this chapter. What do you notice? What will you need to keep in mind as you plan your lessons? Record your thoughts and concerns below.
>
> _____
> _____
> _____
> _____
> _____

CHAPTER 2

YOUR 6–8 BLUEPRINT
Planning Mathematics Lessons for Coherence, Rigor, and Purpose

I was working as a long-term substitute in a sixth-grade mathematics class. During my first day, the class was very unruly. The plans I was given said to teach area, perimeter, volume, and surface area and to use certain pages in the text. With these instructions, I assumed I should go to the text and give the students the exercises on those pages. Needless to say, my lesson flopped and the students were more unruly than before. I knew I had to do something different. I was going to be there for a few weeks. That night, I went online and found a video of a teacher who had the students explore volume by giving them graph paper to fold up into a rectangular prism. The teacher in the video used centimeter cubes to fill the prism and asked questions such as, "How many cubes fill the prism?" and "How does the number of cubes that cover the base of the prism compare to the number of boxes on the graph paper?" I was so excited about this video that I set out to write a lesson for the next day that used the ideas from this video. I intentionally let the students work in pairs, each pair with their own graph paper and set of cubes. I wrote out the questions that were at the heart of what I wanted them to discover such as, "How many cubes do you think will fill your prism?" I was intentional about every step. Student involvement was a priority for me.

The next day, I implemented the lesson and the students were so involved! I was amazed how their behavior improved when they became engaged with a question to explore and a hands-on experience.

Diane Civerchia
Middle School Substitute Teacher
Kentucky

When Diane took charge as the architect of her instruction, she experienced how designing your blueprint is perhaps one of the most important jobs you can do. Throughout this book, you will have the opportunity to build grade-level mathematics lessons for your students by following the many examples presented. Together, we will explore the answers to questions such as these:

- What is coherence?

- What is rigor?

- What is the purpose of a lesson?

- How can you ensure that you plan lessons for coherence, rigor, and purpose?

Let's begin by looking at foundational planning principles of coherence and rigor. As you read, reflect upon how you currently think about your own lesson planning.

WHAT IS COHERENCE?

Coherence is probably the most crucial step in providing a quality mathematics education to students (Schmidt, Wang, & McKnight, 2005). Coherence is a logical sequencing of mathematical ideas. When lessons are coherent, they have a logical flow and are well organized to promote sense making. Lesson coherence should be both vertical and horizontal. For **vertical coherence**, you can look at the standards at the grade level before and after yours. How does your content fit in with what your students have already been taught, and how can you bridge that knowledge to what they will be learning next year? You need to consider what prior knowledge students are likely to have and where they'll be going next so that you can ensure a vertical coherence—planning lessons logically, allowing students to make sense of the mathematics across the grades. For example, Figure 2.1 shows a vertical articulation of selected 6–8 standards.

Figure 2.1

Sixth Grade	Seventh Grade	Eighth Grade
Write and evaluate numerical expressions involving whole-number exponents. Write, read, and evaluate expressions in which letters stand for numbers.	Apply properties of operations as strategies to add, subtract, factor, and expand linear expressions with rational coefficients.	Know and apply the properties of integer exponents to generate equivalent numerical expressions. For example, $3^2 \times 3^{-5} = 3^{-3} = \frac{1}{3^3} = \frac{1}{27}$.

Horizontal coherence refers to daily lesson planning. Do your daily lessons follow a logical order, a gradual building up of a concept and/or skill over time? For example, in seventh grade, understanding that the probability of a chance event is a number between 0 and 1 comes before finding the probabilities of compound events. Teaching expressions on Monday, geometry on Tuesday, and probability on Wednesday is not a logical, coherent sequence.

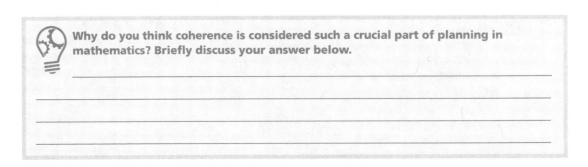

Why do you think coherence is considered such a crucial part of planning in mathematics? Briefly discuss your answer below.

_____

_____

_____

_____

WHAT IS RIGOR?

Some teachers believe planning for **rigor** means providing more difficult material or asking students to complete more problems. This is not correct. Some even say that rigor means mathematical content is accelerated. However, as Hull, Harbin Miles, and Balka (2014) explain, mathematical rigor within a classroom is actually

a direct result of active participation in deep mathematical thinking and intensive reasoning. There are dual meanings for rigor when planning great lessons. First, *content rigor* is the depth of interconnection concepts and the breadth of supporting skills students are expected to know and understand. Next, *instructional rigor* is the ongoing interaction between teacher instruction and students' reasoning and thinking about concepts, skills, and challenging tasks that result in a conscious, connected, and transferable body of valuable knowledge for every student. (p. 22)

Since rigor results from active student participation and deep mathematical thinking and reasoning, let's compare two sixth-grade examples of what it is and what it is not.

Anthony and Alex are teaching area of right triangles.

Example: Anthony

Anthony gives the following task (Figure 2.2) to his students and states, "Calculate the area of the triangles using the formula at the top of the page."

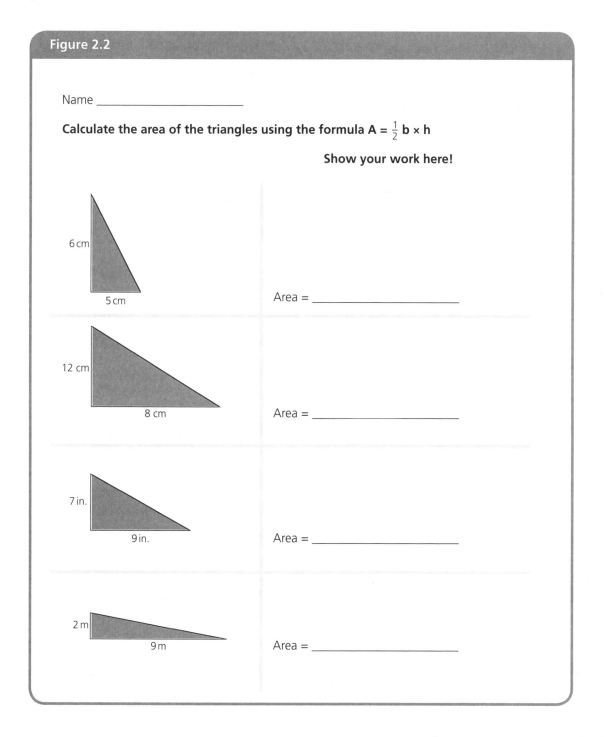

Figure 2.2

Name _____

Calculate the area of the triangles using the formula $A = \frac{1}{2} b \times h$

Show your work here!

6 cm
5 cm

Area = _____

12 cm
8 cm

Area = _____

7 in.
9 in.

Area = _____

2 m
9 m

Area = _____

Example: Alex

Like Anthony, Alex is teaching area of right triangles. He begins the lesson by asking each pair of students to draw a rectangle on graph paper. Then he gives the following set of instructions prepared on a worksheet as in Figure 2.3.

Figure 2.3

Name _____

1. Draw a rectangle on graph paper.

2. Find the area of your rectangle. Write the formula and answer here _____.

3. Draw a diagonal to divide your rectangle into two right triangles.

4. Predict the area of one of the triangles. _____ Justify your prediction. _____

5. Check the area of your triangle by counting the squares inside the triangle. How close was your prediction? _____

6. What do you notice about the area of the rectangle and the area of the right triangle? _____

7. How can we use this information to help us develop a formula for the area of a right triangle? _____

After Alex's students complete the task and discuss their thinking, Alex asks follow-up questions such as, "So what did you notice about the area of the rectangle compared to the area of the triangle?" and "How can we use that information with the formula for the area of a rectangle to generate a formula to find the area of a right triangle? Do you think this formula will work for all triangles? Why or why not?"

Both of these teachers are working with the area of a right triangle. However, Alex's lesson is more rigorous. Students in Alex's class are encouraged to think and use reasoning as they develop a conceptual understanding of area. Through the task, they have the opportunity to actively delve into the concept and have discourse that results from a shared experience. They also move from conceptual understanding of the area of a right triangle to the beginning stages of procedural fluency as they figure out the formula for the area of a right triangle. Alex then extends the thinking by asking if this works with all triangles.

On the other hand, Anthony's task does not require any reasoning. Students are simply plugging numbers into a formula, a lower-level skill that will not extend beyond the task as written. Obviously, students need the skill of calculating area from a formula, but is that all we expect? Or do we want students to go beyond calculating to understanding area and why the formula $A = \frac{1}{2} b \times h$ makes sense. Anthony's task does not encourage students to reason. His task is not rigorous.

Think about a rigorous lesson you have taught, observed, or read recently. Identify the parts of the lesson that make it rigorous. Briefly discuss your findings here.

_____

_____

_____

_____

WHAT IS THE PURPOSE OF A LESSON?

We can trace the purposes of mathematics lessons back to the National Research Council's (2001) conclusions in *Adding It Up: Helping Children Learn Mathematics*. The authors cite **conceptual understanding** and **procedural fluency** as two major strands that must be integrated into the teaching and learning of mathematics. It is important to note that not all mathematics lessons have the same purpose.

What Is Conceptual Understanding?

Conceptual understanding means comprehension of mathematical concepts, operations, and relations. It involves knowing that mathematics is more than a set of rules or procedures and really understanding what is happening in different mathematical concepts. For example, students can recognize, interpret, and generate examples of concepts and identify and apply principles, facts, definitions, and so forth. The different approaches of two more teachers, Jordan and Rashad, show what a conceptual lesson looks like and what it does not. Both are eighth-grade teachers working on the topic: Subsets of the Real Number System.

Example: Jordan

Jordan wants her students to know the subsets of the real number system. She plays a matching game with her students. Students are divided into pairs, and each pair receives a deck of cards. Students shuffle the cards and place them face down in an array. In turn, each student selects two cards to find a match between the name of a subset and a number that is part of that subset. For example, Julio chose the following two cards (Figure 2.4).

Figure 2.4

2.6	Rational number

Since 2.6 is a rational number, Julio keeps the two cards. His partner draws next and gets a –5 card and a card that says whole number. Since –5 is not a whole number, this student replaces the cards and it is Julio's turn again. Students play until all cards have been matched.

Example: Rashad

Rashad has been using Venn diagrams all school year to teach various concepts. He gives his students a list of numbers (Figure 2.5) and asks them create a Venn diagram of the real number system and place these numbers and headings where they belong.

Figure 2.5

Names of Subsets	Numbers to Place in Venn Diagram	
Natural numbers	0	$\sqrt{2}$
Whole numbers	−4	$\sqrt{9}$
Integers	100	−9.5
Rational numbers	85	π
Irrational numbers	$\frac{6}{8}$	$\frac{1}{2}$
	$7\frac{2}{3}$	−14
	89.6	
	0.3 …	

Figure 2.6 shows an example created by one student pair.

Figure 2.6

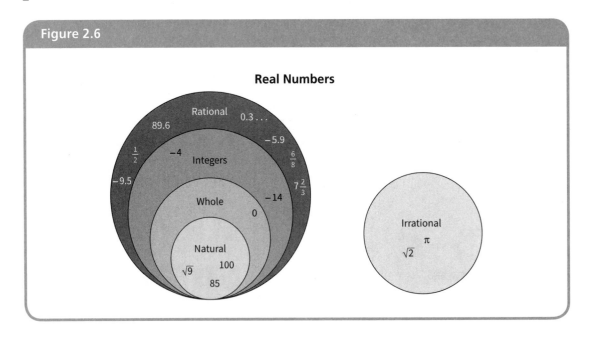

Both teachers have an eighth-grade lesson working with the subsets of the real number system. However, when you compare the lessons to the criteria of conceptual understanding—which involves students recognizing, interpreting, and generating examples of concepts, as well as identifying and applying principles, facts, and definitions—you see that only Rashad's lesson fits the criteria. His lesson was more than memorizing rules. His students could apply principles, facts, and definitions, as well as find the relationships among the subsets of real numbers.

On the other hand, Jordan's activity can be completed by students using only memorization. A more in-depth discussion of conceptual-understanding lessons appears in Chapter 5.

What Is Procedural Fluency?

Procedural fluency describes the ability to use procedures accurately, efficiently, and flexibly. Students demonstrate procedural fluency when they refer to knowledge of procedures and have skill in performing them. They transfer procedures to different problems and contexts, and they know when a strategy or procedure is more appropriate to apply to a particular situation.

A lesson that develops procedural fluency is one in which students leverage their conceptual understanding and flexibly use various strategies that they find work best for the types of problems they are solving. **Distributed practice** over time helps students become proficient with the procedures so that they are more able to understand and manipulate more complex concepts in future learning.

When you start with lessons for conceptual understanding, you use representations to help students see the meaning behind the mathematical concept. A representation that helps students understand a concept can be a reliable tool that helps them understand procedures and thus develop procedural fluency.

Example: Kathleen

Kathleen, a sixth-grade teacher, is working on integer operations with her students. She knows that some of her colleagues teach rules for adding integers and move on to the next operation, but Kathleen knows students do not always remember rules. She facilitates a conceptual-understanding lesson using two-color chips. The red side represents negative and the yellow is positive. She places them on a mat and, through questioning, has the students discover that when you put a negative with a positive, you make zero. Kathleen calls this a zero pair. Then she asks students to show 6 red and 2 yellow chips. She asks them what this represents. One student replies, "I have 2 zero pairs and 4 red chips." Kathleen agrees and further asks, "So what is the value of your chips?" Another student answers, "4 negatives." Kathleen continues the class discussion using –4 to represent 4 negative chips. She leads the students to see that they just solved the equation –6 + (+2) = –4 by showing the integers that are represented by the chips (Figure 2.7). Kathleen knows that students will refer back to this conceptual understanding of addition of integers and use this representation to support their procedural fluency.

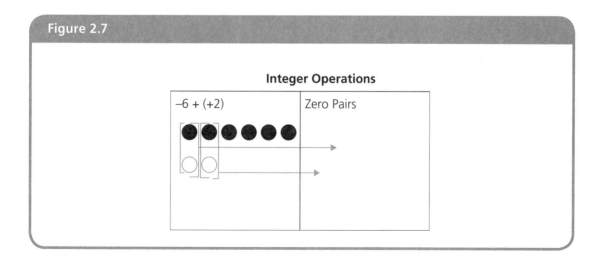

Figure 2.7

Integer Operations

–6 + (+2)	Zero Pairs

Procedural fluency lessons are discussed in more detail in Chapter 5.

What Is Transfer?

A third purpose of a lesson in mathematics is **transfer.** A transfer lesson is a lesson in which students demonstrate transfer of learning; that is, they show that they are able to effectively use content knowledge and skill in a problem situation. According to Hattie and colleagues (2016), a transfer task should encourage connections. It is a task that can be open-ended with **multiple entry points.** Hattie and colleagues (2016) also point out that transfer, as a goal, "means that teachers want students to begin to take the reins of their own learning, think metacognitively, and apply what they know to a variety of real-world contexts" (p. 175).

In a lesson designed for transfer, students make sense of a problematic situation, think about how they can apply their skills and foundational understandings to solve the problem, and reflect on their own **problem-solving** process.

Example: Shayla

To create a transfer lesson, Shayla begins with the following seventh-grade standard:

Use proportional relationships to solve multi-step ratio and percent problems.

From this standard, she decides to create a transfer lesson that asks students to demonstrate their understanding of proportional relationships and percents. She creates the following task:

You are the manager of the local smartphone store. Your boss tells you that the phone store across town has just sold 35% more phones with their new advertising campaign. To keep your job, your boss wants to see the data that show that your advertising campaign helped your store sell 35% more phones, too. Create a short report for your boss showing him the sales result from the new advertising campaign. Be sure to defend your job. Your data are summarized in the chart below (Figure 2.8). You began your advertising campaign on Monday of this week.

Figure 2.8

Day of Week	# Phones Sold Two Weeks Ago	# Phones Sold This Week
Monday	25	26
Tuesday	27	36
Wednesday	15	25
Thursday	18	24
Friday	20	27
Saturday	35	70
Sunday	30	45

For this transfer lesson, students must make sense of the data in the chart to solve the problem and use it to justify keeping their job. There are multiple entry points for this task as well as an endless number of correct responses. Students need to relate their content knowledge about multistep ratio and percent problems to their conceptual understanding of percents in order to solve the problem. This is a **metacognitive** thought process because the students must reflect on everything they have learned and pull it all together to perform the task.

Tasks in a transfer lesson may be similar to or even the same as those in a conceptual-understanding lesson. The difference is in the learning intention of the lesson. When a task is used to develop conceptual understanding, students do not have a set of efficient strategies to solve the problem. They explore, use their background knowledge, and try to figure out how to solve the problem. They may unearth new ideas and test them. When the task is used to determine if students have mastered a concept and skill at the end of a unit, students bring the conceptual understandings and skills learned in the unit and use them efficiently and effectively to solve the problem.

Transfer lessons are discussed in more detail in Chapter 5.

> **Do you think teachers plan more conceptual, procedural, or transfer lessons? Why?**
> _____
> _____
> _____
> _____

HOW CAN YOU ENSURE THAT YOU PLAN LESSONS FOR COHERENCE, RIGOR, AND PURPOSE?

Faced with so many decisions, teachers may feel forced to make daily planning decisions that individually work but, when examined together, do not promote coherence, rigor, and an overall purpose.

Lessons on a given mathematics topic need to be connected to enhance learning. They must involve a mix of conceptual understanding, procedural fluency, and transfer. When several coherent lessons on a topic come together as a whole, it is called a **unit plan.**

Eighth-grade teacher Mario was planning an equations unit. He was short on time and gathered resources from several sources to cover the 15 lessons he would need for the unit, as directed by the district's pacing guide. He found two fun activities from last year that involved graphing points to make pictures. Then he found three lessons on Pinterest where students use a graphing calculator that he knew his students would love doing and two more lessons in the textbook that asked students to solve equations. His teaching partners gave him six more lessons on using a tile manipulative for balancing equations, so he assembled a total of 13 lessons. He left two lessons open for review.

After teaching the unit, Mario reviewed the collection of lessons and reflected on the instruction. He asked himself these questions:

- Did these lessons bring rigor to the study of equations?
- Did the lessons meet/match grade-level standards?
- Did the lessons sequentially build students' mathematical understanding?
- Did the lessons connect the big ideas of equations?

While Mario felt that he did teach some successful lessons, he found that when he reviewed them as a unit, the lessons did not connect to enhance the students' learning. There was no coherence. Lessons did not build on one another but jumped from topic to topic. He decided that for next year, he will ensure that his teaching of equations is rigorous, coherent, and purposeful by redesigning the entire unit with those goals in mind.

The lesson template in this book was designed to help you plan individual lessons. As you use this template to create successive lessons, be sure to keep big ideas and standards in mind. These steps will help ensure that you create a coherent unit plan. Each chapter in Part II of this book will have a discussion on unit coherence.

Big Idea(s):

Essential Question(s):

Content Standard(s):

Mathematical Practice or Process Standards:

Learning Intention(s) (mathematical/language/social):

Success Criteria (written in student voice):

Purpose:

☐ Conceptual Understanding   ☐ Procedural Fluency   ☐ Transfer

Task:

Materials (representations, manipulatives, other):

Misconceptions or Common Errors:

Format:

☐ Four-Part Lesson   ☐ Game Format   ☐ Small-Group Instruction

☐ Pairs   ☐ Other _____

Formative Assessment:

Launch:

Facilitate:

Closure:

PART II

DRAFTING YOUR 6-8 BLUEPRINT

CHAPTER 3

LAYING YOUR FOUNDATION
It Starts With Big Ideas, Essential Questions, and Standards

As the science and mathematics teacher on my team, I am responsible for practical math, prealgebra, and Algebra I along with my science classes. At lunch the other day, I was sitting with my math and science colleagues. I mentioned to Mo, another science teacher, that I had just come up with a great essential question for our unit on matter. "How about the question, 'Does matter behave predictably?'" Mo responded that she liked it. Then Jamel, a fellow prealgebra teacher, piped in, "I didn't know you had essential questions in science, too!"

"What do you mean by 'too'? You do them in math?" I exclaimed.

"We sure do," said Jamel. "Don't you do them for your math classes? It sounds like you are really good at them!"

This conversation at lunch really had me thinking. I don't use essential questions in math. But why not? They guide my science lessons, and I always share them with my students so that we know why we are studying and doing the labs we are doing. Why did I never make that connection to math? My lessons always go fine, but I think about math skills as being needed to do the next step in mathematics. The skills build on one another. It never occurred to me that there is an overarching purpose to the mathematics skills. If I had essential questions in mathematics, it would sure help me tie the lessons together. I am going to try this!

Kim McCormick
Middle School Mathematics and Science Teacher
New Hampshire

Many teachers think about mathematics as skills, like Kim, or simply find it difficult to write essential questions for mathematics. In this chapter, we will focus on big ideas, essential questions, and standards as the building blocks of a lesson taught at the 6–8 grade levels. We will also address the following questions:

- What are state standards for mathematics?
- What are essential questions?
- What are process standards?

WHAT ARE STATE STANDARDS FOR MATHEMATICS?

For many years, research studies of mathematics education concluded that to improve mathematics achievement in the United States, standards needed to become more focused and coherent. The development of common mathematics **standards** began with research-affirmed **learning progressions** highlighting what is known about how students develop mathematical knowledge, skills, and understanding. The resulting document became known as the *Common Core State Standards for Mathematics (CCSS-M)* (National Governors Association Center for Best Practices & Council of Chief State School Officers, 2010). The landmark document was intended to be a set of shared goals and expectations for the knowledge and skills students need in mathematics at each grade level. The overall goal was college and career readiness.

Currently, the majority of states have adopted the *Common Core State Standards for Mathematics* as their own state standards. However, it is important to note that while many states adopted the *CCSS-M*, others have updated, clarified, or otherwise modified them, adopting the updated set as their new state standards. A few states have written their own standards.

Most standards documents are composed of **content standards** and **process standards** of some kind. It is important to recognize that no state standards describe or recommend what works for all students. Classroom teachers, not the standards, are the key to improving student learning in mathematics. The success of standards depends on teachers knowing how to expertly implement them. It is important as a teacher to be very knowledgeable about your own state standards and what they mean, not only at your grade level but also at the one above and below the one you teach. They are at the heart of planning lessons that are engaging, purposeful, coherent, and rigorous.

Regardless of whether your state has adopted *CCSS-M*, has modified the standards, or has written their own, the **big ideas** of 6–8 mathematics are universal. Big ideas are statements that describe concepts that transcend grade levels. Big ideas provide focus on specific content. Here are the big ideas for algebraic thinking in Grades 6 through 8.

Sixth Grade

The study of algebraic thinking focuses on variable expressions and equations. Students write and evaluate numerical expressions. Sixth graders also solve simple one-step equations such as $4x = y$ to describe relationships. This study of expressions and equations lays the foundation for the transition to algebraic representation and problem solving in later grades.

Seventh Grade

Properties of operations in Grade 7 are used to generate equivalent expressions. Students use the arithmetic of rational numbers to create expressions and equations in one variable and use these equations to solve problems. The focus on solving real-world and mathematical problems using algebraic equations lays the groundwork for eighth-grade equation work and contributes to the understanding for writing nonlinear expressions and equations in later grades.

Eighth Grade

Eighth grade builds on previous experiences and focuses on more complex equations by learning about and applying the properties of integer exponents, square and cube roots, and scientific notation. Students connect previous understandings about proportional relationships to linear equations. Systems of two linear equations in two variables are introduced with three solution strategies.

While the major topics in 6–8 algebraic thinking are the same, states may have a slightly different focus at a grade level. Compare your state standards for your grade level with the summary previously stated. Are there any differences? If so, what are they? Briefly describe them here.

_____

_____

_____

_____

WHAT ARE ESSENTIAL QUESTIONS?

It is estimated that over the course of a career, a teacher can ask more than two million questions (Vogler, 2008). If teachers are already asking so many questions, why do we need to consider essential questions? An **essential question** is a building block for designing a good lesson. It is the thread that unifies all of the lessons on a given topic to bring the coherence and purpose discussed previously. Essential questions are purposefully linked to the big idea to frame student inquiry, promote critical thinking, and assist in learning transfer. (See Chapter 5 for more information on essential questions in transfer lessons.) As a teacher, you will revisit your essential question(s) throughout your unit.

Essential questions include some of these characteristics:

- *Open-ended.* These questions usually have multiple acceptable responses.
- *Engaging.* These questions ignite lively discussion and debate and may raise additional questions.
- *High cognitive demand.* These questions require students to infer, evaluate, defend, justify, and/or predict.
- *Recurring.* These questions are revisited throughout the unit, school year, other disciplines, and/or a person's lifetime.
- *Foundational.* These questions can serve as the heart of the content, such as a basic question that is required to understand content to follow.

Not all essential questions need to have all of the characteristics. Here are some examples of essential questions for Grades 6 to 8.

- How can equations and inequalities be used to solve, model, and/or analyze mathematical situations?
- How can geometric properties be used to describe, model, and analyze situations?
- How are the situations described by equations different from the situations described by inequalities?
- How does the type of data collected affect the choice of graph used to display data?
- How do we use probability and data analysis to make predictions?
- Where are integers used in the real world?

Look at the list of sample 6–8 essential questions. Decide which characteristics describe which question. Note any thoughts or comments below.

_____

_____

_____

_____

WHAT ARE PROCESS STANDARDS?

Up to this point, we have been discussing content standards. However, every state also has a set of standards that define the **habits of mind** students should develop through mathematics. In 1989, the National Council of Teachers of Mathematics (NCTM) introduced these standards as process standards, stating that "what we teach [in mathematics] is as important as how we teach it" (NCTM, 1991), encouraging us to teach mathematics through these processes. Those standards are the following:

1. **Problem Solving:** Students use a repertoire of skills and strategies for solving a variety of problems. They recognize and create problems from real-world situations within and outside mathematics to find solutions.

2. **Communication:** Students use mathematical language, including terminology and symbols, to express ideas precisely. Students represent, discuss, read, write, and listen to mathematics.

3. **Reasoning and Proof:** Students apply inductive and deductive reasoning skills to make, test, and evaluate statements to justify steps in mathematical procedures. Students use logical reasoning to analyze and determine valid conclusions.

4. **Connections:** Students relate concepts and procedures from different topics in mathematics to one another and make connections between topics in mathematics and other disciplines.

5. **Representations:** Students use a variety of representations, including graphical, numerical, algebraic, verbal, and physical, to represent, describe, and generalize. They recognize representation as both a process and a product.

The Common Core State Standards have the eight **Standards for Mathematical Practice** (SMPs), which also describe the habits of mind students should develop as they do mathematics (National Governors Association Center for Best Practices & Council of Chief State School Officers, 2010). The following SMPs are the same across all grade levels.

1. **Make sense of problems and persevere in solving them.** Students work to understand the information given in a problem and the question that is asked. Students in Grades 6 to 8 formulate equations and inequalities to model a given situation using information in the problem and use a strategy to find a solution. They check to make sure their answer makes sense.

2. **Reason abstractly and quantitatively.** Students make sense of quantities and their relationships in problem situations. They use real numbers and variables in mathematical expressions, equations, and inequalities to represent a wide variety of real-world contexts. They examine patterns in data and assess the degree of linearity of functions. Quantitative reasoning involves creating a representation of a problem, understanding the units involved, and attending to the meaning of the quantities, not just how to compute them.

3. **Construct viable arguments and critique the reasoning of others.** Students make conjectures and build a logical progression of statements to support their conjectures. They justify their conclusions, communicate them to others, and respond to the arguments of others. They construct arguments using verbal or written explanations accompanied by expressions, equations, inequalities, models, graphs, tables, and other data displays.

4. **Model with mathematics.** Students use representations, models, and symbols to connect conceptual understanding to skills and applications. Students can apply the mathematics they know to solve problems in their everyday lives. They analyze relationships mathematically to draw conclusions and interpret mathematical results in the context of the situation and decide if the results make sense.

5. **Use appropriate tools strategically.** Students use tools when solving a mathematical problem. These tools may include pencil/paper, concrete models, ruler, protractor, calculator, spreadsheet, computer algebra system, a statistical package, or dynamic geometry software.

6. **Attend to precision.** Students learn to communicate precisely with each other and explain their thinking using appropriate mathematical vocabulary. They also calculate accurately and efficiently and express numerical answers with a degree of precision.

Standards

LI and SC

Purpose

Tasks

Materials

Student Thinking

Lesson Structures

Form. Assess.

Lesson Launch

Lesson Facilitation

Closure

7. **Look for and make use of structure.** Students discover patterns and structure in their mathematics work and use it to their advantage when solving problems. They can also articulate what they discover to share with their peers and teachers.

8. **Look for and express regularity in repeated reasoning.** Learners notice repeated calculations and begin to make generalizations. By recognizing what happens when using positive and negative exponents, students extend that understanding to more difficult problems. This standard mentions short-cuts. However, short-cuts are only appropriate when students discover them by making generalizations on their own and understand why they work.

The SMPs are not intended to be taught in isolation. Instead, you should integrate them into daily lessons because they are fundamental to thinking and developing mathematical understanding. As you plan lessons, determine how students use the practices in learning and doing mathematics.

Both sets of standards overlap in the habits of mind that mathematics educators need to develop in their students. These processes describe practices that are important in mathematics. Not every practice is evident in every lesson. Some lessons/topics lend themselves to certain practices better than others. For instance, you might use **classroom discourse** to teach a content standard through important mathematical practices.

Example: Manuel

Manuel, an eighth-grade teacher, creates a problem using exponents to have his students engage in constructing viable arguments and critiquing the reasoning of the others. He displays the following (see Figure 3.1):

Figure 3.1

$$3^0 = ?$$

$$3^1 = 3$$

$$3^2 = 9$$

$$3^3 = 27$$

$$3^4 = 81$$

Manuel then asks his students the following: "Using what you see, figure out what 3^0 is and justify your thinking." Students work in pairs to analyze the display. After a few minutes, Manuel calls the class back together for a discussion.

Manuel: So who would like to tell us something they discovered?

Betty: Well, the exponents are all in order, 0, 1, 2, 3, 4, but I never saw a zero exponent before.

Jimmy: The answers go up by multiples of 3.

Shaq: Those aren't multiples. You would have a 6 in there. But they do go up by multiplying the answers by 3. $3 \times 3 = 9$, $9 \times 3 = 27$, 27×3 is 81.

Janine: It works backward, too. $\frac{81}{3}$ is 27. $\frac{27}{3}$ is 9. $\frac{9}{3}$ is 3.

Betty: So 3^0 must be 0 because $3^1 = 3$, and if you take away another 3, you get 0.

Manuel: Does anyone else agree with Betty's thinking?

Shaq: I don't think I do. We are not subtracting; we are dividing. If you keep going backward like Janine said with division, you go $\frac{9}{3} = 3$, and $\frac{3}{3} = 1$. So 3^0 must be 1.

Through classroom discourse, Manuel asked a carefully selected question to have his students engage in constructing viable arguments and critiquing the reasoning of the others. He did not point out his students' misconceptions. He let them critique each other's reasoning. This is an example of how content can be taught through important mathematical practices.

> **Think about the process standards/mathematical practices included in your state standards. Select one and reflect on how you weave it into your lessons.**
>
> _____
> _____
> _____
> _____
> _____
> _____
> _____
> _____
> _____
> _____
> _____
> _____
> _____
> _____
> _____
> _____
> _____
> _____
> _____

It is important to note that the decision to start with a big idea, essential question, or standard is up to you. Some school systems have **pacing guides** and **district-wide curricula,** which dictate the order in which the standards must be taught. In that case, you need to do the following:

- Look at your standards and decide which big ideas it covers.
- Identify the common thread or essential question you want to weave through your lessons on this big idea.

If your district does not have a pacing guide, you may first want to select a big idea to teach and then select the state standards you will cover in the lessons.

Building Unit Coherence

One of the best ways to build coherence between and among lessons within your unit is through the big ideas, essential questions, and standards. Keep in mind that connecting individual lessons through these three main elements promotes in-depth conceptual understanding, supports coherence, and unifies individual lessons. In fact, your lessons will share big ideas, essential questions, and shared standards within one unit. A big part of creating a coherent unit is strategically deciding how these three elements will be connected. Consider mapping the three components for the entire unit as you develop the lesson plan (Figure 3.2).

Figure 3.2

Unit-Planning Template

Unit Topic:

Unit Standards	Unit Big Ideas	Unit Essential Questions

 Download the Unit-Planning Template from resources.corwin.com/mathlessonplanning/6-8

Big Ideas, Essential Questions, and Standards

The sixth-grade team, Josh and Jeff, are developing lessons to teach algebraic expressions. After discussing the ups and downs of last year's instruction, they decided to write an essential question to help focus the lesson. Josh said, "You know, Jeff, I think we may have our answer for an essential question. Remember how the students are always asking, 'When are we ever going to use this?' Why not focus our lessons on real-world situations so that our students will be able to answer their own question?" Jeff replied, "What a great idea!"

Big Idea(s):

Arithmetic concepts extend to understanding of algebraic expressions and equations.

Essential Question(s):

What are some everyday situations that can be expressed as algebraic expressions and equations?

Content Standard(s):

Write, read, and evaluate expressions in which letters stand for numbers.

Mathematical Practice or Process Standards:

Reason abstractly and quantitatively.

Attend to precision.

Look for and make use of structure.

See the complete lesson plan in Appendix A on page 188.

What kinds of essential questions can you ask that encompass big ideas in your class? Record some of your responses below.

_____

_____

_____

_____

_____

_____

_____

_____

_____

_____

The seventh-grade math team, Alix, Kyle, and Bryan, had been collaboratively planning for almost a year when a new teacher, Kia, joined them. Alix explains, "We like to start by talking about the standard first. We have noticed over the past year that we were interpreting the standard differently. Now, we take a few minutes to talk about the standard and then move onto the big ideas for the standard. This effort has kept us on the same page." Kia responds, "I appreciate that you take the time to talk about what the standard means. I know the math, but it is different when we talk about the big ideas from the standard. And I am interested in hearing everyone else's ideas."

Big Idea(s):

Students use prior understanding of the four operations with rational numbers and apply the operations in measurement contexts to solve real-world problems.

Essential Question(s):

Can an expression or equation be written to represent a real-life mathematical problem?

Content Standard(s):

Solve multistep real-life and mathematical problems posed with positive and negative rational numbers in any form (whole numbers, fractions, and decimals), using tools strategically. Apply properties of operations to calculate with numbers in any form, convert between forms as appropriate, and assess the reasonableness of answers using mental computation and estimation strategies.

Mathematical Practice or Process Standards:

Model with mathematics.

Look for and make use of structure.

Critique the reasoning of others.

See the complete lesson plan in Appendix A on page 192.

What kinds of essential questions can you ask that encompass big ideas in your class? Record some of your responses below.

_____

_____

_____

_____

_____

_____

_____

_____

_____

Eighth-Grade Snapshot

Big Ideas, Essential Questions, and Standards

Serena is the only person on her team who teaches eighth-grade math. The other core math teacher has Algebra I and geometry classes. Serena finds this difficult when planning because she always likes to bounce ideas around. Right now, she is thinking about essential questions for her graphing unit. Her standards and pacing are determined by her district curriculum and pacing guides. She participated in a workshop this summer on essential questions and remembered that the instructor offered to help anyone in the class via e-mail. Serena immediately sent an e-mail and was pleased to hear back so quickly. After she and her instructor chatted online about the role of graphing in algebra, Serena knew just what she should do.

Big Idea(s):

Functions can be represented verbally, graphically, symbolically, physically, and in a table.

Essential Question(s):

What do different shapes of graphed data tell us?

Content Standard(s):

Understand the connections between proportional relationships, lines, and linear equations.

Mathematical Practice or Process Standards:

Model with mathematics.

Look for and make use of structure.

See the complete lesson plan in Appendix A on page 203.

Are there other topics in your grade level that could be guided by an essential question? Give some examples below.

_____

_____

_____

_____

_____

_____

_____

_____

_____

Now it is your turn! You need to decide what big idea, essential question, and standards you want to build a lesson around. Start with your big idea and then identify the remaining elements.

Big Idea(s):

Essential Question(s):

Content Standard(s):

Mathematical Practice or Process Standards:

Download the full Lesson-Planning Template from resources.corwin.com/mathlessonplanning/6-8
Remember that you can use the online version of the lesson plan template to begin compiling each section into the full template as your lesson plan grows.

CHAPTER 4

REINFORCING YOUR PLAN
Learning Intentions and Success Criteria

My math team read *Visible Learning for Mathematics, Grades K–12: What Works Best to Optimize Student Learning* (Hattie et al., 2016) for a book study this year and I have to say one of the biggest impacts on our practice was the way we developed learning intentions and success criteria. We have been posting objectives for years but frankly we hadn't really engaged the students in understanding their role in learning the objectives. We realized that we need to spend some time developing learning intentions and success criteria that middle school students can understand. Bryan, a team member, brought up a great point. He said,

> We are not helping our kids see themselves in the math we are teaching. They need to be more engaged—but really we need to figure out how to engage them in owning their learning. I know we need to do more things than just this, but I think it starts with the learning intentions.

The team really came together. We decided to try them out and ask our students if they liked this. Middle school students love to be asked their opinion! The results were amazing. They really liked the success criteria. One of Bryan's students said, "I feel like I don't have to wait until the test to know how I am doing!"

Megan Murray
Primary Maths Education Instructor
England

Just as builders decide on the impact of structural changes, upgrades, and the timeline for completion, they must also envision how each of these decisions will affect the completed house. Just as builders need short- and long-term goals, teachers and students need specific learning intentions, or learning goals, that describe what you want the students to know, understand, and be able to do as a result of the learning experiences (Hattie et al., 2016). This chapter will explore the following questions:

- What are learning intentions?
- What are mathematics learning intentions?
- What are language and social learning intentions?
- How do you communicate learning intentions with students?
- What are success criteria?
- How do learning intentions connect to the success criteria?
- When should learning intentions and success criteria be shared with students?

WHAT ARE LEARNING INTENTIONS?

You begin the lesson-planning process by identifying the **learning intention**. The learning intention is "a statement of what students are expected to learn from the lesson" (Hattie et al., 2016). The learning intention serves two purposes. First, it informs your design of the learning experience by focusing you and students on deep learning rather than on completing activities. Second, it provides clarity to your students about their goal for the lesson. When students know the learning intention, they are more likely to focus on the lesson and take ownership for learning (Hattie et al., 2016). To ensure that the learning is rich and purposeful, students need to be active participants in discussing and understanding how the mathematics task or activity connects to the learning intention. Teachers design mathematics, language, and social learning intentions.

WHAT ARE MATHEMATICS LEARNING INTENTIONS?

Mathematics learning intentions are aligned to the content standards. They focus on mathematics knowledge, skills, and/or concepts. The National Council of Teachers of Mathematics' (NCTM's) (2014b) *Principles to Action: Ensuring Mathematical Success for All* identifies the importance of mathematics learning intentions in the first Exemplary Teaching Practice:

> Establish mathematics goals to focus learning. Effective teaching of mathematics establishes clear goals for the mathematics that students are learning, situates goals within learning progressions, and uses the goals to guide instructional decisions. (p. 10)

The mathematics learning intention is not a restatement of the standard. Rather, it is a scaffolded, student-friendly statement that reflects the part of the standard you are currently teaching. To design a mathematics learning intention, first begin with the standard and then construct one or more learning intentions using student-friendly language written from the students' point of view (see Figure 4.1).

Figure 4.1

Standard	Mathematics Learning Intention
Recognize and represent proportional relationships between quantities. a. Decide whether two quantities are in a proportional relationship. b. Identify the constant of proportionality (unit rate) in tables, graphs, equations, diagrams, and verbal descriptions of proportional relationships. c. Represent proportional relationships by equations. d. Explain what a point (x, y) on the graph of a proportional relationship means in terms of the situation, with special attention to the points (0, 0) and (1, r), where r is the unit rate.	I can compute unit rates. I can determine whether two quantities represent a proportional relationship. I can recognize, represent, and explain proportions using tables, graphs, equations, and diagrams. I can verbally describe proportional relationships.

You can also connect prior knowledge to mathematics learning intentions as you prompt students to share and talk about what they have already learned and how this connects to what they will be learning next. Some middle school teachers prompt students to ask questions and pose "wonders" about what they will be learning, activating students' prior knowledge and creating curiosity about new learning (Figure 4.2).

Figure 4.2

I Wonder . . .

How are the formulas for volumes of cones, cylinders, and spheres related?

How does an increase in the radius or height affect the volume?

If a sphere and a cylinder had the same radius, which would have a greater volume?

Who uses these formulas in their jobs?

WHAT ARE LANGUAGE AND SOCIAL LEARNING INTENTIONS?

Language Learning Intentions

Language learning intentions connect to the Standards for Mathematical Practice (National Governors Association Center for Best Practices & Council of Chief State School Officers, 2010), state process standards, and mathematical vocabulary. Students are expected to develop and defend mathematical arguments, understand and explain their reasoning, and critique each other's reasoning.

When you create language learning intentions in addition to the mathematics content learning intentions, you help your students develop and use rich mathematics vocabulary (Hattie et al., 2016). Middle school students need to use new mathematics vocabulary often so it can be learned, integrated, and applied. Furthermore, English Language Learners are better supported with additional opportunities to speak about mathematics.

One way you can prompt language opportunities is to encourage your students to explain and justify their thinking. By providing specific language intentions, you create expectations for all of your students for using mathematical language in your classroom. You can develop the language learning intentions for the unit and then revisit them daily as they align to the mathematics learning intentions (Figure 4.3).

Standards

LI and SC

Purpose

Tasks

Materials

Student Thinking

Lesson Structures

Form. Assess.

Lesson Launch

Lesson Facilitation

Closure

Figure 4.3

Standard	Mathematics Learning Intentions	Language Learning Intentions
Compare properties of two functions each represented in a different way (algebraically, graphically, numerically in tables, or by verbal descriptions)	I can • Compare and contrast multiple representations of (tables, graphs, equations) of two functions • Determine whether the relationship is a function • Identify the rate of change and y-intercept for a linear function	I can • Describe, compare, and explain tables, graphs, and equations • Use mathematical vocabulary like *linear function, rate of change,* and *y-intercept* accurately and in context

Social Learning Intentions

Social learning intentions also connect to the Standards for Mathematical Practice (National Governors Association Center for Best Practices & Council of Chief State School Officers, 2010) and state process standards. Social learning intentions focus on particular social skills that students need to exhibit as they work together to collaboratively solve problems and communicate their thinking. Middle school students naturally construct learning through games, collaboration, and problem solving in formal and informal settings. Since learning is socially constructed through communication and collaboration with others (Vygotsky, 1978), you can tailor these social learning intentions to reflect what your students specifically need. For instance, you can construct your social learning intentions to highlight the social skills your students need so they can work together to solve problems (Hattie et al., 2016). As with the language learning intentions, you can develop social learning intentions for the unit and specify the particular intentions you want students to work toward.

Example: Andy

Andy, a sixth-grade teacher, has been steadily working on helping his sixth graders solve problems in cooperative problem-solving groups. He decides to include four social learning intentions (Hattie et al., 2016) to target his sixth graders' listening skills (see Figure 4.4).

Figure 4.4

Learning Intentions for Cooperative Group Problem Solving

We are learning to do the following:

• Listen when others are speaking

• Look at our group members when they are speaking

• Ask a question about what our group members shared with us

• Summarize what we heard our group members say

Example: Bianca

Bianca is one of many teachers responsible for integrating the Standards for Mathematical Practices (National Governors Association Center for Best Practices & Council of Chief State School Officers, 2010) and other state process standards that ask students to "construct viable arguments and critique the reasoning of others" (para. 3). To address this, she regularly arranges her seventh graders in pairs to help solve a "debate" between two fictitious students who cannot agree on a mathematical solution. This debate was inspired by Ridgeway, Swan, and Burkhardt's (2001) thinking routine, Always, Sometimes, or Never True (Figure 4.5).

Figure 4.5

Who Wins the Debate?

Mariella and Mona were having a debate. Mariella says that she has a trick for comparing number values. She says that when comparing two numbers, the one with the greater number of digits ALWAYS has the greater value. Mona disagrees and says this is SOMETIMES true. Who is right? Be prepared to present your thinking to another pair of students.

Bianca's students must work together to understand the reasoning presented by the students in the example, explain their own reasoning to each other, come to an agreed-upon decision, and present their solution to another pair of students. Without such clear social and language learning intentions, the students might become confused about Bianca's expectation for this learning activity and miss out on important learning.

HOW DO YOU COMMUNICATE LEARNING INTENTIONS WITH STUDENTS?

As you think about how to share learning intentions with your students, consider the way in which you communicate how the learning intentions reflect your beliefs about your students. By using positive and accessible language to frame what the students will learn, you can use learning intentions "as a means for building positive relationships with students" (Hattie et al., 2016, p. 48).

Consider two ways in which you might discuss the following place value standard and learning intentions.

Standard: Understand that the probability of an event is a number between 0 and 1 that expresses the likelihood of the event occurring. Larger numbers indicate greater likelihood. A probability near 0 indicates an unlikely event, a probability around $\frac{1}{2}$ indicates an event that is neither unlikely nor likely, and a probability near 1 indicates a likely event.

Learning Intentions: We are learning to do the following:

- Explain why the numeric probability of an event must be between 0 and 1
- Explain the likeliness of an event occurring based on probability

Now look at Figure 4.6. Which dialogue would you use to convey the intentions to students?

Standards

LI and SC

Purpose

Tasks

Materials

Student Thinking

Lesson Structures

Form. Assess.

Lesson Launch

Lesson Facilitation

Closure

Figure 4.6

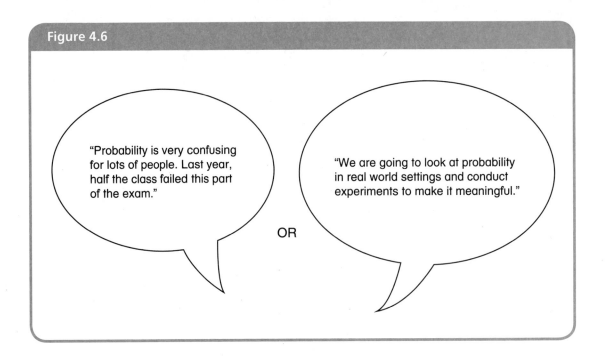

You can develop and post the language and social learning intentions for a series of lessons or the unit. Some teachers like to post the language and social learning intentions as they introduce the unit to the students. It can be particularly beneficial to focus on these learning intentions at the beginning of the year as you develop students' collaborative problem-solving and communication skills.

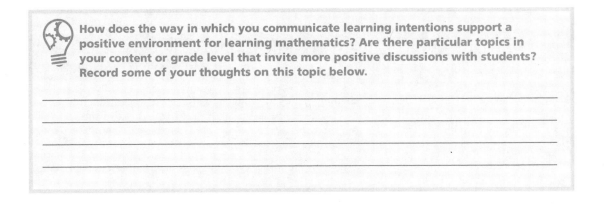

How does the way in which you communicate learning intentions support a positive environment for learning mathematics? Are there particular topics in your content or grade level that invite more positive discussions with students? Record some of your thoughts on this topic below.

WHAT ARE SUCCESS CRITERIA?

Students also need to know how to tell when they have learned the mathematics. While learning intentions provide the purpose of the learning, the **success criteria** describe what the learning looks like when students understand and can do the mathematics they are learning. Clear success criteria can increase learner motivation because students know when they have learned and do not need to rely on a sticker, smiley face, or checkmark. Success criteria also prompt deeper, more meaningful learning because teachers can make sure that the success criteria mirror the learning intentions and their students' learning needs. While all students are guided by the same learning intentions, you can differentiate the success criteria to match your learners (Wiliam, 2011).

HOW DO LEARNING INTENTIONS CONNECT TO THE SUCCESS CRITERIA?

It is also critical for you to include the students in understanding, monitoring, and celebrating achievement of the success criteria. Hattie and Yates (2013) identify five learning components that are valuable to determining learning intentions and success criteria:

1. *Challenge.* Teachers must construct learning experiences that appropriately mix what students know with what they do not know.

2. *Commitment.* Teachers should also develop lessons that engage students' commitment to the learning.

3. *Confidence.* Students and teachers need to have confidence that the students will be able to learn the material. Confidence can be generated from the students' prior learning experiences, the teacher's skill in listening and providing targeted feedback, the selection of appropriate lesson tasks, and appropriate peer feedback.

4. *High expectations.* Teachers need to have high expectations for all students and believe that they can and will learn.

5. *Conceptual understanding.* Students need to be able to develop rich understanding of mathematics content.

As you write success criteria, be sure to use student-friendly language that focuses specifically on indicators of success.

Example: Rodrigo

When Rodrigo writes success criteria for his sixth graders, he uses the same success criteria stem ("I know I am successful when …") to purposely trigger students' ownership. He then revisits the success criteria in individual progress conferences with students who struggle. During these conferences, he first focuses the students on the successes they have achieved. Then he identifies one or two criteria they have not *yet* achieved. Rodrigo emphasizes the word *yet* to help his students understand that they are on their way. Together, Rodrigo and his students determine strategies for improvement.

WHEN SHOULD LEARNING INTENTIONS AND SUCCESS CRITERIA BE SHARED WITH STUDENTS?

Your decisions about when to share the learning intentions and success criteria with your students should depend solely on the purpose of your lesson. If you are presenting a problem or task for students to investigate because you want them to explore mathematics concepts first, then you should withhold the mathematics learning intention until later in the lesson. Once the mathematics learning intention is revealed, you can and should refer to the learning intention throughout the lesson.

Example: Maria

Maria, an eighth-grade teacher, posts the mathematics learning intention for problem-solving lessons but keeps it covered up until the point in the lesson when students begin to develop conceptual understanding and make connections. When her students see that a new learning intention has been posted and covered up, they get excited because they know they will be exploring and problem solving. In a very strategic way, Maria is communicating to the students that they are expected to solve the problem using multiple solutions, representations, and explanations. Once the mathematics learning intention is revealed, you can and should refer to the learning intention throughout the lesson.

Standards

LI and SC

Purpose

Tasks

Materials

Student Thinking

Lesson Structures

Form. Assess.

Lesson Launch

Lesson Facilitation

Closure

How can you communicate success criteria with your students? Record a few of your ideas below.

_____

_____

_____

_____

Building Unit Coherence

The focus on learning intentions and success criteria provides another good way to construct coherence across your lesson plans. Many of your learning intentions, particularly the language and social learning intentions, will be reflected over a longer time period, making this an ideal way to support coherence across your unit plan. As you design your lesson, keep a running list of those learning intentions and success criteria that students accomplish throughout the unit. Many teachers post the success criteria for the entire unit to help students see and understand what they are working toward.

Notes

_____

_____

_____

_____

_____

_____

_____

_____

_____

_____

_____

_____

Josh and Jeff are discussing their success criteria. Jeff says, "I really want our sixth graders to be aware when they have successfully achieved the objectives for the algebra unit." Josh replied, "Last year we wrote our success criteria and let our students know what they were but we did not really focus on them throughout our teaching of algebra."

Jeff responded, "I agree with you. We wrote the success criteria in our plans but barely mentioned them as we were teaching our lessons. What about posting them as we start our unit? And, because our social learning intentions are almost the same for several topics, this will help us to spotlight our success criteria and stay focused." Josh agrees, "I like your idea! Let's do it!"

Learning Intention(s):
Mathematical Learning Intentions

We are learning to:
- Write expressions that record operations with numbers and letters standing for numbers. For example, "subtract y from 5" as 5 - y.

Language Learning Intentions

We are learning to:
- Use the terms algebraic expression, sum, term, product, factor, quantity, quotient, coefficient, constant, like terms, equivalent expressions, and variables appropriately

Social Learning Intentions

We are learning to:
- Listen to the ideas of others
- Respectfully disagree with the mathematical arguments of others

Success Criteria
(written in student voice):

I know that I am successful when I can:
- Read and write expressions with letters standing for numbers
- Evaluate expressions for specific values
- Apply the order of operations to algebraic expressions
- Use the terms algebraic expression, sum, term, product, factor, quantity, quotient, coefficient, constant, like terms, equivalent expressions, and variables appropriately in writing and speaking
- Listen to the ideas of others
- Respectfully disagree with the mathematical arguments of others

See the complete lesson plan in Appendix A on page 188.

How could you communicate learning intentions and success criteria with your students? Record some of your ideas below.

_____

_____

_____

_____

_____

Standards

LI and SC

Purpose

Tasks

Materials

Student Thinking

Lesson Structures

Form. Assess.

Lesson Launch

Lesson Facilitation

Closure

The seventh-grade math team, Kia, Alix, Kyle, and Bryan, has been working on bringing forward the language learning intentions. All of them have been working hard on developing students' use of vocabulary and increasing discourse opportunities. They know that when students have more time to talk about their ideas, they are more engaged and seem to remember more. Kyle suggests, "What if we have the students reflect on their development regarding the language learning intentions? We could ask them to think about how they engage in discourse!" Alix replies, "Love this! I think our students are ready for this!"

Learning Intention(s):
Mathematical Learning Intentions

We are learning to:

- Represent equivalent forms of numbers
- Write an equation to represent a real-world problem
- Apply properties of operations

Language Learning Intentions

We are learning to:

- Use the terms relationship and equation
- Explain how an equation represents a real-world problem

Social Learning Intentions

We are learning to:

- Listen to the ideas of others
- Respectfully disagree with the mathematical arguments of others

Success Criteria (written in student voice):

I know that I am successful when I can:

- Write an equation, table, and graph for a linear relationship
- Recognize a linear, nonlinear, and no relationship from a graph
- Use the terms relationship and equation
- Explain how an equation represents a real-world problem
- Listen to the ideas of others
- Respectfully disagree with the mathematical arguments of others

See the complete lesson plan in Appendix A on page 192.

How could you communicate learning intentions and success criteria with your families? Briefly write some ideas below.

_____

_____

_____

_____

_____

_____

Learning Intentions and Success Criteria

Serena's team attended a workshop on learning intentions and success criteria last summer. While no one teaches the same content as Serena, she knows that the idea is the same for all content, so she is happy that her team leader, Bruce, has scheduled learning intentions as the topic for their next team meeting. She has been feeling alone lately with no one teaching her content and wondering if her students feel like her math classes are part of the team.

At the meeting, Bruce shared, "My students have been a little confused about my learning intentions and success criteria. Last week, one asked me if they were being tested on them and said in other classes they didn't have learning intentions." Maria, the team English teacher, commented, "Maybe we should have a standard team practice. We could devote one bulletin board in each of our rooms for the intentions and criteria. I am willing to design the boards and then all we have to do is add our own intentions and criteria and change them as needed." Serena exclaimed, "I think that is a great idea! It would make my classes feel more a part of the team by adding this consistency. It would also help if we framed our statements in the same manner." Everyone agreed.

Learning Intention(s):

Mathematical Learning Intentions

We are learning to:

- Write an equation, table, and graph for a linear relationship
- Recognize a linear, nonlinear, and no relationship from a graph

Language Learning Intentions

We are learning to:

- Use the terms relationship, linear equation, and nonlinear relationship appropriately

Social Learning Intentions

We are learning to:

- Listen to the ideas of others
- Respectfully disagree with the mathematical arguments of others

Success Criteria (written in student voice):

I know that I am successful when I can:

- Write an equation, table, and graph for a linear relationship
- Look at a graph and tell if there is a linear, nonlinear, or no relationship
- Use the terms relationship, linear equation, and nonlinear relationship appropriately when I communicate with others in writing or speaking
- Listen to the ideas of others
- Respectfully disagree with the mathematical arguments of others

See the complete lesson plan in Appendix A on page 203.

Consider the process standards that you are required to use. How could you communicate the success criteria to your students? Write some of your ideas below.

_____

_____

_____

_____

Standards | LI and SC | Purpose | Tasks | Materials | Student Thinking | Lesson Structures | Form. Assess. | Lesson Launch | Lesson Facilitation | Closure

Your turn! Construct learning intentions and success criteria for the standard you previously identified.

Learning Intentions (mathematical/language/social):	Success Criteria (written in student voice):

online resources ☞ Download the full Lesson-Planning Template from resources.corwin.com/mathlessonplanning/6-8
Remember that you can use the online version of the lesson plan template to begin compiling each section into the full template as your lesson plan grows.

DECIDING ON PURPOSE
Why Are You Building This Lesson?

I was very specific about the purpose of a lesson I taught recently. This is a heterogeneous, 50-minute, seventh-grade mathematics class, and the topic was generating linear equations from tables. In the past, creating a table and then using the data in the table to create an equation was difficult for the students. This year, I was very deliberate in giving the students a model of a function machine to simulate the input and output data to place in the table. I used a shoebox that was lying around in my classroom. We put in a number and the "machine" shot a number out. For example, when we put in a 12, out came a 24. When we input a 9, the output was 18. When we put in an x, the output was 2x. The students understood exactly what to do, and they were able to determine what was happening "inside the function machine" in order to generate equations. I intentionally took the lesson slow, step by step, and was rewarded with the students understanding the process. When a few were struggling, the others took it upon themselves to help. As an added reason for wanting to learn this material, I told the students that they would be responsible for teaching this material to the one student, Chris, who was absent the day of the lesson.

I am thinking that the time I took to examine what I had done to teach this lesson in the past and the time to try to come up with a purposeful lesson using a model the students could see was worth it.

Shelley Rea Hunter
Mathematics Instructor
New Brunswick, Canada

Writing a series of learning intentions and success criteria from your standards is only the beginning of lesson planning. Your learning intentions inform the *purpose* of each lesson. As mentioned in Chapter 2, there are three types of mathematics lessons organized by purpose: conceptual understanding lessons, lessons that bring about procedural fluency, and transfer lessons. Think of each of these as a room in the house you are building. Just as each room in a house has a different purpose (e.g., a kitchen is built for food preparation), each lesson should have a purpose (e.g., a transfer lesson is designed to let students pull together and apply the previous learning).

This chapter will focus on answers to the following questions:

- What is the role of a conceptual understanding lesson?

- What is procedural fluency, and how does it build from a conceptual understanding lesson?

- How do you know if you need a conceptual understanding or procedural fluency lesson?

- How do you create a transfer lesson?

The National Research Council (2001) recommends five strands of proficiency that should be integrated into the teaching and learning of mathematics. These include the following:

Conceptual understanding. Comprehension of mathematical concepts, operations, and relationships

Procedural fluency. The skill in carrying out procedures flexibly, accurately, efficiently, and appropriately

Strategic competence. The ability to formulate, represent, and solve mathematical problems

Adaptive reasoning. The ability to think logically, reflect, explain, and provide justification

Productive disposition. The inclination to see mathematics as sensible, useful, and worthwhile, coupled with a belief in diligence and one's own efficacy

These five strands of proficiency underlie the three types of mathematics lessons: conceptual understanding, procedural fluency, and transfer.

WHAT IS THE ROLE OF A CONCEPTUAL UNDERSTANDING LESSON?

As described in Chapter 2, conceptual understanding involves comprehension of mathematical concepts, operations, and relations. The National Assessment of Educational Progress's definition of conceptual understanding includes students demonstrating that they can recognize and generate examples of concepts using multiple representations (Braswell, Dion, Daane, & Jin, 2005). In addition, students compare and contrast concepts, operations, and relations.

Conceptual understanding lessons focus on providing opportunities for students to make sense of the mathematics they are learning. Students need an abundance of time and contexts to develop conceptual understanding. Therefore, your lessons need to provide time for students to build ideas, engage in discourse about the mathematics they are learning, represent their thinking in multiple ways, and translate **representations** to abstract ideas.

Your learning intentions, which come from your standards, help you decide if you need a conceptual lesson. For example, learning intentions that include verbs such as *understand, explain, relate, compose/decompose, represent,* and so forth imply that you want your students to show evidence that they can recognize, label, and generate examples of concepts. Your learning intentions indicate that you want a conceptual lesson to involve students' reasoning in settings where they must make sense of concepts, relations, or representations. What follows are examples of learning intentions for Grades 6 to 8 that call for a conceptual lesson along with a conceptual task.

Sixth-Grade Standard: Represent three-dimensional figures using nets made up of rectangles and triangles and use the nets to find the surface area of these figures. Apply these techniques in the context of solving real-world and mathematical problems. See Figure 5.1.

Figure 5.1

Learning Intentions	Conceptual Tasks
Students understand that a net is a two-dimensional representation of a three-dimensional figure.	**What Is It?** Show students nets of pyramids and prisms and have them visualize what the net could be. Distribute paper copies of nets for triangles and rectangles and have students cut, fold, and tape the nets into three-dimensional figures. Ask the students how their visualizations matched up with the final figures.

Figure 5.1 *(Continued)*

Learning Intentions	Conceptual Tasks
Students use nets to understand the meaning of surface area.	**Deconstructing a Box** Working in pairs, students take commonly used boxes (cereal boxes, shoe boxes, etc.) and cut them apart on the edges. The faces then open to form a net of the box. Have students calculate the area of each face and add them together. Ask the students to discuss what the final sum represents.
Students solve mathematical problems using nets.	**How Many Can You Find?**  Provide each small group with a cube and graph paper. Ask them to hypothesize how many different nets fold up to create a cube. After the hypothesis, groups work to find as many nets as they can that fold up to create a cube. How many are there? Can you generalize a rule to recognize if a net will fold into a cube?
Students solve real-world problems using surface area.	**Justify Your Response** Leo was told that the net has a surface area of 100 cubic centimeters. Is this true? Justify your response. 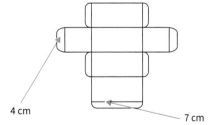 4 cm 7 cm

Standards

LI and SC

Purpose

Tasks

Materials

Student Thinking

Lesson Structures

Form. Assess.

Lesson Launch

Lesson Facilitation

Closure

Seventh-Grade Standard: Understand that rewriting an expression in different forms in a problem context can shed light on the problem and how the quantities in it are related. *For example, a + 0.05a = 1.05a means that "increase by 5%" is the same as "multiply by 1.05."* See Figure 5.2.

Figure 5.2

Learning Intentions	Conceptual Tasks
Students understand that expressions can be written in different forms.	**Match Me** Have students work in pairs to cut out and match the equations and expressions with their equivalent forms. Have students justify each matching.

2x	(x + 2) – 9	Increase by 5%	Ratio of 8 more than a number to the number
x – 7	Twice a number	8 more than a number divided by the number	The ratio of a number to 3
1.05x	$\frac{x}{3}$	$\frac{x + 8}{x}$	The quantity of 2 more than a number minus 9
x + 0.05x	Multiply a number by 1.05	A number divide by 3	Double a number

Learning Intentions	Conceptual Tasks
Students understand that rewriting a problem is a tool for making sense of a problem.	**The Parking Lot Problem** The length of the school parking lot is 40 yards longer than its width. The maintenance department wants to put a fence around the lot. Express the perimeter of the parking lot as an expression. Students rewrite this as: Find the distance all the way around the parking lot. Length is 40 yds. + w. (Width is w.)

Eighth-Grade Standard: Construct and interpret scatter plots for bivariate measurement data to investigate patterns of association between two quantities. Describe patterns such as clustering, outliers, positive or negative association, linear association and non-linear association. See Figure 5.3.

Standards

LI and SC

Purpose

Tasks

Materials

Student Thinking

Lesson Structures

Form. Assess.

Lesson Launch

Lesson Facilitation

Closure

Figure 5.3

Learning Intentions	Conceptual Tasks
Students interpret graphs.	**Where Is This Plane Going?** 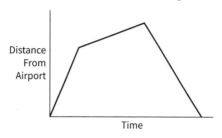 A. A plane takes off from the airport and climbs to 30,000 feet. Once at this altitude, it makes a slow and steady climb to 35,000 feet. At 35,000 feet, engine problems dictate that the pilot make a quick landing at the nearest airport. B. A plane takes off from the airport and climbs to 30,000 feet. Once at this altitude, it makes a slow and steady climb to 35,000 feet. At 35,000 feet, engine problems dictate that the pilot return to the airport.
Students analyze patterns of association.	**Sorting Graphs** Randomly display 12 different scatterplots. Three of the scatterplots should show a positive linear association, 3 should show a negative linear association, 3 should show a nonlinear association, and 3 should show clustering. Ask the students to work with a partner to sort the plots. Have a class discussion where students justify their sorts. At the end of class, you can label the graphs with the correct vocabulary.

While conceptual knowledge is an essential foundation, procedural fluency has its own prominent place in the mathematics curriculum. For years, there was debate in the mathematics education community over which is more important, conceptual understanding or procedural fluency. When procedural fluency involves more than simply memorizing formulas and performing steps to an algorithm, conceptual understanding and procedural fluency have a balanced role to play in a student's mathematics education. All students need to be flexible in their thinking and know more than one way to perform a procedure. In addition, they should be able to select the most appropriate procedure for the situation (National Research Council, 2001). For example, Juliane, a seventh-grade teacher, gives her students this problem:

> The inside of a closet needs to be painted. The closet is 12 feet tall × 10 feet wide × 8 feet deep. Calculate the area that needs to be painted, including the ceiling and floor. Be prepared to defend your method.

After the students complete the work, Juliane leads a whole-class discussion where students defend the method they used to calculate the surface area.

Juliane: Who would like to share their solution and strategy?

Marco: We calculated 592 square feet. We did it by doing 2(8 × 10) + 2 (12 × 10) + 2 (8 × 12).

Juliane: Thank you, Marco. Did anyone else do it differently?

Cesar: We got 592 square feet too, but it took us a lot longer.

Juliane: Explain it to us.

Cesar: First we drew a picture so we would not forget anything and put the 12, 10, and 8 in it. Then we did the front of the closet 12 × 10 = 120. Then we did the back, which was also 12 × 10 = 120. Next was the ceiling, which was 12 × 8 = 96, and the floor, which was also 12 × 8 = 96. Finally, we did the side walls and got 8 × 10 = 80 and 8 × 10 = 80. Then we added up all the areas and got 120 + 120 + 96 + 96 + 80 + 80 = 592 square feet. (Note: Cesar displayed his group's work.)

Juliane: Thank you. We have two different methods but the same answer. Anyone want to comment on these two methods?

Ian: Marco's was shorter.

Lisel: It was shorter but wasn't it really the same thing?

Juliane: What do you mean by that?

Lisel: I think when Cesar's group adds 120 and 120 that is like when Marco's group wrote 2 (12 × 10) because 12 × 10 is 120.

Juliane: Because Cesar's was longer, does that make it wrong?

Micah: No, he still got the same answer but it just took longer.

Juliane: Since both methods work, which method would you rather use if you had a job to figure out surface area all day long?

Marco: I'd rather use my way because it is quicker. (The rest of the class nods and murmurs in agreement.)

The students demonstrated that there are two different ways to calculate surface area. However, Juliane leads the discussion toward discovering that Marco's method is the more efficient of the two. From here, she will encourage students to use the more efficient method, especially since there is an understanding that the two methods are really the same.

In their 2014 position statement on procedural fluency, the National Council of Teachers of Mathematics (NCTM) defines procedural fluency as "the ability to apply procedures accurately, efficiently, and flexibly; to transfer procedures to different problems and contexts; to build or modify procedures from other procedures; and to recognize when one strategy or procedure is more appropriate to apply than another" (NCTM, 2014b).

This definition involves more than memorization and more than knowing when to apply a given algorithm in a particular situation. From our example, we can see that Juliane's students were able to recognize when one strategy was more efficient than another.

To develop procedural fluency, students need to experience integrating concepts and procedures. According to the mathematical teaching practices listed in *Principles to Actions: Ensuring Mathematical Success for All* (NCTM, 2014b), procedural fluency builds from conceptual understanding:

> Effective teaching of mathematics builds fluency with procedures on a foundation of conceptual understanding so that students, over time, become skillful in using procedures flexibly as they solve contextual and mathematical problems.

In Juliane's example, it is clear that her class had experience drawing figures, finding the area of each face, and then adding them together to determine surface area, as evidenced by Cesar's solution. This shows a conceptual understanding of what is meant by surface area, the sum of the areas of all the faces of a figure. Lisel discovered that this could be simplified into the formula that Marco used. As Juliane continues to move the discussion in the direction of efficiency, she reiterates that both methods work but has the students question which they would rather use for efficiency. Marco's method, as Lisel pointed out, was rooted in the conceptual understanding of surface area. Research backs up this sequencing of lessons, suggesting that once students memorize and practice a particular procedure or **algorithm**, they have little interest in learning how the procedure ties back to any concepts (Hiebert, 1999). Conceptual understanding lessons provide the foundation for flexible thinking with procedures, as in the example with Juliane. For this reason, conceptual understanding lessons precede procedural fluency lessons. However, it is possible that you will need to go back and forth between conceptual and procedural lessons to help students make the connections.

Effective procedural fluency lessons connect procedures with the related concepts. Representations and discourse are the mortar that binds the lessons together. For example, let's look at a procedure that students in Grade 6 would be familiar with: order of operations. One example of a procedural lesson for order of operations involves asking students to complete a worksheet of 20 equations that involve applying the order of operations. A different lesson might center on the task shown in Figure 5.4.

Figure 5.4

Thomas solved the following equation. Here is his work:

$$20 + 3 \,(2.6 - 1.2)$$
$$23 \,(2.6 - 1.2)$$
$$23 \times 1.4$$
$$32.2$$

Thomas made a mistake. Find the correct answer. Write Thomas a letter explaining his error and how to correct it.

Student response:

Thomas,

You made a big mistake. Don't you know your order of operations? We always multiply before adding. You added 20 and 3 first but the problem is asking for three groups of what is inside the parentheses. You were supposed to go inside the parentheses first and subtract the 1.2 from the 2.6. You get 1.4 like you did, but then you multiply 1.4 times 3 to get 4.2. Then add 20 + 4.2 and get 24.2 as your final answer.

Standards

LI and SC

Purpose

Tasks

Materials

Student Thinking

Lesson Structures

Form. Assess.

Lesson Launch

Lesson Facilitation

Closure

In the Thomas task, the student used discourse to connect his procedural knowledge to his understanding of equations. He explained what he knows. At the same time, the teacher can be investigating any common errors/misconceptions about order of operations and solving equations. Students have an opportunity to justify their procedures and practice at the same time. This practice is brief, engaging, and purposeful. **Discourse** (written or spoken) allows students to link their conceptual understanding to the procedure.

The other lesson, the worksheet of 20 equations, does not tie into students' conceptual understanding of equations. The lesson may be ineffective and lead to **math anxiety** as per the findings of Isaacs and Carroll (1999). Computational methods that are overpracticed without understanding are forgotten or remembered incorrectly. This leads to student **misconceptions** (see Chapter 8).

The 20-equation worksheet scenario is an example of a traditional drill. **Drill** and **practice** are assignments often given to students to develop their procedural fluency. Traditionally, the terms *drill* and *practice* have been used synonymously. However, there is a difference. Practice, as noted previously, should be brief, engaging, and purposeful. Practice involves spreading out tasks or experiences on the same basic idea over time. Practice allows students the opportunity to solidify the conceptual understanding as the foundation for the procedures. The Thomas problem is an example of practice; students are being asked to solidify their reasoning of the procedure for solving equations. There is only one problem as opposed to 10, 20, or more, which is characteristic of drill. Drill refers to repetitive exercises designed to improve skills or procedures already known. It is a myth that drill is a learning tool. Drill is intended to be repetitive practice of what a student already knows.

> 💡 **Think of a computation lesson you have read in a textbook or other source. How does it fit (or not fit) this summary on mathematical fluency? Note your answer here.**
>
> _____
>
> _____
>
> _____
>
> _____

HOW DO YOU KNOW IF YOU NEED A CONCEPTUAL UNDERSTANDING OR PROCEDURAL FLUENCY LESSON?

Your standards and learning intentions give you direction as to whether a lesson should be for conceptual understanding or procedural fluency. Standards and learning intentions that focus on understanding mathematics call for a conceptual lesson. A few examples of how the standard dictates the type of lesson are shown in Figure 5.5.

Figure 5.5

Standard	Conceptual Understanding	Procedural Fluency
Compute fluently with multi-digit numbers.		✓
Use random sampling to draw inferences about a population.	✓	
Analyze linear equations.	✓	
Find common factors and multiples.		✓

Notice that some standards easily point to a purpose because they use the words *analyze* or *compute*. However, other standards are not as obvious. Let's look at a standard that does not make the choice of a conceptual or procedural lesson clear:

Graph proportional relationships interpreting the unit rate as the slope of the graph.

For this standard, we need to look at our learning intentions. We can unpack this standard into several learning intentions:

- Understand proportional relationships.
- Graph linear equations.
- Understand unit rate mathematically and in real-world situations.
- Interpret slope as a unit rate.
- Calculate slope using a formula.

These mathematical learning intentions indicate that for students to master the standard, they must engage in conceptual understanding *and* procedural fluency lessons.

> **Look at the standards you are about to teach. Collaborate with a colleague and decide what the purpose of the lessons should be to meet those standards. Note the key points from your discussion here.**
>
> _____
> _____
> _____
> _____
> _____
> _____
> _____
> _____
> _____
> _____
> _____
> _____

How Do You Create a Transfer Lesson?

Transfer is the primary goal of all instruction: to ensure that students are able to use what they have learned in the real world. This goal informs the third type of lesson in mathematics: transfer. While there are many different interpretations of transfer, we refer to a transfer lesson as one in which students demonstrate a transfer of learning (their ability to effectively use conceptual knowledge and procedural fluency skills in a problem situation). In Chapter 1, we discussed the definition by Hattie et al. (2016) of a transfer task as one that should encourage connections and be open-ended with multiple entry points.

So, the question you must ask yourself in planning for transfer is, "What is the understanding that my students will need in the future when they are no longer in school?" This should remind you of the essential questions discussion in Chapter 3. While your conceptual understanding and procedural fluency lessons are based on your learning intentions, your transfer lessons are based on your essential questions. After all, if you don't design lessons for transfer, why design lessons at all? If people know how to use a hammer and nails, it does not mean they can build a house. Likewise, if students know how to add or subtract, it does not mean they can balance a checkbook.

Standards

LI and SC

Purpose

Tasks

Materials

Student Thinking

Lesson Structures

Form. Assess.

Lesson Launch

Lesson Facilitation

Closure

To decide if you have created a transfer lesson, use the checklist in Figure 5.6.

Figure 5.6

Rubric for Creating a Transfer Lesson

Does the lesson allow students to	Yes or No
• make sense of a real-world problem as opposed to a contrived word problem?	
• persevere in solving the problem?	
• apply mathematical reasoning?	
• reason abstractly and quantitatively?	
• use appropriate tools strategically?	
• work with content of the big ideas or essential questions of the topic taught?	
• construct viable arguments or critique the reasoning of others?	

 Download the Rubric for Creating a Transfer Lesson from
resources.corwin.com/mathlessonplanning/6-8

Figure 5.7 shows examples of transfer tasks for Grades 6 to 8 based on essential questions.

Figure 5.7

Sixth-Grade Essential Question	Transfer Task
How does the study of ratios and proportions help solve real-world problems?	Janelle regularly purchases ginger ale at Sav-A-Lot for $0.99 a liter bottle. This week, Sav-A-Lot announces a sale on ginger ale at 3 one-liter bottles for $5.00. Advise Janelle. Should she take advantage of the sale? Or should she complain to management about the sale? Put your advice in writing with your reasoning.

Figure 5.7 *(Continued)*

Seventh-Grade Essential Question

How does statistics help us answer real-world questions?

Transfer Task

Begin with a question that you are curious about. Conduct a statistical study by collecting, organizing, and analyzing your data to answer your question. Prepare a presentation to the class that includes your question and identifies your population, your sampling method, your graph, and the justification for your conclusion.

Eighth-Grade Essential Question

What are the advantages of representing the relationship between quantities symbolically, graphically, verbally, or in a table?

Transfer Task

Nicolai is starting his own delivery business. He will pick up and deliver anything! He charges a flat fee of $200 for use of the truck with an additional $0.60 per mile charge from the pickup to the delivery location. Nicolai hires you to advertise his new business and prices. Use the information on his pricing and represent it in graphic, symbolic, verbal, and chart form. Decide which form has the most advantages to get Nicolai's business the most customers. Create an advertising poster using this form and write Nicolai a report justifying your reasons for selecting this form.

Go back to the essential question and transfer task for your grade level. Apply the checklist and reflect on how each item fits the task. Summarize your thoughts below.

_____
_____
_____
_____
_____
_____
_____
_____
_____
_____

Standards

LI and SC

Purpose

Tasks

Materials

Student Thinking

Lesson Structures

Form. Assess.

Lesson Launch

Lesson Facilitation

Closure

Building Unit Coherence

Connecting lesson purposes across a unit develops coherence because you are strategically linking conceptual understanding, procedural fluency, and transfer lessons to build comprehensive understanding of the unit standards. As you develop a lesson, consider the purposes of the lessons that come before and after the lesson you are constructing. Over the course of one unit, you should develop and facilitate lessons with all three purposes, bearing in mind how and when the lesson purposes should be positioned within the unit. Some teachers map out their unit with lesson purposes in mind to ensure that they are developing coherence within lesson purpose (Figure 5.8).

Figure 5.8

Unit:

Day 1	Day 2	Day 3	Day 4	Day 5
Conceptual	Conceptual	Conceptual	Procedural fluency	Procedural fluency

Day 6	Day 7	Day 8	Day 9	Day 10
Conceptual	Conceptual	Conceptual	Procedural fluency	Transfer

Now that you have been introduced to the three lesson purposes, reflect on the lessons in your curriculum guide, textbook, or supplemental materials. Can you categorize the lessons into these three categories? Do you notice one type being more prevalent than the others? Note any thoughts or concerns here.

_____

_____

_____

_____

_____

_____

_____

_____

_____

_____

_____

Sixth-Grade Snapshot

Lesson Purpose

Josh and Jeff are glancing at their last year's lesson plans. Josh comments, "In thinking back to last year's instruction, I know we should have spent more time practicing translating word problems into algebraic expressions. That is what they missed the most on the end of the year exam." Jeff commented, "I am not sure we need more time with the concept, but we could help those students in a small group setting that were struggling with the procedure." "I think that's what was missing!" exclaimed Josh.

Purpose:

☐ Conceptual Understanding   ☑ Procedural Fluency   ☐ Transfer

See the complete lesson plan in Appendix A on page 188.

How do you decide on the purpose for your lessons? Write your thoughts below.

_____

_____

_____

_____

_____

_____

_____

_____

_____

_____

_____

_____

_____

_____

_____

_____

_____

_____

_____

_____

_____

_____

Lesson Purpose

Kyle shared, "I am comfortable with planning conceptual and procedural lessons. All of the lessons we planned have turned out well. It seems like I never get to these transfer lessons. Could we plan a transfer lesson for one of the problem-solving standards? If we built some time in now, we could make sure that students have an opportunity to apply what they have learned in a real-world problem." Bryan responded, "I think this will help them connect their learning to real-world problems, which will motivate them and help them remember the concepts."

Purpose:

☐ Conceptual Understanding   ☐ Procedural Fluency   ☑ Transfer

See the complete lesson plan in Appendix A on page 192.

How do you decide on the purpose of your lessons? Write your thoughts below.

_____

_____

_____

_____

_____

_____

_____

_____

_____

_____

_____

_____

_____

_____

_____

_____

_____

_____

_____

_____

_____

_____

Standards

LI and SC

Purpose

Tasks

Materials

Student Thinking

Lesson Structures

Form. Assess.

Lesson Launch

Lesson Facilitation

Closure

Eighth-Grade Snapshot

Lesson Purpose

Serena believes that middle school students need to understand mathematics before they learn procedures. She adopted this philosophy over her 15 years of teaching. She used to teach very traditionally with only procedures. After attending professional development activities provided by her district, she slowly tried new things in the classroom: problem solving, exploration, and hands-on lessons. Now she understands that students need to connect understanding to procedures, so she decides that this first lesson in the unit needs to be conceptual.

Purpose:

☑ Conceptual Understanding   ☐ Procedural Fluency   ☐ Transfer

See the complete lesson plan in Appendix A on page 203.

This eighth-grade unit begins with a conceptual lesson. Would there ever be a time when you might begin with a procedural fluency or transfer lesson? Why? Explain your thinking below.

_____

_____

_____

_____

_____

_____

_____

_____

_____

_____

_____

_____

_____

_____

_____

_____

_____

_____

_____

_____

_____

_____

_____

_____

Chapter 5 ■ Deciding on Purpose **65**

Now it is your turn. Decide on the purpose of the lesson you are designing.

Purpose:

☐ Conceptual Understanding   ☐ Procedural Fluency   ☐ Transfer

online resources Download the full Lesson-Planning Template from resources.corwin.com/mathlessonplanning/6-8
Remember that you can use the online version of the lesson plan template to begin compiling each section into the full template as your lesson plan grows.

Notes

CHAPTER 6

CHOOSING TASKS
The Heart of a Lesson

As a beginning sixth-grade mathematics teacher, I remember that my main concern was always behavior. After that, my next recollection is teaching numerous lessons on ratios, proportion, and percents. Much emphasis, back then, was placed on mentally calculating percent of a number using 10%, 25%, and 50% as anchors. For example, a typical question would be, "What is 30% of 35?" Students who were able to do this mentally would respond, "I know that 10% of 35 is 3.5 so I multiplied 3.5 three times and got 10.5."

I realize now I was on the right track by helping my students understand how percents related to one another. Unfortunately, my method of helping the students who struggled was to generate more drill problems for them to practice. When I reflect back on these lessons, I realize my lessons must have been tedious for many of my students. We practiced percent examples day after day until I thought every student had mastered the skill. Not only was this boring for me (and probably my students) but not everyone actually did master the skill. What could I have done differently? I wish now that I could have written or found problems that all students

could work, that is, with multiple entry points. As a beginning teacher, where could I find these types of problems?

Karen Dorgan
Retired Math Instructor
Alabama

> **Karen has many good questions. What she is searching for are worthwhile tasks. A worthwhile task is the heart of a lesson. In fact, selecting the task is the most important decision teachers make that affects instruction (Lappan & Briars, 1995; Smith & Stein, 2011).**
>
> **This chapter will address the following questions:**
>
> - Why are tasks important?
> - What is a worthwhile task?
> - How do you adapt a task?
> - What are some sources for worthwhile tasks?

WHY ARE TASKS IMPORTANT?

Effective teachers understand that the **tasks** they choose influence how their students make sense of mathematics. Tasks should challenge students to explore mathematical concepts; they should not be designed simply as work to get the right answer. Getting students to use **higher-order thinking skills**, such as those from Bloom's Taxonomy (create, evaluate, apply, etc.), is a hallmark of a worthwhile task. As you plan your lessons, be sure to select tasks to reach this goal. Consider the following two examples.

Example 1: Jose

Jose gives his eighth-grade students this problem (see Figure 6.1):

Figure 6.1

Find the volume of a cylinder with a height of 7 ft. and a circumference of 3.5 ft.

Find the volume of a cone with a base circumference of 3.5 ft and a height of 7 ft.

Example 2: Carin

Carin asks her eighth graders to do the following:

She gives pairs of students nets for cones and cylinders and a bag of rice. Each paired cone and cylinder have the same base and height measurements. Students are asked to fold the nets and then estimate how many times you can fill the cone with rice and pour into the cylinder to fill the cylinder. Students record their estimates and then perform the experiment. Students then complete the recording sheet in Figure 6.2.

Figure 6.2

Name _____

Cylinders vs. Cones

1. Estimate how many cones filled with rice are needed to fill up the cylinder. _____

2. How many actual times did you fill the cone to fill the cylinder? _____

3. The formula for the volume of a cylinder is the area of the base times the height. B × h = V (cylinder)

4. Using what you learned in this experiment, write a formula for the volume of a cone. Justify your formula.

These two examples illustrate the types of questions that teachers ask about formulas for volume. Only one is an example of a worthwhile task. The following section will identify the characteristics of a worthwhile task. Keep Jose and Carin's problems in mind as you read through the characteristics to determine for yourself who had the worthwhile task.

WHAT IS A WORTHWHILE TASK?

There are seven characteristics of worthwhile tasks:

1. Uses significant mathematics for the grade level
2. Rich
3. Problem solving in nature
4. Authentic/interesting
5. Equitable
6. Active
7. Connects to process standards and/or mathematical practices

   Let's take a look at each feature in more detail.

Uses Significant Mathematics for the Grade Level

The big ideas, essential questions, and standards from your lesson should be your guiding light for finding a worthwhile task; these three elements keep your lesson plan coherent. Tasks based on significant mathematics focus on students' understandings and skills, and they stimulate students to make sense of the mathematics they are learning. A task should take into account students' prior knowledge and the understandings and skills already taught at this grade level or previous grades.

Rich

Each task should be challenging, requiring students to use higher-order thinking skills. Smith and Stein (1998) refer to this kind of task as a **high-cognitive-demand task**. According to Van de Walle et al. (2013), "A high cognitive demand task is a task that requires students to engage in a **productive struggle** that challenges them to make connections to concepts and to other relevant knowledge" (p. 37). A high-cognitive-demand task encourages students to represent their thinking in multiple ways, explore various solution pathways, and connect procedures to mathematics. These tasks always call for some degree of higher-level thinking, and students cannot routinely solve them. Students often use multiple representations such as manipulatives or diagrams to help develop the meaning of mathematical ideas and to work through the task to develop the understanding (Smith & Stein, 2011). If students immediately know the answer, then the task was not challenging.

Problem Solving in Nature

When a task is problem solving in nature, students will not know how to immediately and routinely solve it. They will need to reason and develop a new strategy or try previously learned strategies to seek a solution. Simply applying an algorithm to arrive at the answer is not problem solving. Productive struggle is a hallmark of problem solving. This means that students wrestle with a solution strategy and must apply effort to make sense of the mathematics—to figure something out that is not obvious. The challenge may not come easy to them, but they persevere. Good problems have multiple entry points so that all students have an opportunity to learn. It is important to point out that all worthwhile tasks are problems, but not all problems are worthwhile tasks.

Authentic/Interesting

An authentic and interesting task is one that represents mathematics as a useful tool for navigating the real world. It captures students' curiosity and invites them to make conjectures. Authentic/interesting tasks prompt classroom discourse and pique student interest either through the topic or the method of engagement.

Standards

LI and SC

Purpose

Tasks

Materials

Student Thinking

Lesson Structures

Form. Assess.

Lesson Launch

Lesson Facilitation

Closure

Equitable

When a task is equitable, it has multiple entry points and representations so that students of all levels, abilities, and skills can access the task. NRICH (McClure, Woodham, & Borthwick, 2011), from the University of Cambridge, describes these kinds of tasks as having low threshold and high ceilings (LTHC), and Jo Boaler (2015) describes them as having low floors and high ceilings. Essentially, this means that when a task is equitable, "everyone in the group can begin and then work at their own level, yet the task also offers lots of possibilities for learners to do much more challenging mathematics, too" (McClure, Woodham, & Borthwick, 2011, para. 6). The content can be fairly simple, but the processes and the thinking that students do are much more complex. Some students may solve a task using manipulatives or drawing pictures while others apply symbols at a more abstract level. The task is also nonbiased, meaning it does not contain information that stereotypes individuals or groups of people, and it is culturally sensitive. The teacher honors and respects all students' ideas and solution pathways. Everyone has an opportunity to learn.

Active

With an active task, students are engaged in doing the mathematics. They are decision makers. An active task requires more than simply applying an algorithm. Students must develop reasons, offer explanations, and actively figure things out to make sense of the task and its solution.

Connects to Process Standards and/or Mathematical Practices

The tasks you select should be designed to encourage students to exhibit process standards. Sometimes, teachers believe the way to challenge learners is by presenting them with higher-level content. However, this act alone does not necessarily support all students to reason, communicate mathematically, use and apply representations, see and use patterns, and recognize the underlying structure of the mathematics they are learning. By ensuring that a task incorporates opportunities for students to demonstrate process standards, you support their learning.

To determine if a task is worthwhile for you to use in a lesson, use the rubric shown in Figure 6.3. The first column identifies the characteristic, and the next three columns allow you to rate the degree to which you feel the task has met that characteristic by checking the box, with three being not acceptable and one being a good example of that characteristic. The final column is for any comments you would like to discuss with your colleagues. Note, you may deem a task worthwhile even if you do not rate all of the characteristics as a one. Not all worthwhile tasks will have all of the characteristics.

Figure 6.3

Determining a Worthwhile Task Rubric

Characteristic	1 (Highest Rating)	2	3 (Lowest Rating)	Notes
Uses significant mathematics for the grade level				
Rich				

Figure 6.3 (*Continued*)

Characteristic	1 (Highest Rating)	2	3 (Lowest Rating)	Notes
Problem solving in nature				
Authentic/ interesting				
Equitable				
Active				
Connects to Standards for Mathematical Practice or Process Standards				

online resources Download the Determining a Worthwhile Task Rubric from
resources.corwin.com/mathlessonplanning/6-8

> Thinking about Jose and Carin and their tasks, rate the tasks using the checklist in Figure 6.3. Discuss your results with a colleague. Whose example is a worthwhile task and why? Note your thoughts below.
>
> _____
> _____
> _____
> _____

HOW DO YOU ADAPT TASKS?

You may have experienced a time when you encountered a textbook or school district task that did not match the multiple needs of your learners. Many teachers choose to adapt tasks to increase the cognitive demand (Smith & Stein, 2011) and to provide more entry points for students to reason mathematically. Here are a few examples.

Example: Michael

Michael, a sixth-grade teacher, found the task in Figure 6.4 in his textbook and adapted it to incorporate process standards.

Figure 6.4

Original Task	Adapted Task
Use the data below to answer each question. 20 21 23 24 27 33 34 35 36 38 40 41 42 43 46 52 53 1. What is the median? 36 2. What is the mode? none 3. What is the range? 33	The sixth graders in Mrs. Hernandez's three math classes were fundraising for a field trip. Each class collected a mean of $80.00. There are 15 students in each class. Mrs. Hernandez noticed that while the means were the same, there was a big difference in the distribution of money collected by each student. Some students collected more money than others. Write three possible sets of data that could represent the money collected by the students in each of Mrs. Hernandez's three classes.

Example: Marina

Marina, a seventh-grade teacher, was given the task in Figure 6.5 by her school district. She wanted to design a low-floor, high-ceiling task to provide more entry points for her students.

Figure 6.5

Original Task	Adapted Task
Rudy rents bicycles at the beach. He charges a flat fee of $15 to get the bicycle and $5 per hour. How much does he charge for 1 hour? 3 hours? 10 hours? N hours?	Miguel's family went to dinner at a local hamburger restaurant. Miguel received his first drink free but had to pay $1.25 for each drink after the first. Miguel told his math teacher, Ms. Houston, about this. She turned it into a math problem for her students to solve. She asked the students to write an expression that models the drink policy at the local restaurant. • Craig wrote $1.25d − $1.25 where d is the number of drinks. • Jenny wrote $1.25d where d is the number of drinks. • Katrina wrote $1.25 (d − 1) where d is the number of drinks. Who is correct? How do you know?

Example: Antoine

Antoine, an eighth-grade teacher, found the original task in Figure 6.6 after an Internet search.

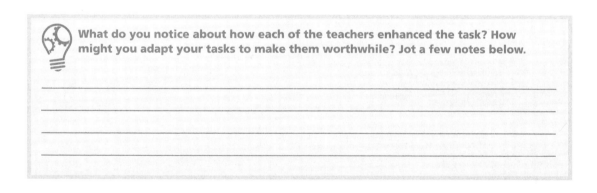

Figure 6.6

Original Task	Adapted Task
Find the volume of the cylinder:	Pictured is a cylinder with a volume of 180π cubic inches.
	What is one possible set of dimensions for this cylinder? Justify your conclusion.

What do you notice about how each of the teachers enhanced the task? How might you adapt your tasks to make them worthwhile? Jot a few notes below.

_____

_____

_____

_____

WHAT ARE SOME SOURCES FOR WORTHWHILE TASKS?

Tasks can be problems, short- or long-term projects, or games. In Chapter 5, we listed many tasks as they relate to 6–8 learning intentions. Some other reliable sources for 6–8 worthwhile tasks are as follows:

Books

Markworth, K., McCool, J., & Kosiak, J. (2015). *Problem solving in all seasons.* Reston, VA: NCTM.

Ray-Reik, M. (2013). *Powerful problem solving: Activities for sense making with the mathematical practices.* Portsmouth, NH: Heinemann.

Schrock, C., Norris, K., Pugalee, D., Seitz, R., & Hollingshead, F. (2013). NCSM *great tasks for mathematics 6–12.* Reston, VA: NCTM.

Van de Walle, J., Karp, K., & Bay-Williams, J. (2016). *Elementary and middle school mathematics: Teaching developmentally.* New York, NY: Pearson.

Standards

LI and SC

Purpose

Tasks

Materials

Student Thinking

Lesson Structures

Form. Assess.

Lesson Launch

Lesson Facilitation

Closure

Mathematics Assessment Resource Service http://map.mathshell.org/tasks.php

Balanced Assessment http://hgse.balancedassessment.org/packetms.html

Dan Meyer's Three-Act Tasks https://docs.google.com/spreadsheets/d/1jXSt_CoDzyDFeJimZxnhgwOVsWkTQEsfqouLWNNC6Z4/edit#gid=0

Robert Kaplinsky http://robertkaplinsky.com/lessons

Illuminations at NCTM https://illuminations.nctm.org

Illustrative Mathematics https://www.illustrativemathematics.org

Inside Mathematics, Problem of the Month http://www.insidemathematics.org/problems-of-the-month/download-problems-of-the-month

Mathcounts https://www.mathcounts.org

Math Pickle http://mathpickle.com

NRICH http://nrich.maths.org

Michigan Council of Teachers of Mathematics www.mictm.org

You Cubed https://www.youcubed.org/tasks

Mathalicious http://www.mathalicious.com/lessons

Phet Interactive Simulations https://phet.colorado.edu

Rich Maths Tasks to Engage http://emmaths.jfcs.org.uk/index.php/tasks

North Carolina Middle School Mathematics Course of Study http://maccss.ncdpi.wikispaces.net/MS+Mathematics

NZ Maths: The Home of Mathematics Education in New Zealand https://nzmaths.co.nz/other-resources

Rich Mathematics Tasks Exemplars http://educationaldesigner.org/ed/volume1/issue3/article9/pdf/burkhardt_09_fig3.pdf

Building Unit Coherence

Tasks are another great way to build coherence and ensure rigor throughout a unit. As you look across the unit, you can connect the tasks that you construct, select, or adapt. Some 6–8 teachers do this by extending tasks over two or three days so students have plenty of time to dive into the concept.

Notes

Sixth-Grade Snapshot — *Task Selection*

Josh and Jeff are talking about the instructional tasks they have used to teach their sixth graders. Jeff says, "I am not sure the tasks we used last year for translating expressions were rigorous." Josh replies, "I agree with you. I think we need to find or adapt some of the tasks. Remember the Soccer Kicks! worksheet we used last year? What we did with that was low level and boring. We basically just told them to look for key words."

"That's right," agreed Jeff. "What we need to do is adapt that task. Use those situations in a way that allows the students to attack those from where they are. Multiple entry points! Because we know that the mathematics is important and that our students love everything to do with soccer!"

"We could start a conceptual lesson with Algebra Tiles and then go to a procedural lesson that lets them work at their own pace to move to the abstract. Last year we just started abstractly and it was not successful."

Josh responds, "I'm in!"

> **Task:**
>
> Each small group of students will solve the problems on the worksheet entitled, Soccer Kicks! (see Figure A.1). Students may rely upon the use of Algebra Tiles early in the lesson but should move to the pictorial and abstract stage by the end of the lesson.

See the complete lesson plan in Appendix A on page 188.

 This task can be downloaded for your use at resources.corwin.com/mathlessonplanning/6-8

Why do you think this is a good sixth-grade task? Use the task checklist to help you decide. Write any thoughts or concerns below.

_____

_____

_____

_____

_____

_____

_____

_____

_____

_____

_____

_____

_____

_____

_____

"So we need to develop a task that reflects our problem-solving standard. What if we developed a series of mini-tasks and gave ourselves two days for students to solve real-world problems and apply what they learned?" Kia replied, "I love it! Do you think we could write some tasks around a pet-sitting business? Several of my students just developed their own pet-sitting business for the summer!" Kyle shared, "That is a great idea! Many of my students are talking about how they are going to babysit or mow lawns to earn money for the summer." Alix responded, "Let's get started!"

Task:

Taking Care of Teddy

Congratulations! You have just been hired for your first pet-sitting job! You have agreed to take care of Teddy the Toy Poodle for four days. You never imagined a 10-pound toy poodle would cause so many problems! You must solve every problem before Teddy's owners get back from vacation. However, Teddy's owners are very intense about Teddy's care. Each day they will text you to make sure you know what you are doing. They have also asked you to keep a journal for them to read when they get back. You must be able to answer their questions or they will find a new pet sitter!

Day One: Teddy Gets a Haircut

Today, Teddy has an appointment with the groomer to get his fur trimmed. Teddy's owners left $50 for you to pay the groomer. The cost of the grooming is $35.50. You have been instructed by the owners to leave a 15% tip on the cost of the grooming. You also want to buy a chew toy for $5.99. The tax rate in Teddy's state is 7.5%. Do you have enough money to get the chew toy? Write an equation to represent this situation. Then explain how the equation matches the story.

Teddy's owner texts to check on how you are doing. You tell her all about the grooming and chew toy. She texts:

New Message

To:
There is no sales tax in the state we are visiting. How much more money would you have? Prove how you know!

Day One

Day Two: Keeping Teddy Out of the Living Room

Every time you leave Teddy, he chews up something in the living room. Yesterday, it was a pillow in the living room. Today, he knocked over a picture frame. You notice a dog gate in a box and decide to put up a gate to block Teddy from getting into the living room. You need to make sure the gate is centered correctly in the middle of the doorway. The doorway is $34\frac{3}{4}$ inches wide. The gate is $22\frac{1}{2}$ inches. How long will the bars that attach to the gate need to be? Write an equation to represent this situation. Then explain how the equation matches the story.

Teddy's owner texts to check on how you are doing. You tell her all about the gate!

Day Three: Teddy's Special Food

Teddy needs special food to stay healthy. You must mix his food in just the right way or Teddy will have terrible tummy troubles.

Directions: Get the 3-gallon container of DOGGY dry dog mix, which has 20% chicken, which is Teddy's favorite ingredient. Then, add the bag of PUPPY dry mix that has 30% chicken. You should now have a 10-gallon container mixed with DOGGY and PUPPY dry mix. Write an equation to describe the relationships between the different dog mixes. Then explain how the equation matches the story. What percent of the final dog food mixture is chicken?

Teddy's owner texts to check on how you are doing.

(Continued)

Standards

LI and SC

Purpose

Tasks

Materials

Student Thinking

Lesson Structures

Form. Assess.

Lesson Launch

Lesson Facilitation

Closure

Day Four: Teddy Goes to the Dog Park

You promised Teddy's owners you would take Teddy to the dog park, but you have been warned that Teddy cannot walk more than three miles or his little joints will ache. The owners want Teddy to walk as close to three miles as possible. When you get to the dog park, there are four paths.

- Path A: 0.24 mile
- Path B: $\frac{1}{2}$ mile
- Path C: 0.6 mile
- Path D: 500 yards

Select the paths or combination of paths that will allow you to walk Teddy as close to 3 miles as possible.

Write an equation to represent this situation. Then explain how the equation matches the story.

Teddy's owner texts to check on how you are doing. You tell her all about dog walk. She texts:

New Message

To:
Do you mind finding a couple other combinations for me? I would love to have some variety on our walks. Prove how you know.

Day Four

See the complete lesson plan in Appendix A on page 192.

 This task can be downloaded for your use at resources.corwin.com/mathlessonplanning/6-8

Why do you think this is a good seventh-grade task? Use the checklist to help you decide. Write any thoughts or concerns below.

_____

_____

_____

_____

_____

_____

_____

_____

_____

_____

| Standards |
| LI and SC |
| Purpose |
| **Tasks** |
| Materials |
| Student Thinking |
| Lesson Structures |
| Form. Assess. |
| Lesson Launch |
| Lesson Facilitation |
| Closure |

Eighth-Grade Snapshot
Task Selection

Serena knows that middle school students need to be actively engaged in their learning. They do well with authentic problems and exploratory activities, so she went online to some trusted sources and found a task that she felt met all the criteria of a worthwhile task. She modified it to be exploratory because this type of lesson meets the needs of the early adolescent.

She did this by adding questions to the lesson such as, "Can you sort these graphs? Do you see any similarities?"

> **Task:**
>
> Each pair of students graphs data from one of nine different situations (see situations in Figure A.5). Three situations are linear relationships, three are nonlinear, and three have no relationship. Pairs post the graphs of their situations. In pairs, students sort the graphs based on the shape of the data. After sorting, there is a class discussion about what the shape of the data means.

See the complete lesson plan in Appendix A on page 203.

 This task can be downloaded for your use at resources.corwin.com/mathlessonplanning/6-8

Why do you think this is a good eighth-grade task? Use the checklist to help you decide. Write any thoughts or concerns below.

_____
_____
_____
_____
_____
_____
_____
_____
_____
_____
_____
_____
_____
_____
_____
_____
_____
_____
_____
_____

Using your lesson plan that is under construction, add a task. Be sure it follows from your previous work and matches your instructional purpose.

Task:

 Download the full Lesson-Planning Template from resources.corwin.com/mathlessonplanning/6-8
Remember that you can use the online version of the lesson plan template to begin compiling each section into the full template as your lesson plan grows.

CHAPTER 7

CHOOSING MATERIALS
Representations, Manipulatives, and Other Resources

According to the Virginia Mathematics Standards, students learn that the procedure to multiply fractions is numerator times numerator and denominator times denominator. Last week, my class used visual arrays to show how and why this standard algorithm works. A few kids were not getting the visual of using arrays, so we tried folding paper. For example, if you have the problem $\frac{1}{2} \times \frac{3}{4}$, you are really asking yourself, "What's $\frac{1}{2}$ of $\frac{3}{4}$?" I asked the kids to take a piece of paper and fold it into fourths. Then I had them fold a piece back to show $\frac{3}{4}$ of the whole.

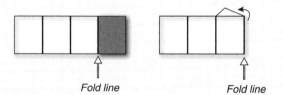

Fold line   *Fold line*

I asked my students to find $\frac{1}{2}$ of what they had by folding the $\frac{3}{4}$ in half.

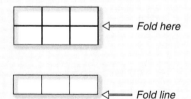

← Fold here

← Fold line

"How many pieces do you see?" They answered, "Three." We opened up the paper to see how many pieces made a whole, which was 8. Eyes lit up when students realized that they could actually represent a multiplication problem through folding a piece of paper. They really enjoyed uncovering the meaning of multiplication of fractions and asked to do a few more examples (although kids really struggled when it came to folding things into thirds!). They also learned that the denominators represented the area of the whole and that the numerators represented the area of what was shared.

When the class was over, I realized I had three or four students who still did not understand the concept of multiplying fractions. What other hands-on resources are there that I can use to reach my students? Are there visual models? I wonder what technology is available that I can use. Should I use another model with all of my students or just the ones that are struggling to understand?

Denika Gum
Sixth-Grade Teacher
Virginia

Resources vary. They can include anything from models or manipulatives, the amount of time devoted to mathematics, or your district-wide textbook. Resources can include teacher aides or special education collaborative teachers who join your class for certain lessons. Technology can vary from hardware, such as calculators, laptops, tablets, and document cameras, to software and applications. Likewise, models and manipulative materials can vary from school to school. This chapter focuses on the resources that can help you create a rigorous and coherent set of math lessons. This chapter will answer these questions:

- What is the role of representations in mathematics lessons?

- What is a manipulative/model?

- How are manipulatives/models used?

- What are other resources?

The Annenberg Learner Foundation (2003) offers this definition:

> "Mathematical representation" refers to the wide variety of ways to capture an abstract mathematical concept or relationship. A mathematical representation may be visible, such as a number sentence, a display of manipulative materials, or a graph, but it may also be an internal way of seeing and thinking about a mathematical idea. Regardless of their form, representations can enhance students' communication, reasoning, and problem-solving abilities; help them make connections among ideas; and aid them in learning new concepts and procedures. (para. 2)

Mathematical concepts are abstract and can be difficult to get across to students. Representations of these concepts can be helpful. Representations can be thought of as a broad category of models. According to Van de Walle, Karp, and Bay-Williams (2016), there are seven ways to represent or model mathematical concepts:

1. Manipulatives

2. Pictures or drawings

3. Symbols

4. Language (written or spoken)

5. Real-world situations

6. Graphs

7. Tables

Selecting a representation is a vital part of your decision making while lesson planning. You must decide, "What representations will help me achieve the learning intentions of today's lesson?" Here is an example of a teacher using a representation to help students make sense of absolute value.

Example: Alfonso

Alfonso, a sixth-grade teacher, showed his students this number line to teach that **absolute value** is the distance from zero on the number line.

Alfonso asks his students to work with a partner to answer the following questions using the number line:

What is the opposite of a?

What is the opposite of f?

What is the opposite of h?

What is the opposite of c?

After the students share and discuss their responses, Alfonso asks this follow-up question: What do you notice about the relationship of your pairs of opposites to the number line? During the class discussion of this question, Alfonso guides his students to discover the concept that each number in a given pair of opposites is the same distance from zero on the number line. Once students have this understanding, Alfonso introduces the symbol | | for absolute value using the letters along with the vocabulary term *absolute value*. For example, he shows that $|a| = 2$ and $|e| = 2$. He then replaces the letters on the number line with integers and encourages the students to use the absolute value symbol with the integers such as $|-6| = 6$, $|9| = 9$, $|5| = 5$.

In this example, Alfonso used a number line with letters as a representation for students to discover the concept of absolute value.

The charts in Figures 7.1, 7.2, and 7.3 show examples of representations that can be used with selected standards.

Standards
LI and SC
Purpose
Tasks
Materials
Student Thinking
Lesson Structures
Form. Assess.
Lesson Launch
Lesson Facilitation
Closure

Figure 7.1

Sixth Grade

Selected Sixth-Grade Standards	Representation/Tools
Use a visual fraction model and equation to represent division of fractions in a story problem such as: How much pizza will each person receive if 3 people share $\frac{1}{2}$ of a pizza?	**Pattern Blocks: Hexagon Represents the Whole Pizza** 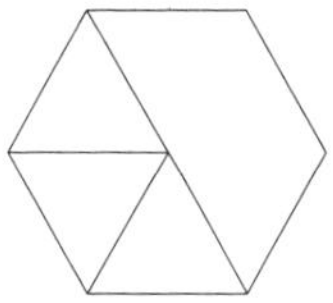
Represent inequalities on a number line.	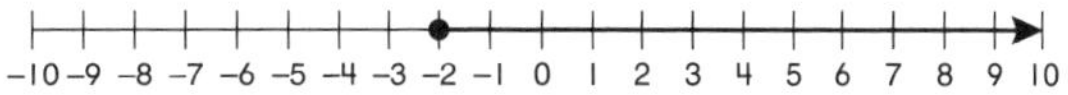
Represent 3-dimensional figures using nets.	**Net of a Triangular Prism** 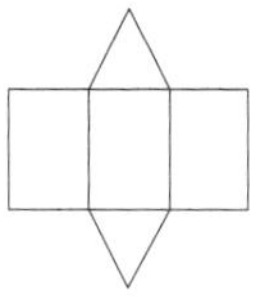
Understand positive and negative numbers as integers.	**Two-Color Counters** 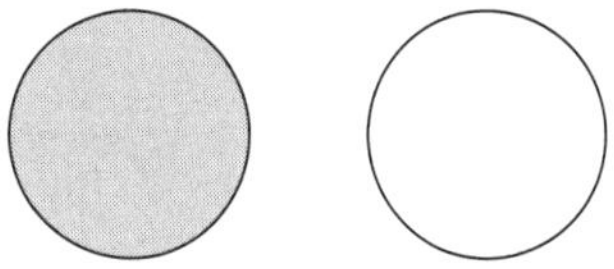
Understand the volume formula V = bhw.	**Cubes** 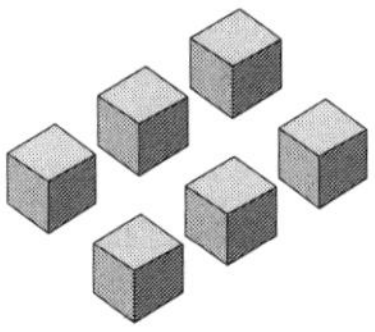

Figure 7.2

Seventh Grade

Selected Seventh-Grade Standards	Representation/Tools
Construct geometric shapes using a protractor and ruler.	**Protractor** 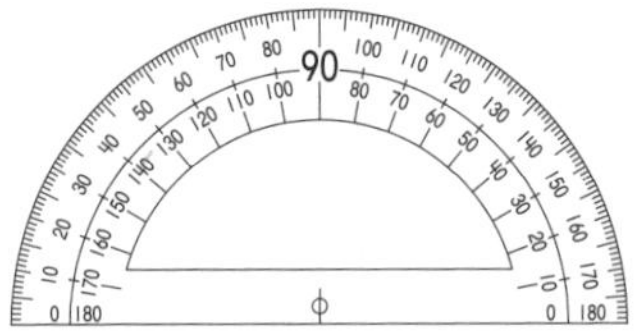
Describe the 2-dimensional figures that result from slicing 3-dimensional figures.	**Foam Cylinder** 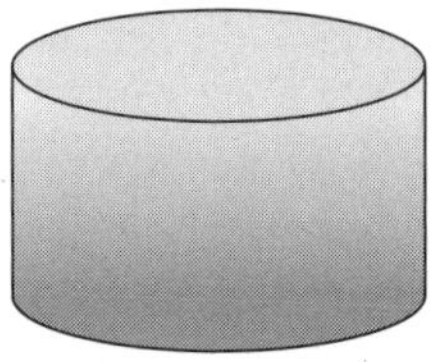
Understand the probability of a chance event.	**Spinners, Cards, and Coins**   

Image sources: Cards: carol_woodcock/iStock.com; Penny: MisterVector/iStock.com

Figure 7.2 (*Continued*)

Selected Seventh-Grade Standards	Representation/Tools
Demonstrate addition and subtraction of integers.	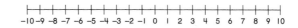
Describe situations where opposite quantities combine to make 0.	**Two-Color Counters**  Source: EAI Education QuietShape Foam Double-Sided Two-Color Counters: Red/Yellow. EAI Education: www.eaieducation.com.

Figure 7.3

Eighth Grade

Selected Eighth-Grade Standards	Representation/Tools
Describe the effects of translations, dilations, rotations, and reflections on 2-dimensional figures by viewing examples in real world context.	**Wallpaper Samples** Image source: S-S-S/iStock.com
Express numbers in scientific notation.	**Place Value Chart**

Place Value Chart

thousands	hundreds	tens	ones	tenths	hundredths	thousandths
10^3	10^2	10^1	10^0	10^{-1}	10^{-2}	10^{-3}
3	2	4	7	5	6	8

(*Continued*)

Figure 7.3 (*Continued*)

Selected Eighth-Grade Standards	Representation/Tools
Estimate square roots.	**Using a Number Line** 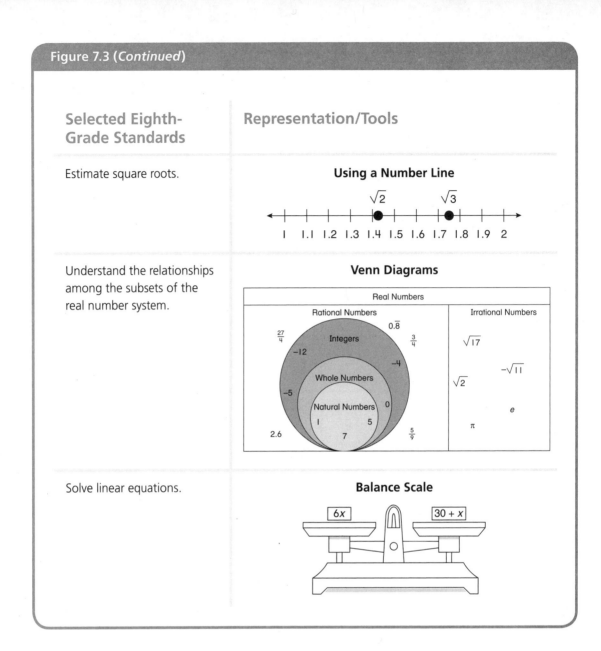
Understand the relationships among the subsets of the real number system.	**Venn Diagrams**
Solve linear equations.	**Balance Scale**

WHAT IS A MANIPULATIVE?

A **manipulative** (also called a model) is one type of representation. Generally, manipulatives are concrete objects that students use to bring meaning to abstract mathematical ideas. Some common manipulatives used in mathematics in middle school include (but are not limited to) two-color counters, pattern blocks, square tiles, wooden cubes, GeoBlocks, and base-ten materials. Figures 7.1, 7.2, and 7.3 include some manipulatives used as representations. Figure 7.4 lists some materials available commercially.

Figure 7.4

Description	Common Use	6	7	8	Picture
Algeblocks: three-dimensional shapes to model algebraic concepts	Integer operations, algebraic operations, simplifying expressions up through polynomials, solving equations	✓	✓	✓	
Algebra Tiles: two-dimensional tiles to model algebraic concepts	Integer operations, algebraic operations, simplifying expressions up through polynomials, solving equations	✓	✓	✓	
Anglegs: plastic strips of varying lengths with brads to connect the strips and create polygons	Investigating properties of polygons		✓	✓	
Base-ten blocks: proportional representations of the base-ten system	Operations with decimals	✓			

(Continued)

Standards

LI and SC

Purpose

Tasks

Materials

Student Thinking

Lesson Structures

Form. Assess.

Lesson Launch

Lesson Facilitation

Closure

Figure 7.4 (*Continued*)

Description	Common Use	6	7	8	Picture
Color cubes, tiles, squares	Volume, modeling word problems for solving equation	✓	✓	✓	
Geoboards: a pegged board for exploring polygons	Transformations, coordinate geometry, right angles	✓	✓	✓	
Hands-On Equations: systematical models solving equations using a static balance	Solving equations; introducing variables (x, 2x, etc.), simplifying equations and expressions	✓	✓	✓	Image source: Hands-On Equations™ Learning System. Copyright © 2016 Borenson and Associates.
Two-color counters	Integer operations	✓	✓		

Not all manipulatives/models need to be commercially produced. For example, marshmallows and straws or toothpicks are useful tools to construct polyhedra, and floral foam cones are very useful when slicing three-dimensional figures to see the two-dimensional shapes that result. A flat piece of wood on top of a coffee cup creates an acceptable stable balance for modeling equations. Templates for pattern blocks and fraction circles can be found online.

Virtual manipulatives are available online for little or no cost. A virtual manipulative is described as "an interactive technology-enabled visual representation of a dynamic mathematical object including all of the programmable features that allow it to be manipulated, that presents opportunities for constructing mathematical knowledge" (Moyer-Packenham & Bolyard, 2016). This includes objects embedded in online games. Virtual manipulatives are not static computer pictures because they are interactive. Research has shown that virtual manipulatives are effective representations to focus on understanding and to practice procedural skills.

Reimer and Moyer (2005) described a study that showed statistically significant gains in students' conceptual knowledge using virtual manipulatives. In an investigation of K–8 teachers, Moyer-Packenham, Salkind, and Bolyard (2008) concluded that "virtual manipulatives provide that additional tool for helping students at all levels of ability to develop their relational thinking and to generalize mathematical ideas" (p. 202). Research by Steen, Brooks, and Lyon (2006) indicates that the use of virtual manipulatives as an instructional tool was extremely effective.

The following sites are free or inexpensive sources for virtual materials:

Algebra 4 All Social Network (http://a4a.learnport.org/page/algebra-tiles)

National Library of Virtual Manipulatives (http://nlvm.usu.edu/en/nav/vlibrary.html)

Math Playground (https://www.mathplayground.com/math_manipulatives.html)

Search online for more virtual opportunities for your students. Note that you need to download JAVA, a free plug-in, to access virtual manipulatives.

HOW ARE MANIPULATIVES USED?

"I hear and I forget. I see and I remember. I do and I understand." This ancient quote from Confucius sums up the current beliefs about using manipulatives in mathematics. It reminds us that we need to provide learning tools to help students make sense of mathematical concepts. In 2009, the U.S. Department of Education's What Works Clearinghouse, a trusted source for scientific evidence of what works in education, made using manipulatives one of its top research-based recommendations. It is important to note that the mathematics is not *in* the manipulatives; rather, students use their interaction with a manipulative to construct the mathematical concepts. In other words, students form ideas about mathematics while working with the manipulatives. They use the manipulatives to test out hypotheses, model/create meaning for algorithms, find patterns and relationships, and so forth, all of which help them construct the abstract concepts.

Teacher perceptions of manipulative use vary. While some teachers value them as indispensable teaching tools, others may view them as play objects, suitable for the primary grades, as Tooke, Hyatt, Leigh, Snyder, and Borda (1992) found in their study. This perception of manipulatives is sometimes shared by middle school students. Alicia, an eighth-grade teacher, wants to use models to introduce linear equations. However, her students have indicated that they only think of manipulatives as something they used in elementary school. Thinking ahead, Alicia opens her first lesson on linear equations with the following story:

"Have you ever heard someone exclaim 'Eureka!' when they get excited about something they just figured out? Does anyone know where that phrase originated? In ancient Greece, in the city of Syracuse, there was a mathematician named Archimedes. He was a brilliant guy but he was working on a problem. He was working with volume and just could not figure out a way to precisely measure the volume of an irregular object. In class, we have learned formulas for volume of regular shapes. So Archimedes took a break from his work and decided to take a hot bath. He stepped in the tub and noticed the water rising. Suddenly it came to him, that the volume of water his body displaced in the tub must be equal to the volume of the part of his body that was in the water. He discovered that the volume of irregular objects could be measured with precision if you submerse them in water. Supposedly, he was so excited to share his discovery that he jumped out of the bathtub and ran through the streets of Syracuse screaming, 'Eureka! I found it!' However, he forgot to get dressed first! Why am I telling you this story? Mathematicians are not people who just sit around with paper and pencil all day thinking math. They use models to help them understand concepts. Archimedes made a huge discovery about volume, but he could not do it with paper and pencil. He had a model—rising water in a bath. We don't learn mathematical concepts easily with paper and pencil either. Sometimes it is helpful for us to work like mathematicians and use models. So for our next unit of study on equations, we are going to use a hands-on model to help us scream 'Eureka!' when we get it."

Alicia likened using manipulatives to the way mathematicians really work and thus laid the groundwork for seeing manipulatives not as an elementary mathematics plaything but as a tool for learning new mathematical concepts.

The most popular use of manipulatives is to introduce a concept. Here is an example.

Example: Elias

Elias, a seventh-grade teacher, wants to introduce probability models, as per his district curriculum guide. He wants the lesson to be one in which students will understand the concept, so he decides to make it interactive.

Elias: Today we are going to collect some data. I have enough paper cups for everyone. [He drops one on the floor.] What do you think is the probability that paper cups will land open-side down [and he shows a cup in that position]? Discuss your ideas with a partner.

Micah: [after discussion with partner] We think it won't happen at all. I have never seen a cup land that way.

Frederica: We think it will land face down sometimes and sometimes not.

Lindsay: Since there are only three ways the cup can land, on its side, open-side up, or open-side down, we think it will land $\frac{1}{3}$ of the time open-end down.

Elias: Some good hypotheses with some justifications. Now let's experiment. Each pair of students will drop a cup 30 times recording results. After you complete the experiment, with your partner discuss the answer to the following question: What is the probability of the cup landing open-side down?

Elias then continued the lesson using different manipulatives/models with experiments to have students develop a probability model. He knew that taking a hands-on approach would be the most effective way to introduce this concept.

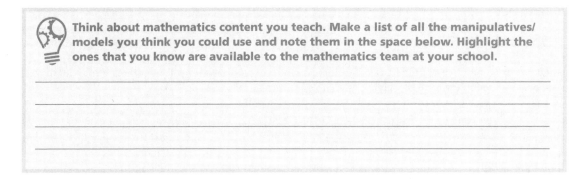

Think about mathematics content you teach. Make a list of all the manipulatives/models you think you could use and note them in the space below. Highlight the ones that you know are available to the mathematics team at your school.

As Thompson and Lambdin (1994) concluded, manipulatives enable students to have a concrete, shared experience upon which the teacher can base a class discussion. "Concrete materials can be an effective aid to students' thinking and to successful teaching."

As Denika demonstrated in the opening reflection, teachers can use representations for assessment as well as instruction because the manipulatives give insight into what students do or do not understand. You can then use this knowledge to help you make decisions about future lesson planning. To begin, you can tie these questions, suggested by NCTM Past President Skip Fennell, into your formative assessment:

• How are students using representation to model and interpret the mathematics presented?

• What do the representations that a student is using tell about that student's understanding of the mathematics?

• What do students provide when asked to use diagrams, sketches, or equations to explain their solution to a problem or task? (Fennell, 2006)

See Chapter 10 for more information on formative assessment and lesson planning.

When students can use different representations to model a concept, they demonstrate their ability to understand the concept. Conversely, when students are introduced to only one representation, their misconceptions may be enhanced. For example, students who are exposed only to an array model of fractions may believe that it is not possible to divide a rectangular sheet of paper into fractional parts. It is good practice to use multiple representations for a concept.

WHAT ARE OTHER RESOURCES?

In addition to representations, you have many other **resources** at your disposal. One of the most common is the **textbook,** but a textbook is only as good as the teacher who uses it. A skilled builder with a hammer and nails can create an architectural masterpiece. In the hands of an unskilled builder, the same blocks of wood made into furniture will fall apart in your living room. As you consider the most effective way to use your textbook for instruction, keep these suggestions in mind:

- Carefully select portions of the text for your students to use. Consider the readability level of what you select and the complexity of the explanations and the level of questions offered. Questions in textbooks are sometimes low level (e.g., recall, carry out an algorithm).

- Discover your students' prior knowledge before preselecting any material based on lessons written for the general middle school population.

- Supplement your lessons with suggestions from the teacher ancillary materials that accompany your text.

Note that there will never be a textbook tailored to meet the individual needs of your students. For this reason, creating your own lessons—incorporating the best of what your textbook has to offer—is advantageous.

Another resource you may have is a district-wide curriculum. Usually, district lesson plans are aligned closely to the state-required mathematics standards. Most plans are based on big ideas, conceptual understandings, real-world applications, and hands-on experiences. The district plans will likely engage your students and keep them excited about learning mathematics; these plans may even have ideas for differentiating instruction. Always prepare the district lesson plans thoroughly, using our guidelines, but in class remember to teach your students, not the plan.

The Internet is an endless source of teaching materials. A word of caution: The learning intentions and success criteria you create for your lessons should be of paramount importance. Before jumping to any website with what appear to be engaging lessons or ideas, be sure to match them with your learning intentions and success criteria and think deeply about your standards, big ideas, essential questions, and the purpose of your lesson.

Using a copy of your textbook, something you found on the Internet, or your district curriculum that you used recently in a lesson, reflect on how closely the lesson matched your big ideas, essential questions, learning intentions, and success criteria. Note your reflections here.

_____

_____

_____

_____

Building Unit Coherence

You can create coherence and appropriate rigor across a unit by carefully attending to how and when you use particular resources, particularly the manipulatives. It can be tempting to use the same manipulative throughout a unit; however, students need to understand a concept through a variety of manipulatives. Think back to how Denika had more than one method to model multiplication of fractions.

Josh and Jeff are discussing whether or not to continue using manipulatives with their procedural knowledge lesson on writing expressions. Jeff asked, "We used Algebra Tiles to introduce our lesson yesterday, so maybe we should put them away for today's lesson. After all, the students will not be able to use the tiles for any tests." Josh responded, "If we make the tiles available, then students who need them can use them and those who do not, won't. Multiple entry points."

Jeff quipped, "Good thinking! Yes, we can walk around and observe who is using them and how!"

Materials (representations, manipulatives, other):

Algebra Tiles

Paper/pencil

Soccer Kicks! Problems Set A and Set B (see Figures A.1 and A.2)

See the complete lesson plan in Appendix A on page 188.

How does the representation for this lesson enhance or further the learning intentions and success criteria of this lesson? Write your thoughts below.

_____

_____

_____

_____

_____

_____

_____

_____

_____

_____

_____

_____

_____

_____

_____

_____

_____

_____

_____

_____

_____

_____

_____

Standards

LI and SC

Purpose

Tasks

Materials

Student Thinking

Lesson Structures

Form. Assess.

Lesson Launch

Lesson Facilitation

Closure

Seventh-Grade Snapshot   *Material Selection*

"I am so excited about this pet-sitting task!" shared Alix. "I think we should make some kind of record for the task so they can keep track of the different kinds of problems." Kyle wondered, "What if we make a journal for them to record their ideas?" Alix, Bryan, and Kia agreed. Bryan offered, "I think the journal is a great idea, but I would also like them to record their solutions on chart paper so they can share their ideas with the whole class." "Yes," shared Alix. "Let's do both!"

Materials (representations, manipulatives, other):

Teddy's Pet-Sitting Problem-Solving Journal (see Figure A.3)

Larger chart paper sectioned into four parts

DAY ONE	DAY TWO
DAY THREE	DAY FOUR

See the complete lesson plan in Appendix A on page 192.

How do the representations for this lesson enhance or further the learning intentions and success criteria of this lesson? Write your thoughts below.

_____

_____

_____

_____

_____

_____

_____

_____

_____

_____

Even though Serena is the only person on her team who teaches the eighth-grade mathematics curriculum, she often discusses lessons with her teammate, Ellen, who teaches the Algebra I and geometry curricula. For this lesson, Serena asked Ellen, "Which representations do you want the students to be familiar with when they get to Algebra I? I am doing a lesson on graphing and want to be sure it aligns with what you do." Ellen responded, "By the time students begin Algebra I, I like them to be aware that situations, usually presented as word problems, can be modeled by equations, graphs, tables, and physical models. So it sounds like your lesson that uses word problems, graphs, equations, and tables should be just what the students need to prepare for Algebra I."

Serena was happy to have the support of her colleague.

Materials (representations, manipulatives, other):

An assortment of pictures of faces that demonstrate emotions such as a baby crying, a woman smiling, a boy angry, etc.; chart-size graph paper; markers; inch or centimeter cubes; pennies; stopwatch; rugs worksheet; a soup can (or any can); and prepared exit slips (see Figure A.6).

See the complete lesson plan in Appendix A on page 203.

How do the representations for this lesson enhance or further the learning intentions and success criteria of this lesson? Write your thoughts below.

Under Construction

Now it is your turn! Decide what representations will help meet your learning intentions and success criteria for the lesson you are building.

Materials (representations, manipulatives, other):

online resources ➤ Download the full Lesson-Planning Template from resources.corwin.com/mathlessonplanning/6-8
Remember that you can use the online version of the lesson plan template to begin compiling each section into the full template as your lesson plan grows.

Standards

LI and SC

Purpose

Tasks

Materials

Student Thinking

Lesson Structures

Form. Assess.

Lesson Launch

Lesson Facilitation

Closure

CHAPTER 8

CEMENTING THE CRACKS
Anticipating Student Thinking

During a recent sixth-grade lesson on writing expressions, I discovered that many of my students had a major misconception. The students had been given a situation similar to the following: "Deandra has $10 less than her brother, Sean. Write an expression to represent how much money Deandra has." Some of my students seemed to struggle! I asked one of my students why writing an expression to represent the money was difficult. He replied, "There isn't enough information here to solve the problem." In reviewing student work, I realized many of the students had the same misconception. In addition, another student said, "We don't know how much money Sean has. We need this information." That is when I realized the idea of a variable for the unknown in an expression did not make sense to many of the sixth graders. With this insight, I would have to reteach this lesson. Maybe I will begin with equations or focus my lesson on variables. That afternoon as I drove home from school, I was thinking about the lesson. "Where did this misconception that you need to be able to 'solve expressions' come from?"

Anne Marie Newhouse
Sixth-Grade Teacher
Ohio

Anne Marie's experience is similar to that experienced by many mathematics teachers. It is a surprise when student thinking is not aligned with what teachers know students should have learned. It is even more astonishing when that thinking is a misconception, as in Anne Marie's case. In this chapter, we will consider the factors that lead to these situations and explore how advance planning and anticipation can be crucial. This chapter will focus on the following questions:

- What are misconceptions, and where do they come from?
- How can you plan to minimize misconceptions?

WHAT ARE MISCONCEPTIONS, AND WHERE DO THEY COME FROM?

One problem that leads to very serious instructional issues for teachers and students is misconceptions. **Common errors** and **misconceptions** occur when students make incorrect or inappropriate generalizations of an idea (Resnick, 1982; Resnick & Omanson, 1987). Misconceptions may result from several sources: preconceptions, informal thinking, or poor memory.

Students do not come to school with a blank slate of knowledge. They come with background knowledge gathered from prior learning experiences both within and outside of school, such as home or social media. Some of this knowledge relates to the topics taught in school (Bransford et al., 2000; Gelman & Lucariello, 2002; Piaget & Inhelder, 1969; Resnick, 1983). Learning builds on and is related to this **prior knowledge**. Prior knowledge is based on intuition, everyday experiences, and what students have been taught previously. Before beginning instruction, you need to know your students' prior knowledge. Your instruction depends on whether this knowledge is accurate or not (Lucariello, 2012).

> Example: DeShawn
>
> DeShawn, a sixth-grade teacher, always asks his students to explain their reasoning. He was surprised to see Paul, one of his students, write the following:
>
> $\frac{1}{4} > \frac{3}{5}$ because fourths are greater than fifths.
>
> Perplexed, DeShawn asked Paul why he used that reasoning. Paul said, "I learned that the bigger the number in the denominator, the smaller the parts."
>
> DeShawn was surprised that Paul was overgeneralizing what he remembered. This misconception about fractions was so strong that Paul still had the misconception after DeShawn's instruction. Paul continued to look only at the denominator, ignoring the numerator, even after participating in all of DeShawn's engaging comparing fractions activities.

Other misconceptions arrive from everyday experiences. Students form many ideas about numbers, figures, and fractions from what they see on television, social media, computer games, and so forth. It's no wonder some students develop very interesting and perhaps incorrect ideas about mathematical concepts (SanGiovanni & Novak, 2018). For example, the word average is used on television and in social media frequently. Students read about "the average amount of soda Americans drink per day" or "the average amount of hours a person sleeps." This creates confusion in the mathematics class when average is used for the statistical terms *mean*, *median*, and *mode*. Mohyuddin and Khalil (2016) tell us that students become emotionally and intellectually attached to misconceptions because they have actively constructed them. They often find it difficult to accept new concepts that are different from their misconception.

Not all misconceptions come from prior knowledge. Some are the **unintended consequences** of the best-intentioned teaching. Here is an example.

> Example: Angela
>
> Angela, a seventh-grade teacher, asked her students to identify the property used in the following statement:
>
> $(75 + 22) - 37 = (22 + 75) - 37$
>
> Kenny, one of her students, responded, "The associative property."
>
> Angela was puzzled by the answer, particularly since the class had spent considerable time identifying properties. She asked Kenny to explain how he arrived at his answer.
>
> Kenny said, "Whenever I see parentheses, I know that the property is either distributive or associative. This was a short example, so it is associative. Distributive has more parentheses."
>
> Angela was surprised at the misconception Kenny had. Kenny believed that the inclusion of parentheses determined the property. Angela felt she may have contributed to this misconception by exclusively using examples of the commutative property without parentheses in her previous lessons.

To summarize, misconceptions are a problem for two reasons. First, students become emotionally and intellectually attached to the misconceptions because they have actively constructed them, as in the example with averages. Second, they interfere with learning when students use them to interpret new experiences, as in the examples with Kenny and Angela.

For more exploration of unintended consequences, check out "The Thirteen Rules That Expire" (Karp, Bush, & Dougherty, 2014). This National Council of Teachers of Mathematics article highlights 13 generalizations that are often in school because they work for the lesson at hand, but they do not hold true over the long term. For example, teachers often tell students that a larger number cannot be subtracted from a smaller number because they do not want to confuse students by introducing negative numbers. However, students do not have to be taught explicitly about negative numbers to know they exist. The focus of your lessons should always be on developing conceptual understanding instead of adhering to a rule.

> **How do you identify your students' common misconceptions? Note some of the main ones here.**
>
> _____
>
> _____
>
> _____
>
> _____

HOW CAN YOU PLAN TO MINIMIZE MISCONCEPTIONS?

According to Steven Leinwand (2014),

> Effective teachers have always understood that mistakes and confusion are powerful learning opportunities. Moreover, they understand that one of their critical roles is to anticipate these misconceptions in their lesson planning and have at their disposal an array of strategies to address common misunderstandings *before* they expand, solidify, and undermine confidence.

Before we can plan to minimize misconceptions (admitting they can never be eliminated totally), it is helpful to know some of the more common mathematics misconceptions that middle school students form. Note that the table in Figure 8.1 is not an exhaustive list.

Figure 8.1

Misconception	Student Example
When you multiply a number by 10, just add 0 to the end of the number.	$0.35 \times 10 = 0.350$
Subtraction is commutative.	$(-45) - 37 = 37 - (-45)$
Dividing by $\frac{1}{2}$ is the same as taking half of the number.	$40 \div \frac{1}{2} = 20$

Figure 8.1 (*Continued*)

Misconception	Student Example
When plotting points on a plane, the points should be placed in the spaces.	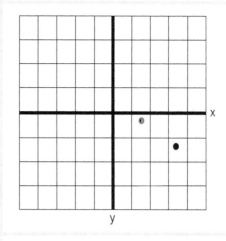
While one positive and one negative make zero, this is only true when you have one of each.	1 + (−1) = 0 5 + (−5) = 10
Multiplication makes numbers bigger.	$\frac{1}{4} \times \frac{1}{2} = \frac{1}{8}$ Students believe $\frac{1}{8}$ is bigger than $\frac{1}{4}$ or $\frac{1}{2}$.
You always divide the larger number by the smaller number.	When given the question "What is 25 divided by 100?" students will write 100 ÷ 25 = 4 instead of 25 ÷ 100 = 0.25.
When using exponents, multiply by the exponent.	$3^3 = 9$
Multiply everything inside parentheses by the number outside parentheses.	23 (4 × 6) = 23 × 4 × 23 × 6 = 12,696
The length of the diagonal in a square is equal to the length of a side of the same square. (Note: This misconception comes into play when students do not use the distance formula to find distance.)	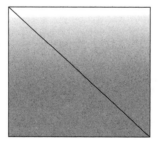

(Continued)

Standards

LI and SC

Purpose

Tasks

Materials

Student Thinking

Lesson Structures

Form. Assess.

Lesson Launch

Lesson Facilitation

Closure

Figure 8.1 (*Continued*)

Misconception	Student Example
The points on a line of best fit must go through some of the data points on a scatterplot.	Student says, "This is not a line of best fit because it does not go through any of the data points."
Categorical data do not include any numbers. All data with numbers are quantitative.	Which of the following represents quantitative data? **a.** A company does research on salaries in their type of business. **b.** A social media outlet gathers data on ZIP codes of their online community. Student mistakenly says both are quantitative because they both deal with numbers.

Because misconceptions tend to be strongly held student beliefs, it does not work well to simply repeat a lesson or tell a student that his or her idea is a misconception. Instead, you need to include in your plan how you will uncover and diagnose student misconceptions.

You can do this through use of anticipation, formative assessment, and questioning techniques. Let's take a quick look at each of these approaches.

Formative Assessment

Formative assessment can include techniques such as observations, interviews, show me, hinge questions, and exit tasks as explained in the book *The Formative 5* (Fennell, Kobett, & Wray 2017). Each of these techniques can be used to uncover prior knowledge, which may include misconceptions. Chapter 10 will focus on using formative assessment strategies.

Questioning

Questioning is another way to uncover misconceptions in prior knowledge. Some questioning techniques that work for this purpose include the following:

1. Prepare and pose questions that probe prior knowledge related to the lesson you are planning.

2. Avoid asking questions that require one-word answers (Kazemi & Hintz, 2014).

3. Ask follow-up questions to both correct and incorrect answers (Moyer-Packenham & Milewicz, 2002; Walsh & Sattes, 2005).

Anticipating

Anticipating misconceptions is another way to minimize them. Here are three ways you can add steps to your lesson plan to anticipate, diagnose, and correct the misconceptions.

1. Use Figure 8.1 to help you anticipate misconceptions and to help you think about those you commonly see in the content of your lessons.

2. Consider your experience with previous students.

3. Discuss the misconceptions with your colleagues to gather additional ideas on how to correct the misconceptions.

> Example: Natalie
>
> Natalie, an eighth-grade teacher, includes this word problem in her lesson plan on inequalities to check for student understanding.
>
>> The eighth-grade class at Sullivan Middle School is going on a field trip. Each bus can hold 72 students. There are already 60 students on the bus. The last group of students gets on and the bus is still not full. How many students could have been in the last group? Write an inequality and solve.
>
> Three students wrote the following response:
>
>> $n + 60 < 72$
>>
>> $n + 60 - 60 < 72 - 60$
>>
>> $n < 12$
>>
>> So there were 12 people in the last group.
>>
>> $n + 60 < 72$
>
> Natalie notices that while these students can do the computation, they have a misconception that is leading to an incorrect conclusion. She asks, "Why can't there be 10 people in the last group?" to which one student replies, "Because n can only be one answer and the work I did says it is 12."
>
> Notice that Natalie does not ask for a one-word answer. Her question probed thinking for a specific piece of prior knowledge.
>
> Natalie discovers that these students share the misconception that variables can only stand for one number. To address this, she adds the following activity to her lesson the next day.
>
> Natalie works with a small group of students who had the misconception. She tells them that they are going to model yesterday's field trip problem with centimeter cubes to represent the students in the problem. Students arrange 60 cubes as specified in the problem. Natalie tasks the students to determine all the different possible groups that could board the bus but still not make 72. One student says 1 will work. Another says 10 will work. A third student models 11 will work. Natalie writes 1, 10, and 11 and asks the students if there are any other possibilities. The students find 2, 3, 4, 5, 6, 7, 8, and 9 also work. Following up on their original responses, Natalie leads the small group to see that $n < 12$ is the same as all the answers they just found and that n can represent more than one number.

Natalie is deliberately providing the students with an additional experience that allows them to reconstruct the concept they misunderstood—that a variable can stand for more than one number. This is a necessary step for students who are truly vested in their misconceptions because they constructed them and used them successfully in the past.

Building Unit Coherence

To increase coherence, you can also identify the misconceptions that students may develop across a unit.

Example: Meiko

Meiko, a sixth-grade teacher, always jots down misconceptions that she anticipates the students may develop or have already developed. This allows her to plan lessons that will help her prevent the misconception from occurring.

Meiko developed this practice after her students insisted that dividing by $\frac{1}{2}$ is the same as dividing in half! She had to interrupt her teaching to plan a lesson that corrected the misconception. She planned a lesson where students had to perform the following two computations and compare results to see that dividing by $\frac{1}{2}$ is not the same as dividing in half. See Figure 8.2.

Figure 8.2

Dividing by $\frac{1}{2}$	$26 \div \frac{1}{2} =$
Dividing in half	$26 \div 2 =$

Now, she lists misconceptions that she anticipates for each unit before she begins teaching so she will be ready.

Notes

Student Thinking

While planning algebra lessons for writing expression, Josh and Jeff discuss how, in the past, sixth graders did not understand how to translate word problems into algebraic expressions. Josh exclaimed, "My students incorrectly translated statements such as '6 less than y' as '6 – y!'" Jeff added, "I know, and my students also incorrectly used the distributive property, only distributing the first term." Both teachers decided to design a lesson to help their students address these misconceptions through real-world scenarios. They adjusted the Soccer Kicks! worksheet to include examples of the distributive property and the less than situation.

Misconceptions or Common Errors:

- Students incorrectly translate statements such as "6 less than y" as "6 - y."
- Students incorrectly use the distributive property and may only distribute the first term.
- Students forget that if a coefficient is not written, the coefficient is 1.

See the complete lesson plan in Appendix A on page 188.

Why do you think that simply informing students of a misconception will not change their thinking? What role does anticipating a misconception play in helping you focus your lesson plan? Record your thoughts below.

Standards

LI and SC

Purpose

Tasks

Materials

Student Thinking

Lesson Structures

Form. Assess.

Lesson Launch

Lesson Facilitation

Closure

The seventh-grade team discussed some of the different misconceptions the students demonstrated in the past week. Alix shared, "One thing I am anticipating is that on the Day Three problem, the students won't expect the mixture to be less than 40%. I like that the solution is below what the problem sets up. We need to throw a few more surprises in there." Bryan agreed, "Yes, and I think that is what is more likely to happen in the real world. This problem will likely be the most difficult, but they can solve it in several ways. Let's think about how we can scaffold for some of the students who struggle." The seventh-grade team agreed!

Misconceptions or Common Errors:

- Students may struggle with multistep problems. You may scaffold the problems by focusing on the first part of the problem.

- Encourage the students to use number lines, such as in the dog park problem. Students can also use drawings to solve.

- Students may struggle to convert measurements. Provide measurement conversions as needed.

- Students may struggle to represent the situation using an equation.

- Students may find the tax on individual items and/or compute tax incorrectly.

- Students might be challenged by the Day Three problem because they will have to buy more to increase the percentage of chicken.

An additional blank text frame is added to the resources for the teacher to add an additional question as an extension for a group that ends early.

See the complete lesson plan in Appendix A on page 192.

Why do you think that simply informing students of a misconception will not change their thinking? What role does anticipating a misconception play in helping you focus your lesson plan? Record your thoughts below.

_____

_____

_____

_____

_____

_____

_____

_____

_____

_____

_____

_____

Standards
LI and SC
Purpose
Tasks
Materials
Student Thinking
Lesson Structures
Form. Assess.
Lesson Launch
Lesson Facilitation
Closure

Eighth-Grade Snapshot

Student Thinking

Serena is always concerned about how her students interpret lessons. She does not want any misconceptions. Her favorite way to analyze her lessons is to talk with the Algebra I teacher who has her students the following year. This year, Serena went to Ellen and asked her if her students arrived with any misconceptions. During their conversation Ellen mentioned, "Jorge did have trouble graphing second-degree equations. He insisted that equations always graph as straight lines. I am not sure where he got that from!" Serena replied, "Neither do I! Though if I think back to last year, we did not graph any curves at all. We only graphed lines. That may be the source. I am just putting together a lesson right now on graphing equations. I will add a few word problems that can be modeled with curves. Thank you for the info!"

Misconceptions or Common Errors:

- Students may try to connect the points on the scatterplot where there is no relationship.
- Some students confuse the x and y axes.

See the complete lesson plan in Appendix A on page 203.

Why do you think that simply informing students of a misconception will not change their thinking? What role does anticipating a misconception play in helping you focus your lesson plan? Record your thoughts below.

_____

_____

_____

_____

_____

_____

_____

_____

_____

_____

_____

_____

_____

_____

_____

_____

_____

_____

_____

_____

_____

Now it is your turn! Decide on whether you are anticipating a misconception or need to probe prior knowledge. Add it to your lesson plan.

Misconceptions or Common Errors:

Download the full Lesson-Planning Template from resources.corwin.com/mathlessonplanning/6-8
Remember that you can use the online version of the lesson plan template to begin compiling each section into the full template as your lesson plan grows.

106 The Mathematics Lesson-Planning Handbook, Grades 6–8

CHAPTER 9

FRAMING THE LESSON
Formats

As a middle school teacher of Family and Consumer Sciences, my seventh-grade class was involved in a lesson on baking. I asked the question, "What amounts of each of the ingredients do we need so that we can double this cookie recipe?" Who would have thought that this simple question would lead to two full math lessons?

As I asked this question, I saw expressions of "I think I know this" to "I haven't a clue!" The only definitive answer everyone could give me was "Two eggs, not one!" So taking out all the measuring cups (both dry and wet), we went to work. Using flour and water, the cups became manipulatives that transformed multiplying and dividing fractions into something they could understand and apply.

I thought it was a simple question that would take five or ten minutes to answer and then we would bake the cookies. Well, that simple question led to two full lessons on fractions before the actual baking took place! In the end, the students all enjoyed the cookies and came to the conclusion that we do use math in our everyday lives.

Thinking back on this lesson, I wonder, "Why couldn't the students make the connection between baking and math? Did they really not know how to double or was it the application? Why couldn't they transfer the knowledge from one class to another? Could we find a way to link our mathematics and career skills classes to emphasize mathematics applications in the real world?"

Susan Hoye Mahoney
Family and Consumer Science Teacher
New York

Lessons need structure. Lesson formats give you that structure and refer to how you organize your class for instruction. Some lessons work better when students are in collaborative groups, and some are more effective when students move around to different centers. In middle school, the master schedule is a critical factor because it determines how much time is allotted for instruction, thus becoming a factor in selecting your lesson format. For instance, some middle schools schedule mathematics classes for 45 to 50 minutes daily while others use a 90-minute block. Lesson format can and should vary depending on your purpose, with consideration for how much time you have to implement a lesson. Mathematics labs and project-based learning are easier to execute in a longer block of time. Sometimes partnering with other disciplines can be an efficient use of instructional time, as Sue suggested in her reflection. This chapter will address the following questions:

- How do middle school schedules affect planning and instruction?

- What are some different lesson formats?

- How do you plan for interdisciplinary instruction?

HOW DO MIDDLE SCHOOL SCHEDULES AFFECT PLANNING AND INSTRUCTION?

Middle schools serve pre-adolescent and young adolescent students between Grades 5 and 9, with most of the students in the sixth- to eighth-grade range (U.S. Department of Education, 2008). Middle schools organize their teachers and students into different configurations. Remember from Chapter 1 that middle school organization takes into account the distinct nature of young adolescents. For young adolescents, the predominant organizational structure is team teaching. **Team teaching** creates instructional cohorts that group two to four teachers of different core disciplines with 50 to 125 students for core content instruction. This configuration promotes student and teacher bonding and closer relationships. It affects planning as the team has common interdisciplinary planning time, which is an advantage for interdisciplinary teaching (Hanover Research, 2015). However, this may create an obstacle for mathematics teachers who do not have a common time to also plan with other grade-level mathematics colleagues. According to Hackmann et al. (2002), it is advantageous to schedule common departmental planning time as well, as it allows for stronger curriculum development. Some middle schools do provide this additional department common planning time along with the interdisciplinary time that was part of Sue's reflection. When this common math planning time is not available, you can use technology to your advantage to communicate with other mathematics teachers at your grade level either in your school or across the country. The National Council of Teachers of Mathematics (NCTM) provides a venue for online communities called "my NCTM" (https://my.nctm.org), where you can enter into mathematical planning discussions and create your own grade-level mathematics planning team. This is helpful for teachers who have the full responsibility for mathematics at a grade level with no grade-level mathematics colleagues with whom to bounce ideas around.

Allocated time is the total amount of time for teacher instruction and student learning. While there are many variations in scheduling across middle schools, the two most common schedules are an hour period (55–60 minutes) for each subject or a block schedule (McLeod, Fisher, & Hoover, 2003). The amount of allocated time affects your format choices. When you have a longer block of time (i.e., 90 minutes), it is possible to work on projects, conduct interdisciplinary lessons, and have more stations and more time to work with struggling learners. However, both time allotments allow for work with multiple representations, rigorous tasks, and formative assessment with a solid lesson launch. Purposeful lesson planning is the key in both time allotments.

WHAT ARE SOME DIFFERENT LESSON FORMATS?

Seemingly, everyone has their own preferred **lesson format**, but the fact is that there is not one mathematics lesson format that should be implemented every day. Adhering to one model can be limiting, and it may not best support your students' learning because the format is taking precedence over the students' needs. Effective teachers use more than one type of lesson format. As you think about selecting lesson formats, ask yourself if the mathematics lesson structure meets the following criteria.

- Does it support student discourse?
- Does it support differentiation?
- Does it place the big ideas front and center in the lesson?
- Does it lend itself to the learning needs of pre-adolescents?
- Does it enhance opportunities for formative assessment?

As you decide on a lesson format, you need to analyze the standards you will teach. In particular, you should consider which of the standards point to developing conceptual understanding and which ones point to procedural fluency.

The following formats are only four of the many ways you might structure your lessons. Flexibility is the key to selecting lesson formats. You should structure your lessons with a deep consideration of your students' pre-adolescent needs and mathematics standards. Note that these lesson formats provide many opportunities to formatively assess students, provide timely feedback, and foster student-to-student interactions.

Four-Part Lesson Plan

Structure your class using this format for problem-solving lessons. The four parts are known as *before*, *during*, *after*, and *reflection* (see Figure 9.1). This is an adaptation of the format from the book *Teaching Mathematics Developmentally K–8* by Van de Walle et al. (2016).

Figure 9.1

Before

| Teacher activates prior knowledge in students | Teacher ensures the problem is understood | Whole group |

⬇

During

| Students work | Teacher provides support | Small group |

⬇

After

| Class discussion | Students present their conclusions/conjecture | Whole group |

⬇

Reflection

| Students make sense of the lesson | Closure | Individual |

Before

In the *before* stage, your students are in a **whole group**. The goal of this part of the lesson is to prepare students for the mathematics to come by having them revisit concepts, procedures, and strategies previously learned. You can do this by focusing on vocabulary, starting with a similar problem, or having students reword, act out, or model the problem. You also introduce the problem during the before stage.

During

In the second part of the lesson, the *during* stage, students work in small groups. They work on solving the problem, and they prepare to present their ideas to the class. They can use manipulatives or any representations they choose. This is when they actively engage with the task. You can use this time to support the groups though questioning. Use several different questioning strategies to support your students' higher-order thinking, such as the following:

- Ask group members to share their strategies with other group members.
- Pose questions to provoke further thinking when groups are at an impasse.
- Ask probing questions.
- Provide extensions when appropriate.

In this part of the lesson, take note of student thinking and the strategies used so that you can begin to organize the *after* part of the lesson. Be as hands-off as possible so that your students can engage in productive struggle.

After

In the *after* part of the lesson, students come back together in a whole group to share their work. The purpose of this part of the lesson is for students to analyze their classmates' thinking. In the *during* stage, you noted the students' strategies so that you can now organize student presentations, posters, or other products in an order that leads to discourse around their work. For example, you may decide to have the students with incorrect solutions make their presentations first so you can ask the class if everyone agrees. This will allow you to start a class discussion on the effectiveness of the strategy used. Alternatively, you may have students do a gallery walk or try another method to share student thinking and encourage discourse. During the *after*, your students make sense of the mathematics. They form conjectures and link the new ideas to their previous understandings.

Reflection

Reflection refers to the process of thinking about learning. In the *reflection* piece of the lesson, students get the time they need to cement their learning individually. It is during reflection that student learning takes place. During reflection, students examine ideas and seek out evidence to support or refute ideas they have previously held. To ensure this reflection, you should provide students with a prompt they can use to reflect on the class discussion and the mathematics involved. Here are some sample prompts for reflection that you might try.

- How was your strategy different from those of your classmates?
- What was your favorite strategy, and why?
- Explain a strategy used by a classmate that was not yours.
- How did this lesson connect to what we did yesterday?

Reflection is a proactive way to support students' mathematical development. You should never skip the reflection portion of the lesson. In fact, you may wish to use reflection time as your closure (see Chapter 13).

Game Format

There are some lessons where you want students to practice what they have learned so they can make connections. The game format works well for this purpose and gives you a chance to assess your students formatively.

During planning, assign all students into groups of two or three, and decide on a game or activity for each group or pair. Select games or activities they are familiar with so they can practice the concept or skill they need. The game Equate is a good example. In this game, students score points by forming equations on the board either across or down as in scrabble. You might select this game for students needing practice with equations. Another game is 24, the integer version. In this game, students form equations that equal 24 using only the four given integers on a randomly selected card. There are many computer-based games such as Green Globs and Graphing Equations, where students try to blast green globs on the screen by writing linear (or quadratic) equations that pass through as many green globs as possible.

Notice that the games referred to are not just matching games where students complete the game in five or ten minutes. These games are engaging and require students to problem-solve along the way.

Rich games and activities lend themselves well to this lesson format.

To begin a lesson structured in the game format, gather the whole group together. Assign groups of two, three, or four students to games and allow them to play. Use this time for you to move from game to game, observing, formatively assessing, and joining in when necessary. Note that students remain with the same game throughout the lesson. This is not a student rotation format; instead, the teacher moves from group to group.

This format works well in classes where the time allotment is 60 minutes. During the longer block schedules, this format may be used for part of the class time and another format for the other part.

Standards

LI and SC

Purpose

Tasks

Materials

Student Thinking

Lesson Structures

Form. Assess.

Lesson Launch

Lesson Facilitation

Closure

Figure 9.2

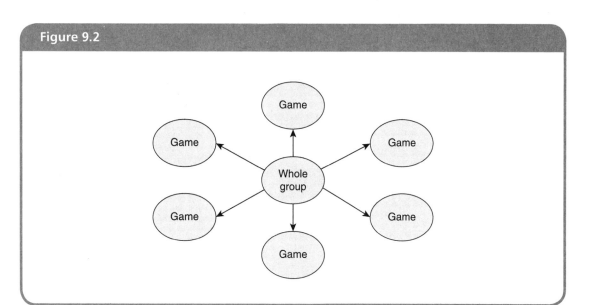

Small-Group Instruction

In this lesson format, you have the opportunity to work with small groups of students for instruction while the other groups work independently. Research shows that students who work in groups on problems, assignments, and other mathematical investigations display increased achievement (Protheroe, 2007).

You begin instruction with a whole-group mini-lesson that takes 10 to 15 minutes. For instance, you might review a previous concept, introduce a new concept or vocabulary, play a short game on the day's topic, and so forth.

After the mini-lesson, you have small groups engage in independent tasks that allow students to explore, practice, apply, and/or review the topic for the lesson. Students can play games, use the computer, solve problems, or explore concepts with manipulatives. While most students are working in small groups independently, another group works with you. Be sure to form the groups in ways that make sense for their learning. For example, you may choose to work with a small group of students with a particular misconception about graphing.

You can vary how you use this format. Figure 9.3 shows how you can move from whole group into small groups and remain in those groups for the entire class period. This works well for students who need time to fill in knowledge gaps or who need extra time on a concept with you. Remember that not all middle school students learn at the same pace. Some need more instructional time to cement concepts or practice procedures. If you work with only one group during the class period, then you reconvene the whole class at the end of the lesson to share ideas from the day. You may use this time to preview the next lesson and/or review the day. See Chapter 13 for more on closure.

Figure 9.3

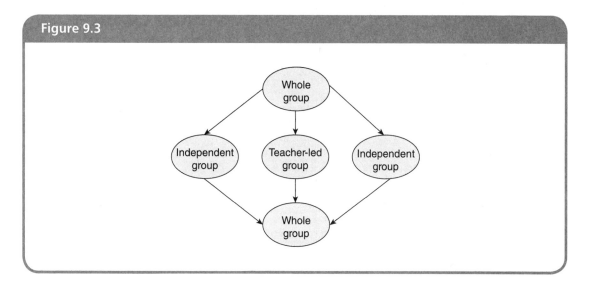

You may need to use this format two or three days in a row if you have a 55- to 60-minute class period, whereas teachers in a block schedule may be able to reach their goal in one class period. Alternatively, you can use the format as shown in Figure 9.4. Here you have the opportunity to work with a rotation of small groups during the class period. For example, you may decide that your introduction to probability needs to be differentiated. You group students accordingly and rotate groups during the class time so that you work with each group and can differentiate the lesson to meet the needs of the group members. Students working independently also get a chance to rotate among two or three different activities or stations. Note that this alternative works best on a block schedule. In a 55- to 60-minute class period, this lesson would need to be carried out over several days.

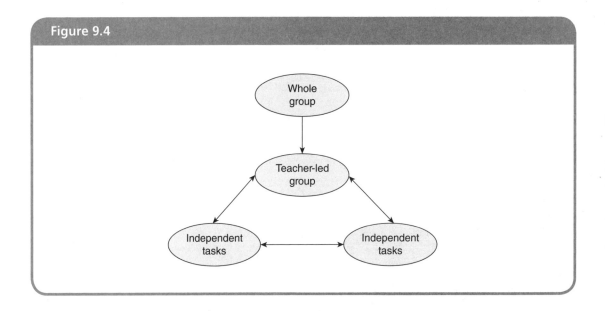

Figure 9.4

This format lends itself to procedural fluency lessons because you can use the small-group instruction time to target students who need additional scaffolding to link the concept to the procedure. On the other hand, you can use this model to reinforce a concept or to practice procedural fluency with a group of students who, based on your formative assessment from the previous day, need additional attention immediately. Students learn concepts at varying rates. Not all students make sense of mathematics at the same pace. This model provides you with the opportunity to bridge this gap.

Overall, the value of this format and its variations is that you can differentiate to meet individual needs. Project-based learning lends itself nicely to this format as you can work with individual groups on specific learning gaps while others work collaboratively on their projects.

Pairs

With this format, students work in pairs to answer questions throughout the lesson. For example, you may begin the lesson by presenting two equivalent numerical expressions (3^{-3} and $\frac{1^3}{3}$) and asking the students to decide with their partners what is the same about them. Students then share their answers as a whole group. Next, you further the discussion by asking pairs to discuss how the expressions are different. After a brief discussion, they share as a whole group. The lesson continues in this fashion. It may involve a series of short tasks or one short task that students engage in with their partner.

You can pair students of similar abilities, different abilities, differing language strengths, and so forth depending on your goals for that particular lesson. Frequently changing the way you pair students is a good practice.

This format encourages student discourse. The smaller the number of students in a group, the more the children get individual opportunities to express themselves. This structure works well for helping students build conceptual understanding. This technique is more appropriate for a 55- to 60-minute class period. In a block schedule, time allows you to vary this technique with others.

These are just a few lesson formats. You may have a few of your own to add to the list, or you may adapt any of these presented as long as the format supports the purpose of your lesson.

HOW DO YOU PLAN FOR INTERDISCIPLINARY INSTRUCTION?

While common team planning in the middle school provides ample opportunities to create interdisciplinary units, it is possible to also plan with teachers who are not part of core instruction such as health and physical education or family and consumer sciences. These teachers are not part of your team but offer exceptional opportunities for transfer and application of mathematical learning to everyday activities, such as what Sue has wondered about in the beginning of the chapter. Here is an example of a conversation between a middle school mathematics teacher, Roberto, and his students' physical education instructor, Tad. They are not planning an interdisciplinary unit but are on their way to reinforcing each other's lessons.

Example: Roberto

Roberto: Tad, I was wondering if you collect any data with your students during the year, such as points scored during intramural basketball games?

Tad: We do collect some data, why?

Roberto: I thought we might be able to reinforce each other's lessons. I do scatterplots in math and always am looking for real-world data that the students can relate to. I was wondering, if I can share your data in my class and use them to make scatterplots, perhaps you could use the scatterplots made by the students to discuss the implications in physical education. What do you think?

Tad: Not a bad idea. I like it! Let's get together and do some coordinating.

This integrated approach also helps teachers better use instructional time. One benefit of interdisciplinary teaching is students have a chance to work with multiple sources of information, thus ensuring they are receiving a more inclusive perspective than they would from consulting one textbook (Wood, 2015).

> **Why do you think more effective teachers use multiple formats? Is there anything inherent in changing formats that might be described as good instruction? Write your responses below.**
>
> _____
> _____
> _____
> _____
> _____
> _____
> _____
> _____

Building Unit Coherence

When using multiple lesson formats, you often create stronger coherence because you are matching the format to the content and to your learning intentions. In other words, you are facilitating your lesson using a format that best meets the needs of your learners. Forcing lessons into the same format day after day chips away at coherence because you are trying to make the lesson fit the structure instead of deciding which structure best suits the lesson content.

Switching to a block schedule this year was a new experience for Josh and Jeff. They struggled with lesson formats most of the year but learned from their mistakes. Josh said, "You know, Jeff. I think this lesson on translating expressions would be perfect if we could pull small groups to work with. Some of our students are going to roll ahead to solving abstractly and some won't want to give up the tiles." "I agree with you completely," said Jeff. "Last year, we did not have enough allotted time to do that but this year it should work great!"

Format:

☐ Four-Part Lesson   ☐ Game Format   ☑ Small-Group Instruction

☐ Pairs   ☐ Other_____

See the complete lesson plan in Appendix A on page 188.

Think of a lesson you recently taught. Which format might best meet the purpose of that lesson? Record your thoughts below.

_____

_____

_____

_____

_____

_____

_____

_____

_____

_____

_____

_____

_____

_____

_____

_____

_____

_____

_____

_____

_____

Standards

LI and SC

Purpose

Tasks

Materials

Student Thinking

Lesson Structures

Form. Assess.

Lesson Launch

Lesson Facilitation

Closure

Seventh-Grade Snapshot

Lesson Format

The seventh-grade team considered the format options. While transfer lessons can be implemented in a variety of formats, they wanted to ensure that the students had plenty of opportunities to make sense of the problem. "I think we should use the four-part lesson plan format because we want them to make sense of the pet-sitting context, work in pairs and groups of four, and then share in a whole-group setting. What do you think?" asked Kia. Kyle agreed, "At first I thought that we should organize them in pairs, but Kia is making a great point. While they will work in pairs, the overall four-part lesson format, stretched out for two days, makes the most sense." The team agreed.

Format:

☑ Four-Part Lesson ☐ Game Format ☐ Small-Group Instruction

☐ Pairs ☐ Other_____

See the complete lesson plan in Appendix A on page 192.

Think of a lesson you recently taught. Which format might best meet the purpose of that lesson? Record your thoughts below.

_____
_____
_____
_____
_____
_____
_____
_____
_____
_____
_____
_____
_____
_____
_____
_____
_____
_____
_____
_____
_____
_____
_____

Serena could not decide if students should work in small groups for this lesson or pairs. She likes small groups because more students are able to share and hear more ideas. She likes pairs because each student has to share more of the responsibility for the work. Thinking back to her discussion with Ellen, the Algebra I teacher, about misconceptions, she decided that the lesson had to include more examples to give students the chance to compare graphs with no relationships, linear relationships, and curves. Serena decided that for students to sort in a meaningful way, there had to be at least three examples of each type of graph. That meant nine examples total. With 18 students, Serena made the decision to have her students work in pairs.

Format:

☐ Four-Part Lesson ☐ Game Format ☐ Small-Group Instruction

☑ Pairs ☐ Other_____

See the complete lesson plan in Appendix A on page 203.

Think of a lesson you recently taught. Which format might best meet the purpose of that lesson? Record your thoughts below.

_____

_____

_____

_____

_____

_____

_____

_____

_____

_____

_____

_____

_____

_____

_____

_____

_____

_____

_____

_____

Under Construction

Now it is your turn! Select the lesson format you would like to use for your lesson that is under construction. Be able to justify for yourself how this format supports the purpose of the lesson.

Format:

☐ Four-Part Lesson   ☐ Game Format   ☐ Small-Group Instruction

☐ Pairs   ☐ Other_____

online resources ► Download the full Lesson-Planning Template from resources.corwin.com/mathlessonplanning/6-8

Remember that you can use the online version of the lesson plan template to begin compiling each section into the full template as your lesson plan grows.

Notes

Standards

LI and SC

Purpose

Tasks

Materials

Student Thinking

Lesson Structures

Form. Assess.

Lesson Launch

Lesson Facilitation

Closure

CHAPTER 10

EVALUATING IMPACT

Formative Assessment

I am conducting my internship in an on-grade level seventh-grade class. As I was planning for the fraction operation standards, I thought it would be helpful to conduct some brief formative assessment interviews to help me better understand the students' conceptual understanding of fraction operations. I selected eight students of varying abilities from several different classes to interview. I designed two prompts:

$$3\frac{1}{8} - 1\frac{5}{8} = ? \text{ and } \frac{4}{5} + \frac{4}{10} = ?$$

I am so glad that I interviewed the students because so many had misconceptions! In the first prompt, students subtracted $\frac{1}{8}$ from the $\frac{5}{8}$ rather than turn $3\frac{1}{8}$ into a mixed number. Other students tried to make a mixed number by combining the whole number with the numerator ($3\frac{1}{8} = 3\frac{1}{8}$). In the second prompt, students added numerators and denominators across ($\frac{4}{5} + \frac{4}{10} = \frac{8}{15}$). Other students multiplied only the denominator in $\frac{4}{5}$ to make $\frac{4}{10}$ and then added $\frac{4}{10} + \frac{4}{10}$.

As a result of these interviews, I decided to spend a few days reviewing fraction concepts before beginning work with operations. This was time well spent as students reconciled some key misconceptions that would have prevented them from fully understanding computation with fractions.

Alli Culp
Middle School Teacher
Maryland

Alli used formative assessment to design two prompts to understand her students' thinking about fractions, gather assessment data, and adjust her planning and instruction. This chapter will explore the following questions:

- What is formative assessment?

- What are specific formative assessment techniques?

WHAT IS FORMATIVE ASSESSMENT?

Formative assessment, also called **formative evaluation** (Hattie, 2009), focuses on collecting information about student learning in the moment—as it is happening—and responding to that information by adapting instruction to improve learning. Consistent and thoughtful formative evaluation can be leveraged to produce the largest student-learning gains (Hattie, 2009). Formative assessment can be thought of as *assessment for learning* because teachers adjust their teaching practices in response to what they learn about student understanding. On the flip side, *assessment of learning* may also be called *summative learning*. Schools use **summative assessment** to determine students' achievement levels at particular points in time, particularly at the end of units, quarters, and even entire grade levels. Wiliam and Thompson (2008) recommend the following five key formative assessment strategies.

1. *Clarifying and sharing learning intentions and criteria for success.* The first step in formative assessment involves letting your students know what they will learn and what it means when they have learned it. This is a critical but often misunderstood part of formative assessment. You will recall from Chapter 4 the importance of establishing and communicating learning intentions and success criteria for every student. When you let students know what they are supposed to be learning and help them determine or self-evaluate their own success, you empower them!

2. *Engineering effective classroom discussions, questions, and learning tasks that elicit evidence of learning.* By posing questions, responding to students' thinking, and designing and conducting tasks that prompt deep mathematical thinking, you set the stage for responsive formative assessment. Chapters 6 (tasks), 8 (student thinking), and 12 (facilitating lessons) emphasize the need for and importance of eliciting student thinking. As the engineer, you carefully plan for these opportunities to formatively assess and adapt your instruction.

3. *Providing feedback that moves learning forward.* Feedback that is built upon student thinking and reasoning is powerful because you are targeting exactly the next right instructional move for your particular students. You are charged with evaluating your students to give some type of grade or score, but grades are not actionable feedback. You take the daily collection of student evidence to the next level by offering explicit feedback to students that builds on prior learning, stretches their thinking, and unpacks misconceptions. This feedback is a key component to formative assessment because you are meeting students where they are and advancing their learning during the lesson without delay. Feedback is not a punitive opportunity to catch students when they are wrong but an opportunity to uncover interesting thinking.

   Consider the following examples:

   > Great job explaining what a function is, Miranda!

   > Miranda, I like how you explained that a function relates an input to an output. Can you show me what you mean by giving the class an example?

   Note how the second example provides explicit feedback to the student and asks for further clarification from the student to represent her thinking using an example.

4. *Activating students as instructional resources for one another.* Students can and do provide each other with instructional support. They often recognize each other's misconceptions and can remediate confusion naturally and effortlessly. Other times, they work together through shared learning and serve as instructional supports to each other by asking questions. They also clarify their own understanding by explaining their thinking to others. When you build this kind of co-construction of learning in your classroom, you empower your entire learning community by equally distributing the responsibility of learning to everyone.

5. *Activating students as the owners of their own learning.* When you stimulate students to own their learning, you communicate confidence to them about their ability to advocate for themselves. Students become "in tune" with their own understanding and can convey their levels of understanding to their classmates, teachers, and families.

Standards

LI and SC

Purpose

Tasks

Materials

Student Thinking

Lesson Structures

Form. Assess.

Lesson Launch

Lesson Facilitation

Closure

Example: Kelsie

Seventh-grade teacher Kelsie displays the image of a stoplight (Figure 10.1) to her students during instruction. At strategic points, she asks students to turn and talk about their readiness to move forward in the lesson. When Kelsie first introduced this approach, her seventh graders expressed reticence to evaluate their own understanding, but she persevered and encouraged them to self-evaluate. Now, they are quite comfortable sharing. One of the students, Lionel, explains, "I was nervous to share my thoughts about my understanding to a partner. Now I know that Ms. Smith wants us to be able to figure out if we are confused and then be able to tell her about it."

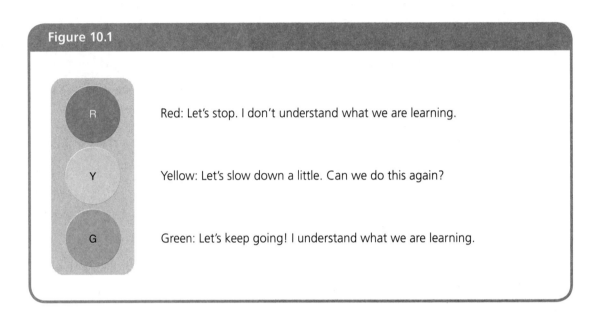

Figure 10.1

Red: Let's stop. I don't understand what we are learning.

Yellow: Let's slow down a little. Can we do this again?

Green: Let's keep going! I understand what we are learning.

As you review these strategies, you may note the shared responsibility that teachers and students hold in the mathematics learning community. You and the students work together to build one another's understanding and probe each other to clarify reasoning. Be sure to communicate that misconceptions are a normal part of every lesson that should be expected and celebrated (Hattie et al., 2016) and express appreciation for their efforts. Also ensure that students understand that they are expected to explain and show their mathematical thinking, ask questions, and evaluate their own understanding.

Which of the formative assessment strategies described so far in this chapter are you currently practicing? Which strategy would you like to develop? Write your intentions below.

_____

_____

_____

_____

_____

_____

_____

_____

_____

_____

_____

WHAT ARE SPECIFIC FORMATIVE ASSESSMENT TECHNIQUES?

The Formative 5 assessment techniques (Fennell et al., 2017) include the following:

- Observation
- Interview
- Show Me
- Hinge questions
- Exit tasks

Each of these techniques includes five important phases:

1. Anticipating student responses
2. Implementing the technique
3. Collecting evidence
4. Adjusting instruction
5. Providing feedback to students

Let's take a close look at each technique, including the five different phases, so you can determine how to implement them in your classroom.

Observation

You observe your students every day! **Observation** is perhaps the most comfortable of all the classroom-based formative assessment strategies because you are constantly informally observing your students as they engage in mathematics activities. Observational evidence is particularly powerful when you document what you observe to inform your instruction (Fennell et al., 2017).

Anticipating Student Responses: How might students respond to the mathematics concepts you are teaching? What will students do during the lessons? What kinds of behaviors or actions will you observe? Think about potential misconceptions (Chapter 8) students might make (Figure 10.2).

Figure 10.2

Mathematics Standard	Anticipate	
	Observations	**Misconceptions**
Understand that positive and negative numbers are used to describe quantities having opposite directions or value.	Use precise mathematical vocabulary to discuss positive and negative numbers.	Students believe that the greater the magnitude of a negative number, the greater the number.
	Use a number line to indicate the position and direction of positive and negative integers.	
	Represent real-world scenarios such as temperature and sea level.	

Standards

LI and SC

Purpose

Tasks

Materials

Student Thinking

Lesson Structures

Form. Assess.

Lesson Launch

Lesson Facilitation

Closure

Implementing the Observations: How and when will you conduct the observation during your lesson? Consider the strategic points during the lesson to conduct observations and collect data.

Collecting Evidence: What kind of tool will you use to record your observations? As you conduct the observation, you will want to use a simple recording tool. Figure 10.3 shows a completed example of a form that seventh-grade teacher Victor used to collect evidence during a lesson.

Figure 10.3

Standard	Solve real-world and mathematical problems involving the four operations with rational numbers.
Prompt	What is the product? Show how you know.
Names	**Observations**
Maria	Recorded multiplication of positive and negative integers on a number line. Discovered that the properties of the operations for multiplication are the same as the properties for rational number multiplication using the number line model.
Kevin	Could not use the number line to model a positive integer multiplied by a negative integer and said, "This does not make sense to me."

Adjusting Instruction: How will you immediately adjust instruction using the feedback from the observation? For example, using the evidence collected in Figure 10.3, Victor prompted Maria to see if she could use what she knows about the properties of multiplication of positive and negative integers to solve division problems. He asked, "How could you use what you discovered about multiplication of positive and negative integers to solve division problems with positive and negative integers?

For Kevin, Victor suggested, "Let's take a look at a situation that might help us make sense of the problem. What if Mrs. Green owed \$5 to her mother and her sister? We could then say that 2 represents her mother and sister and –5 represents the money she owes to each of them." Kevin writes $2 \times -5 = $ ____. Victor then asks, "How much does Mrs. Green owe?"

Providing Feedback to Students: How will you do this during the lesson to move learning forward? It's important to give feedback swiftly, after students have supplied evidence of their learning. Immediate feedback helps students positively connect the feedback with their explanation or representation. You also need to ensure that the feedback is explicit and connects specifically to the student's learning needs. In Victor's example, he said to Maria, "You used the number line to represent your equations. Is it possible to use the number line for division or would another model work better?" In this case, Victor is moving Maria's learning forward to support her strength in making generalizations about her discoveries.

Victor's feedback to Kevin was also careful and thoughtful. He said, "I can see that you started to use a number line to record the equation. How could we use the number line you made to represent the story about Mrs. Green and the equation?" Victor positively reinforced Kevin's effort to use a number line to record the values and the operation for the equation. He then provided a context for the equation to help Kevin make sense of the operation. While Victor could have rushed in to provide a rule, he would have lost a powerful opportunity to help Kevin make sense of the positive and negative operations.

Once again, Victor gave explicit feedback to Kevin and then deftly positioned a new task to move his thinking along. If teachers wait too long to give feedback to students, the magical moment can be lost, and students will not be able to connect the feedback to their actions.

Interview

The formative assessment **interview** is a brief interview that you tuck into a lesson when you want to collect more information about a student's thinking. The interview is brief, is on the spot, and can be conducted as a response to something you observed students doing. Interviews can help you dig deeper into the source of student misconceptions.

Anticipating Student Responses: Consider the kinds of responses students might give you during the interview. You can decide ahead of time that you will interview particular students or a group of students. You might also decide to interview students who respond in particular ways to the lesson. Interview questions include these:

- Why did you decide to solve it that way?
- Can you explain your thinking?

Implementing the Interview: When and how will you conduct it? You can also plan to tuck interviews in a lesson during small-group instruction.

Collecting Evidence: You gather student data to inform your instructional decisions. For example, Anita, a seventh-grade teacher, designed an interview recording sheet to use when students are working in small groups (Figure 10.4). She finds that this is the best time to conduct the interview because she can concentrate on her students' thinking.

Figure 10.4

Group:

Date	Name	Interview Question	Interview Notes

Adjusting Instruction: As you interview students, you can gain insight into those sticky misconceptions that prevent students from learning. For example, during an interview about whole-number exponents, Megan interviewed Ashton by asking him to represent 3^3 using unit cubes and explain his thinking. Ashton showed her the following (see Figure 10.5).

Standards

LI and SC

Purpose

Tasks

Materials

Student Thinking

Lesson Structures

Form. Assess.

Lesson Launch

Lesson Facilitation

Closure

Figure 10.5

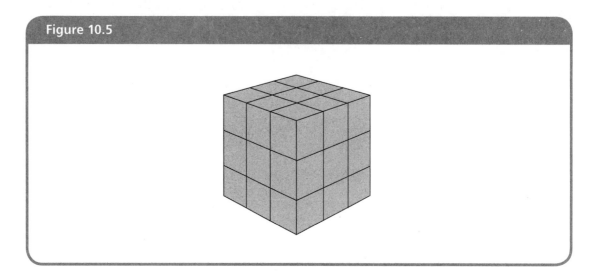

Megan replied, "Now tell me the value of the exponent and how this value is represented in your model."

Ashton explained, "Well, the exponent is 3 and that means that we multiply 3 three times (writes $3 \times 3 \times 3$). So, in my model, the first $3 \times 3 = 9$ is the first layer (points to the bottom of the cube). Then, there are three layers, so that is $9 \times 3 = 27$ (points to each layer of the cube as he explains)."

Megan asked, "You explained how you found the total value of this expression and explained the exponent. What would your model look like if I changed the exponent to 3^4?"

Ashton responded, "Well, then I would have to make three more cubes with 27 in each cube! See, now I would write it as $3 \times 3 \times 3 \times 3 = \_$ because $3 \times 3 \times 3 = 27$ (points to the cube) and then I would multiply 27×3, which would be the same as if I made three more cubes. Can I make two more cubes?" Without waiting for an answer, Ashton built two more cubes (see Figure 10.6).

Figure 10.6

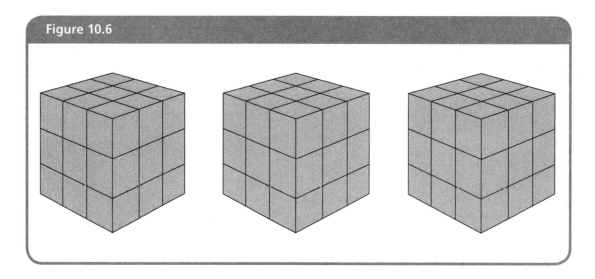

"See, this shows $27 \times 3 = 81$."

Megan asked, "What have you noticed about the exponents?"

Ashton responded, "I noticed right away that exponents get really big really fast. I also noticed that the reason we say the exponent 3 as 'cubed' is because it actually makes a cube when we make a model. At first I thought adding an exponent would add a layer to the cube, but I realized that wasn't going to be big enough."

Megan replied, "Ashton, you are thinking like a mathematician because you are noticing patterns and then applying those patterns. You noticed something important about what happens when an exponent is increased by even one digit and how that affects the value. I would like you to share your ideas with the class because I think it will help everyone understand the power of exponents."

Megan's interview revealed Ashton's advanced understanding of exponents and his ability to make connections and see patterns between the model and the exponent. If she had not interviewed Ashton, she might never have known that he was thinking this deeply about his learning.

Providing Feedback: Once again, timely *feedback* is critical. However, note that in Megan's interview, she did not start providing feedback to Ashton before she gathered evidence of his thinking. She needed to fully understand the extent of his understanding in order to provide appropriate feedback.

Megan next said to Ashton, "You explained to me how your model for 3^3 would change if we increased the exponent value to 3^4. What would happen if we increased the value to 3^5? Can you describe what that model would look like?"

In this example, Megan reflected back what Ashton said and did in the interview, and then she asked a question to prompt more thinking. While it would have been easier for Megan simply to tell Ashton the pattern, she knew that providing feedback by reflecting back to Ashton about his own thinking would promote new learning.

Show Me

The **Show Me** technique is "a performance response by a student or group of students that extends and often deepens what was observed and what might have been asked within an interview" (Fennell et al., 2017, p. 63). This technique is nicely suited for middle school teachers because you can easily integrate the Show Me technique into lessons by asking students to show understanding using manipulatives and/or drawings, digit cards, whiteboards, and/or response cards.

Anticipating Student Responses: As you plan to use the Show Me technique, think about the potential responses students might provide. For example, Gary, a seventh-grade teacher, gave each student a set of Algebra Tiles. He planned to ask the students to show a representation of a polynomial, $2x^2 + 5x$, using the Algebra Tiles and then determine the symbolic form of the polynomial (see Figure 10.7).

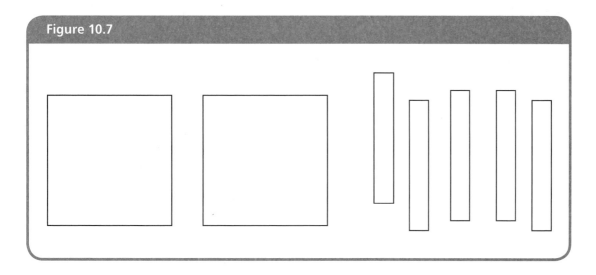

Figure 10.7

He anticipated that some students might struggle and prepared some questions to help the students reason using the relationships of the Algebra Tiles (see Figure 10.8). When a few students struggled, he asked,

Standards

LI and SC

Purpose

Tasks

Materials

Student Thinking

Lesson Structures

Form. Assess.

Lesson Launch

Lesson Facilitation

Closure

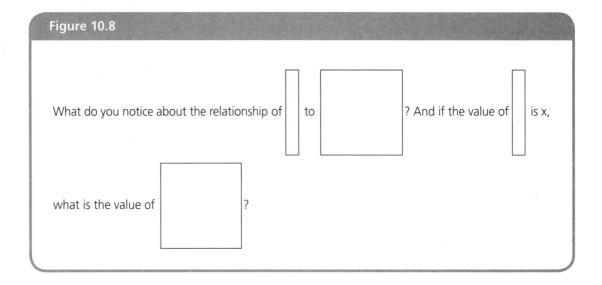

Figure 10.8

What do you notice about the relationship of [ ] to [ ] ? And if the value of [ ] is x,

what is the value of [ ] ?

Implementing Show Me: Consider at what points you will want to use it. Gary planned to implement the Show Me technique during the brief whole-group lesson. He hoped to give them several prompts and ask them probing questions to explain their representations.

Collecting Evidence: You can collect evidence using the Show Me technique by taking photographs, jotting down notes, and using technology applications like Go Formative (Goformative.com), which collects representations of individual students' work. Gary often snaps a photo of the students as they are showing their work.

Adjusting Instruction: As you conduct the Show Me technique, consider how you will adjust instruction using the evidence you are collecting. Show Me prompts, in particular, often reveal trends in student thinking because you can see everyone's response at one time. For example, as Gary was prompting the students with the Show Me technique, he noted that a few students were not able to connect the representation of the polynomial with Algebra Tiles to the symbolic representation. He decided to have the students first show the polynomial and then asked them to discuss the value of what they represented. He thought that this adjustment would help the students focus on the values they saw before writing the symbolic representation.

Providing Feedback: The Show Me formative assessment offers the perfect opportunity for students to provide feedback to each other by explaining their own thinking and probing each other's thinking. For instance, as Gary scanned the room, he noticed that Sierra quickly showed the symbolic representation almost before he even posed the prompt. While she waited for her classmates, she created more Algebra Tile representations and wrote the symbolic form to match. Gary decided to put the students in pairs while he posed the prompts so they could explain their thinking to each other. He purposely paired Sierra with Tommy because he noticed that Tommy was struggling to show the symbolic notation. He heard Sierra say, "Tommy, when Mr. Raymond shows the representation with the Algebra Tiles, just think about what the value of each one is and then write that down. After that, we will put it together."

Hinge Questions

As a teacher, you craft and ask hundreds of questions throughout the course of one day! The **hinge question** is a special kind of question that essentially provides a check for understanding at a pivotal moment in your lesson (Wiliam, 2011). In other words, the next part of your lesson hinges on how students respond. According to Wiliam (2011), students should respond in one minute or less. Fennell et al. (2017) suggest that this could be expanded to two or three minutes, particularly as you consider the developmental needs of your primary students.

Anticipating Student Responses: The key to writing a good hinge question is to anticipate the possible interpretations or incorrect responses that students might give. Hinge questions take several forms, including multiple choice and short, open-ended prompts. For example, Keisha, an eighth-grade teacher, developed a multiple-choice hinge question for the following standard:

> Know that straight lines are widely used to model relationships between two quantitative variables. For scatter plots that suggest a linear association, informally fit a straight line, and informally assess the model fit by judging the closeness of the data points to the line.

Here is Keisha's hinge question:

> The coaches from Meredith School District were arguing about whether more basketball practice increased student wins. The coaches decided to collect some data. They recorded the number of hours they practice and their wins. The graph (Figure 10.9) shows the results of this data collection. Select the choices that match the data.

Figure 10.9

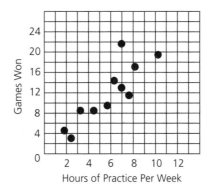

The graph indicates which of the following? Select all that are true.

A. The scatterplot diagram shows a positive correlation between the number of hours of practice per week and the number of games won.

B. The fewest number of hours of practice is four.

C. The scatterplot diagram shows a negative correlation between the number of hours of practice and the number of games won.

D. The number of games won ranges from 4 to 22.

Keisha anticipated that all or most of her students would select A but also thought a handful of students might select C. Some students might still be shaky on understanding how data change when there is a positive or negative correlation. She also wanted to see if the students would be able to explain the correlation they selected on the scatterplot by describing the relationship between the number of practice hours and number of games won.

Implementing Hinge Questions: To implement hinge questions, you can pose them at the beginning, middle, or end of the lesson. The key idea is to pose the question at a strategic point to assess if students are ready to move on to the next concept. For example, Keisha decided to ask her question after a task on analyzing scatterplots, which was at the midpoint of her lesson.

Collecting Evidence: You can collect evidence of students' responses to the hinge questions by using small slips of paper, journals, or technology. For example, Keisha displayed the prompt for her students on a whiteboard and distributed small slips of paper with the same prompt for students to circle and then write a brief explanation.

Adjusting Instruction: Many teachers choose to regroup students to adjust instruction after collecting evidence from the hinge question. Keisha planned to move her students into math stations so she could provide additional instruction for her struggling students in a small group while the other students rotated through the stations, which included a task with analyzing scatterplots. Keisha used the hinge question to flexibly group her students, using real evidence from the lesson. She loved that she was immediately responding to the students' learning needs.

Providing Feedback: You can provide feedback on the hinge question in many ways. Some teachers reveal the correct answer and have students gather in pairs or small groups to discuss the solutions. Other teachers, like Keisha, use the hinge question to provide explicit instructional feedback to the students during the lesson, either in small groups or individually. The key is to take an immediate call to action based on the evidence.

Exit Task

The **exit task** is a "capstone problem or task that captures the major focus of the lesson for that day or perhaps the last several days and provides a sampling of student performance" (Fennell et al., 2017, p. 109). You may be familiar with the term **exit ticket** or **exit slip**. However, an exit task extends beyond a simple question that may assess only a small portion of the student's understanding. Instead, the exit task is a high-cognitive task (see Chapter 6) that includes opportunities for students to connect procedures to concepts, explore mathematical relationships, use representations, and apply self-monitoring and self-regulation skills as they work to solve the problem (Smith & Stein, 2011).

Bryan, a sixth-grade teacher, considered the prompts in Figure 10.10 for his exit task.

Figure 10.10

Task A	Task B
Compare 62% and $\frac{4}{7}$ using <, >, or =.	Plot $\frac{4}{7}$, 123%, 62%, 0.23, $\frac{9}{11}$, $\frac{6}{10}$, and $\frac{57}{100}$ on a number line and then choose two values and explain why you placed them on those points on the number line.

Bryan chose Task B because he wanted the students to use reasoning and provide mathematical evidence to show their thinking. Task A wasn't going to give him good information about the students' understanding of decimal, percent, and fraction comparisons.

Anticipating Student Responses: Once again, it is critical to *anticipate* the results of the formative assessment, particularly as you consider how you will assess your students' understanding of the concept you just taught. You can also differentiate the exit task or design it so that students can enter into the task from different points. For example, students could begin by placing the values they are most comfortable plotting on the number line.

Implementing Exit Tasks: As the description of the task indicated, you can implement an exit task at the end of a concept or lesson. Some teachers design exit tasks to reflect standards that they have been teaching for a long time. Other teachers design and conduct exit tasks toward the end of the lesson. The key is to make sure you give students plenty of time to solve the task!

Collecting Evidence: Review the students' responses to the exit task to collect evidence for overall trends in their understanding. After that, you can examine each group for individual strengths and needs. For example, Bryan likes to use an exit task summary sheet (Figure 10.11) to analyze student work from the whole class. He uses the same format for each exit task and supplies the specific criteria for each task. He then records the names of the students below the appropriate criteria.

Figure 10.11

Exit Task: Plot $\frac{4}{7}$, 123%, 62%, 0.23, $\frac{9}{11}$, $\frac{6}{10}$, and $\frac{57}{100}$ on a number line and then choose two values and explain why you placed them on those points on the number line.

Does Not Meet Expectations (Describe)	Meets Expectations (Describe)	Exceeds Expectations (Describe)
Provides incomplete or incorrect placement of values on the number line.	Provides accurate placement of values on the number line and includes a basic explanation.	Provides accurate placement of values on the number line and provides a thorough explanation.
Raymond	Marcela	Kia
Mia	Sam	Aliyah

Adjusting Instruction: Your exit task evidence is quite important in deciding how you will adjust instruction. For instance, you may decide that your students are ready to move on or, perhaps, that they need additional, targeted instruction. The exit task is particularly suited to differentiation as you see the particular needs of your students. You may be tempted to divide them into same-ability groups, but you might also wish to consider mixed-ability groups, which allow students to share strategies and construct new ideas together. The key is to use student evidence to make your decisions about how you will adjust instruction.

Providing Feedback to the Students: Since the exit task is often conducted at the end of the lesson or series of lessons, you will want to provide feedback that is directly connected to the success criteria. You can do this when you move to your next instructional step, whether you choose to work with students individually, in small groups, or in large groups. Exit task data are also great data to share with families. For example, Bryan collects two exit tasks per quarter to place in the students' portfolios for family conferences. In his school, students lead the conferences by sharing their work, thus providing even more opportunities to receive feedback.

As you can see, formative assessment is intricately tied to your planning and teaching. If you are just beginning to use formative assessment techniques, begin with those that are most comfortable to you, and build your repertoire as you develop ease with the techniques.

> **Which of the formative assessment techniques will you try first? Why? How will you begin integrating this technique into your teaching practice? Record your ideas below.**

As you design and collect daily formative assessment evidence, you develop comprehensive knowledge of your students' mathematical understanding. You can support unit coherence by varying the techniques and kinds of formative assessment data you collect.

Example: Michaela

Michaela, a sixth-grade teacher, realizes that she is primarily using the observation technique for her students. This technique produces a lot of anecdotal evidence, but although it is rich in detail, she wants to use more student work evidence. Consequently, she decides to incorporate more Show Me assessment prompts over the course of the unit. She feels that the combination of anecdotal notes and student work nicely captures her students' mathematical understanding and, over the course of the unit, creates a coherent picture of all of the students' learning.

Notes

Standards

LI and SC

Purpose

Tasks

Materials

Student Thinking

Lesson Structures

Form. Assess.

Lesson Launch

Lesson Facilitation

Closure

Sixth-Grade Snapshot

Formative Assessment

The sixth-grade teachers are deciding which formative assessment technique to use for teaching students how to translate word problems into written expressions. Jeff suggests, "Since we are planning to begin with Algebra Tiles, I would like to use observation and interviews to ensure everyone understands the concept. When I notice my students understand using the tiles, I want to move them to the pictorial level, drawing or illustrating the problem. Then, I will challenge them to write expressions without tiles or drawings." "Good idea," says Josh. "When we observe struggling learners, let's help these students by listening to their thinking and working with them in a small-group setting. Observation is a great way to meet student learning needs."

Formative Assessment:

Observe students as they work on problems. Look to determine if students are drawing pictures of the manipulatives or writing the expressions abstractly. Note that a few students may still need to use Algebra Tiles.

See the complete lesson plan in Appendix A on page 188.

Think of a lesson you taught recently where a hinge question would have been useful. Note the question below.

Bryan wondered, "Since we are teaching a transfer lesson, how can we help the students provide feedback to each other while we also collect formative assessment data?" Kyle agreed, "I think that while we are hoping that the misconceptions are resolved, we still need to be prepared." Alix responded, "What if we also strategically pair them to work together purposefully? Students can then provide feedback to one another!" Kyle added, "In the meantime, we can conduct some interview questions and record responses to learn more about the students' understanding." Kia responded, "Let's write some interview questions!"

Formative Assessment:

Interview:
- How do you know your equation matches the problem?
- Is there another way to represent the problem?

See the complete lesson plan in Appendix A on page 192.

How might you capture students' work while using the Show Me formative assessment technique?

When it came to assessment, Serena knew exactly what she wanted to do. She had just read a synopsis of formative assessment online at the National Council of Teachers of Mathematics website. There were several examples of formative assessment techniques. She was intrigued by the hinge question. She had never used one before, but when she thought about how much time she spent deciding on an essential question, she realized that a hinge question would help her decide if her lesson was meeting the focus she was looking for. She designed a hinge question and could not wait to see what results she would get!

Formative Assessment:

Hinge question (after the sorting): How do each of these graphs reflect the information in the story?

See the complete lesson plan in Appendix A on page 203.

How could you integrate brief formative assessment interviews into your practice? Note your ideas below.

_____

_____

_____

_____

_____

_____

_____

_____

_____

_____

_____

_____

_____

_____

_____

_____

_____

_____

_____

_____

_____

_____

Standards | LI and SC | Purpose | Tasks | Materials | Student Thinking | Lesson Structures | Form. Assess. | Lesson Launch | Lesson Facilitation | Closure

Now it is your turn! Decide on the formative assessment(s) that will best suit the lesson you are building.

Formative Assessment:

Download the full Lesson-Planning Template from resources.corwin.com/mathlessonplanning/6-8
Remember that you can use the online version of the lesson plan template to begin compiling each section into the full template as your lesson plan grows.

PART III

PULLING ALL THE PIECES TOGETHER

CHAPTER 11

PLANNING TO LAUNCH THE LESSON

I love thinking about my lesson launches. I have come to find them as important as the task/lesson itself. I see the launching of a task/lesson similar to a movie. If the opening of a movie is very uninteresting, typically the audience will become distracted and disengage. This will then lead them to missing out on much of the movie until something captures their attention. In the process, they are overlooking details that could bring more meaning to the movie. Similarly, in teaching, if I do not captivate the students in the first five to ten minutes, they are less likely to fully engage in the task/lesson. Students may then miss the opportunity to recognize details, notice patterns, and ask important questions.

On the other hand, if an audience is attracted to the story within the first few minutes, it will anticipate the next twist and turn in the story. I have noticed that if my launch is intriguing, the students will begin to notice, wonder, and predict independently, which, in turn, cultivates an environment of enthusiasm for learning mathematics, making connections, and learning.

Something I have been doing lately is storytelling. Just last week I started a lesson on systems of equations by telling the students the old tortoise and the hare story. I used this story because many of the students have heard the story and are able to tell others about the story if they haven't. However, through the storytelling, I encouraged the students to re-create the story with characters that interested them. They chose a tiger and a greyhound. In my story, the tiger gives the dog a head start. The tiger knows that he runs 7 feet per second and

the dog runs 5 feet per second. The students started calling out questions:

- Who wins the race?
- Who runs the furthest?
- Who is the fastest?
- Can we create an equation to represent the tiger and the dog?

I was thrilled with their questions and knew that they were now ready! I said, "Let's graph the race to represent what is happening in the story." The students excitedly went to work!

Zac Stavish
Middle School Teacher
Maryland

This chapter explores ways to begin your lesson. We will explore the following questions:

- What is a lesson launch?
- How can you launch a problem-solving lesson?
- What kinds of lesson launches focus on mathematics concepts?
- What are number routine lesson launches?
- What do you anticipate students will do?

WHAT IS A LESSON LAUNCH?

Imagine you are opening to the first page of a book or turning to a new television show. How quickly do you decide whether you will continue to read or watch or abandon? In a similar way, students may also make conscious or unconscious decisions about whether they will engage in a lesson. This possibility highlights the importance of the **lesson launch.**

Your lesson launch can be implemented in many ways and should be designed with just as much purpose and planning as the main body of your lesson. For example, lesson launches may include a number sense routine to help students think and talk about numbers, equations, and computation. Or, your lesson launch might introduce a specific problem-solving task. Your lesson launch can be tied directly to the big idea and learning intention for the day, particularly if you plan to use the lesson launch to set up the lesson you are about to teach. Or you might use the lesson launch to circle back to a big idea or concept that the students previously learned because you want to make sure the children continue to build understanding of that concept. This is called **interleaving,** and it increases the students' retention and performance on assessments (Rohrer, 2012).

The way that you construct how your lesson will be launched will depend greatly on your students' learning needs, the content standards, Standards for Mathematical Practice or process standards, learning intentions, and lesson purpose. Lessons can be launched by creating interest around a problem-solving task (like in the vignette at the start of this chapter), connecting to prior knowledge or previous lessons, or implementing a number routine. Lesson launches can be facilitated in 5 to 15 minutes and are typically conducted in a whole-group setting.

Many teachers use the same routine, like a warmup, to launch a lesson every day. While there are benefits to building a routine into your mathematics lesson, such as a warmup, teachers report that most students passively watch one or two students answer the warmup exercises. Rather than beginning your mathematics lesson in the same way every day, vary your lesson launch as it connects to the students' learning and math content needs. As you read this chapter, consider ways you might launch your mathematics lessons to stimulate *all* students' interests and boost conceptual understanding.

HOW CAN YOU LAUNCH A PROBLEM-SOLVING LESSON?

Launching a lesson with a focus on problem solving gives you an opportunity to help students unpack a problem before trying to solve it. The following problem-solving lesson launches also nicely connect to the Standards for Mathematical Practice or process standards. You can focus on helping students make sense of problems, develop ways to communicate their ideas, ask questions of their peers, and critique each other's reasoning and thinking.

See, Think, and Wonder Lesson Launch

The See, Think, and Wonder (STW) (Ritchhart, Church, & Morrison, 2011) routine summons students to carefully observe, make some predictions, and expand the predictions into questions. Along with Notice and Wonder (Math Forum, 2015), which is described later in this chapter, STW capitalizes on students' keen observational skills and natural curiosity about what they are learning. When you use this launch, you invite students to bring their own thoughts and questions forward before you instruct them to engage in particular ways with the content. Both strategies can help students draw on prior knowledge, and they motivate students to reason before receiving formal instruction, which is particularly useful for English Language Learners (ELLs) or other learners who struggle. The two strategies have slight but important variations.

> Example: Lucita
>
> Lucita, a sixth-grade teacher, has always noticed that her sixth graders are very inquisitive, and she likes to engage their curiosity as much as possible. Instead of giving the students the definition and area formula of a right triangle, she decides to capitalize on their natural curiosity to engage and motivate them.
>
> To launch the lesson, Lucita shows students the illustration in Figure 11.1 and asks them to SEE quietly.

Figure 11.1

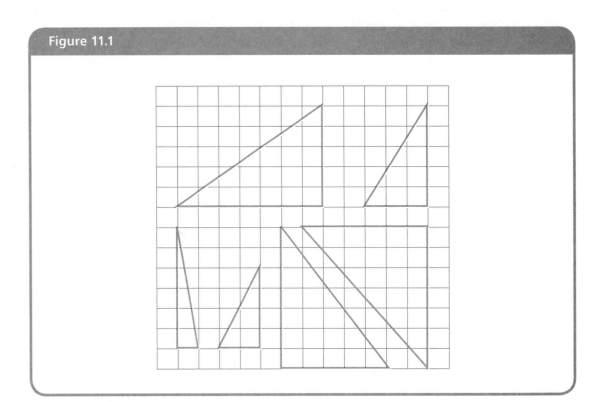

This quiet reflection time allows students an opportunity to make observations without being hindered by another student's thoughts. Lucita makes sure that students have enough time to notice important details in the picture. She then asks the students to share with a partner what they saw. She reminds them that she wants them to share by making "I SEE" statements. She then asks the student pairs to share something their partners noticed that they didn't. She records their answers in a chart that everyone can view (Figure 11.2).

Figure 11.2

I SEE

Triangles on grid paper

Right angles

Two triangles that almost match

Some of the triangles have more boxes than the other.

Skinny triangles

Wider triangles

Acute angles

Some of the boxes are cut in half.

Lucita then asks the students to THINK. To remind her students that this is when they make predictions about what they are seeing, she says, "Using what you observe, make a prediction about what you are seeing. What do you think is going on here?" She again gives them quiet time to think. This time, she calls on students to share their ideas. Then she records their answers (Figure 11.3).

Standards

LI and SC

Purpose

Tasks

Materials

Student Thinking

Lesson Structures

Form. Assess.

Lesson Launch

Lesson Facilitation

Closure

Figure 11.3

I THINK

That the two triangles might match up.

That the angles equal 180 degrees.

That they all have a least a right angle.

Maybe they have two acute angles?

Lucita then asks students what they WONDER after Seeing and Thinking about the shapes. She records the Wonders (Figure 11.4). Students may also record their own Wonders on individual whiteboards and then post them for everyone to see.

Figure 11.4

I WONDER

If we are going to measure the angles.

If we are going to find the perimeter.

If we are going to find the area.

Lucita then uses the Wonders to launch into her lesson about finding the area of right triangles. She gives the students the same paper with the triangles and asks, "How can you find the area?" By igniting their curiosity, Lucita is able to build on what they already know to advance their understanding before developing the formula for finding the area of a right triangle.

Notice and Wonder Lesson Launch

While similar to the See, Think, and Wonder approach, the Notice and Wonder protocol, developed by the Math Forum (2015), simplifies the process into two distinct steps. It was originally designed to focus students on unpacking word problems to enhance students' understanding of "the story, the quantities, and the relationships in the problem" (p. 2). The Math Forum suggests the following steps:

Notice

- Display or read a portion or complete problem to students.
- Ask the students, "What do you notice?" Be sure to encourage wait time.
- Record all of the students' ideas without commenting.

Wonder

- Ask the students, "What are you wondering?"
- Record all of the students' ideas without commenting.
- Ask the students if they have additional questions or clarifications.

At the conclusion of the Notice and Wonder, you can encourage students to tell the story in partners or small groups before solving the problem.

Example: Kelsie

Seventh-grade teacher Kelsie often uses Notice and Wonder to introduce routine and nonroutine word problems. Her students are so accustomed to this approach that they can even conduct their own Notice and Wonder sessions in small groups. One day she shares the following problem with her seventh graders:

Karlo had 240 baseball cards. He decided that he wasn't interested in collecting anymore, but he didn't want to give them all away. So, he decided to give some away. He gave half of them to his younger cousin. He found five doubles in his collection and gave that five to his friend. Of the amount left, he gave $\frac{1}{5}$ to his younger brother, who was just starting his collection. Now both his cousin and brother were upset because each thought the other got more. Who ends up with more baseball cards? ▮▮▮▮▮▮▮▮▮▮▮▮▮▮? (Note that the question is covered.)

The seventh graders notice the following:

- Karlo had 240 baseball cards.
- He gave half to his cousin.
- He gave $\frac{1}{5}$ to brother.
- He gave 5 to a friend.

They wondered the following:

- Why is he giving away all these cards?
- Shouldn't he try and sell some?
- Who ends up with the most cards? Karlo, the cousin, or the brother?

Kelsie then reveals the question: "Who ends up with more baseball cards?" How many cards does each person have?

Kelsie often uses the Notice and Wonder technique to encourage the students to engage with the problem before seeing the question. She notices that the students often ask the question in the problem themselves, which enhances student comprehension and heightens their interest in solving the problem.

Numberless Word Problem Lesson Launch

Students may be so distracted by the numbers in the word problem that they are tempted to perform any operation regardless of what makes sense. The **numberless word problem** launch encourages the students to make sense of the word problem without the numbers.

Example: Denzyl

Denzyl, an eighth-grade teacher, displays and reads the following problem to his students:

Ellie and Tia are running a 10K marathon. Ellie and Tia started out together. Ellie runs every mile faster than Tia. What is happening to the distance between the two runners? Create a graph that represents the story.

Denzyl has purposely selected a word problem to help students visualize what the graph would look like without the number values and think about the equation that would represent the story ($d = t + ?$).

Denzyl asks student pairs to talk with each other and share their ideas about what is happening in the word problem. As he looks around the classroom, he notices that the students are talking about how much faster Ellie might run than Tia. He also notices that students are discussing that the graph depends on how much faster Ellie runs than Tia. Prior to the lesson, he anticipated that the students might supply numbers and begin trying to solve the problem. He is pleased to see that this is happening!

After about five minutes of paired discussion, Denzyl asks, "What is this word problem asking us to solve?" Here are the students' replies.

Maria: I think we are doing that distance/time formula?

Mabel: I agree, but we really can't solve this until we know how fast the girls are running.

Raymond: Yes, and the graph will go up!

Leo: Right, but we don't know how much until we know how fast they run each mile.

Maria: Ya, but the lines will get farther apart no matter what because Ellie runs faster.

Leo: Ohhh! You mean because they start out kinda close together, but Ellie goes faster so then they are farther apart?

Denzyl smiles. This is exactly the kind of discussion he had hoped to elicit. Without the numbers in the problem, the students are able to reason about the problem, supply their own numbers, and visualize what the graph might look like to test their ideas.

 What do you notice about the lesson launches? How might you integrate these kinds of lesson launches into your lesson planning? Record some of your ideas here.

_____

_____

_____

_____

WHAT KINDS OF LESSON LAUNCHES FOCUS ON MATHEMATICS CONCEPTS?

You can use the following lesson launch routines to focus students on recalling, using, and applying prior knowledge; using, developing, and applying appropriate vocabulary; and noticing and examining the structure of mathematics.

One of These Things Is Not Like the Others

You may remember the old *Sesame Street* song:

> One of these things is not like the others,
> One of these things just doesn't belong. (Raposo & Stone, 1972)

In this lesson launch, students examine numbers, pictures, and graphs and try to determine why one of the choices does not belong. Students must select one of the options and then construct a viable argument about why they believe a particular picture, number, or graph does not belong. The key to this launch is to provide examples that offer different entry points for students.

Standards

LI and SC

Purpose

Tasks

Materials

Student Thinking

Lesson Structures

Form. Assess.

Lesson Launch

Lesson Facilitation

Closure

Example: Diamond

Diamond's students have been working diligently on interpreting graphs. She wants to see if the students will be able to interpret a graph by describing a story that matches the direction and movement of the line in the graph.

Diamond designs the prompt in Figure 11.5 to elicit conversation about the graphs. Whenever Diamond uses this type of prompt, she typically displays it and then gives the students time to think about and prepare a mathematical argument for which one is not like the others. Sometimes she even challenges the students to create a mathematical argument for all of the choices. In this case, she ensures that any of the choices can be selected as the one not like the others if students can explain their reasoning.

Figure 11.5

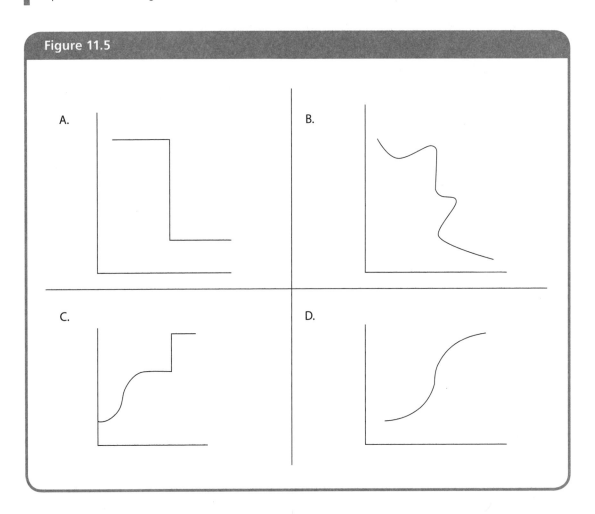

Diamond asks, "Which one of these things is not like the others?"

Diamond's students quickly notice that two of the graphs are showing increases and two are showing decreases. Also, Graph A and Graph C show horizontal lines.

This lesson launch offers Diamond good insight into her students' thinking about interpreting graphs. She is able to use the student work from this lesson launch to transition to her lesson that focuses on understanding functions to interpret and draw graphs.

You can also tailor this lesson launch to focus on particular kinds of reasoning that your students exhibit. For more examples like this, you can check out the Which One Doesn't Belong website (http://wodb.ca) created by Mary Barousa with contributions by teachers from all over the country. Also, check out Christopher Danielson's (2016) book, *Which One Doesn't Belong?* which focuses on shapes, numbers, and other mathematics concepts.

WHAT ARE NUMBER SENSE ROUTINE LESSON LAUNCHES?

Number sense routines focus on strategies that help students understand number concepts and build computational fluency. Most important, you are providing opportunities for students to derive their own strategies, hear the strategies their peers use, and develop fluency using those strategies. Number sense routines also offer opportunities for students to engage in **spaced practice**, which occurs when you expose students to an idea over several days and then *space* opportunities to practice the learned skill (Hattie et al., 2016). Select your number sense routines purposely, either as a launch to link to the content you are about to teach or as an opportunity to provided spaced practice. The following number sense routine lesson launches encourage the students to develop understanding and reasoning about numbers, flexibility with numbers, and number fluency.

Estimation

> Example: Marcus
>
> Marcus, a sixth-grade teacher, uses estimation both as a lesson launch and as a station in his classroom. He uses estimation as a launch when he wants to create a discussion with students about efficient ways to reason about numbers. For a lesson on decimal multiplication, Leo launches the lesson by posing the two different scenarios in a visual format (Figure 11.6).

Figure 11.6

How much?

12.2 pounds of apples
$2.75 per pound

How many students?

Mountain Range College
24,900 enrolled

Sea Level College
0.43 as many students at Mountain Range

Image sources: Apples: drmakkoy/iStock.com; Mountain: ser_igor/iStock.com; Sea: gyener/iStock.com

---

Standards

LI and SC

Purpose

Tasks

Materials

Student Thinking

Lesson Structures

Form. Assess.

Lesson Launch

Lesson Facilitation

Closure

He first asks them to make an estimate for the apple problem and the college problem and record their estimates on sticky notes. He posts the new sticky notes from least to greatest and asks the students to make observations about the estimates. Then he asks the students to pair up and discuss the range of estimates and come up with a new estimate and record it on a sticky note and post for everyone to see. Students quickly note which estimates are too high and too low. They also notice that their estimates are now much closer together. He elicits reasoning from the students and encourages them to make friendly numbers to estimate. This launch sets the stage perfectly for Marcus to build on their decimal estimation to make sense of the standard algorithm.

For more estimation examples, pictures, and lessons for Grades 6, 7 and 8, check out the Estimation 180 website (http://www.estimation180.com/lessons.html) created by Andrew Stadel.

Number Lines

The number line is ideally suited to support students as they develop meaning about rational numbers and the relationships between rational numbers. The number line offers endless opportunities to differentiate according to students' content and learning needs. You can change the start and end points, include particular benchmarks, and provide or encourage students to connect concrete or pictorial representations to the placement of values on the number line. You display a number line and ask students to post sticky notes to show where it belongs. You can also put different number lines in stations around the room and ask students to move through the stations.

You can use the number line in a number sense launch routine to help students construct conceptual understanding, reason about number patterns and relationships, and develop fluency.

Example: Becca

Seventh-grade teacher Becca uses an interactive number line to encourage students to reason about where to place $\frac{1}{3}$, –0.1, –4, $\frac{1}{100}$, and 2 on a number line. She poses the prompt and distributes laminated number lines and markers to the students. Students then record their thinking using dry erase markers. Finally, she posts the students' ideas and has the students discuss what they notice about the placement of the rational numbers (Figure 11.7).

Happily, she notes that many students are thinking about value of each of the rational numbers and the associated placement on a number line.

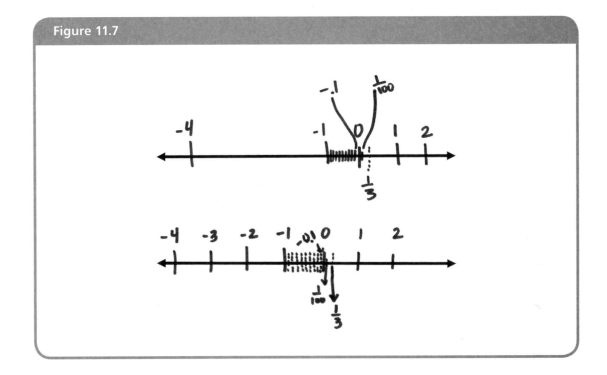

Figure 11.7

Always, Sometimes, or Never True

This lesson launch is ideally suited to help students confront rules they have previously learned that no longer can be applied or explore a common misconception. Students are presented with a prompt and then must prove whether it is Always, Sometimes, or Never True by providing examples and a verbal or written explanation.

> Example: Caite
>
> Caite asks students to be prepared to provide examples and counterexamples to justify their reasoning. She selected the following prompt because students seemed to have forgotten the role of parentheses in equations and wanted to encourage a discussion that would challenge their own errors. Caite poses the following prompt:
>
> $$4(x + 2) = 4x + 2$$
>
> Ray calls out, "Sometimes!" Others yell out in agreement.
>
> Caite notices that *Sometimes* is often the default answer when students are unsure. She pressed them for an explanation, "If you believe it is sometimes, then you must be able to find an example and a counterexample." Her students engage in a spirited discussion as they try to find an example when this prompt might be true.
>
> Alane says, "I don't think it is ever true. We have tried ten different examples and we can't make it work."
>
> Caite smiles, "I appreciate your effort to find these examples to justify your reasoning. How does working out some examples help support your reasoning?"

Splats

Developed by Steve Wyborney, Splats are visual number sense routines that build students' mathematical reasoning by presenting them with a combination of visual **subitizing**, visual patterns, and hidden values. Jose uses Splats to foster understanding about writing expressions and finding variables by determining the hidden values under the splat when given the total. He presents the Splat to the students and reminds them that when the splat is the same color, the hidden values are the same, and when the splat colors are different, the hidden values are different (Figure 11.8).

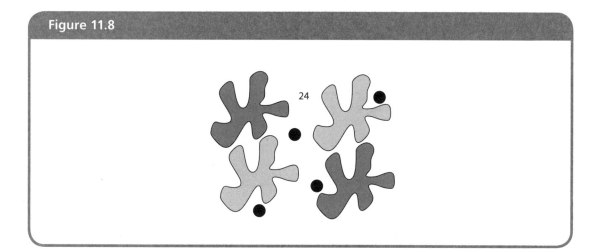

Figure 11.8

> Example: Jose
>
> Jose asks, "What might an expression look like for this splat? What could the variables be?"
>
> Jose's students immediately notice that there are four Splats and four dots showing. They know that the equation must equal 24.

Standards

LI and SC

Purpose

Tasks

Materials

Student Thinking

Lesson Structures

Form. Assess.

Lesson Launch

Lesson Facilitation

Closure

Amonte says, "I see 24 is the total so first I subtract the 4 because of the four dots and get 20. Then I know there are two light gray Splats that are equal and two dark gray splats that are equal, so this means I am going to try different values for those splats."

Jose asks, "How would you write that as an expression?"

Amir says, "Hmmmm 2x + 2y + 4 = 24?"

Jose asks, "What could the variables be? Is there only one possibility?"

Lisa says, "I can think of one! What about x = 4 and y = 6?"

Emelio says, "Ya, I think there are a ton! Especially if we make a pattern!"

Jenna asks, "The variables can represent negative numbers, right? Or fractions?"

Jose says, "What a great question, Jenna! Let's see what you can find! How about if you work with a partner to see if you can find more possibilities for the variables. We will share in about five minutes."

Jose is pleased with the students' thinking. The Splats encourage the students to write expressions, think flexibly, manipulate variables, look for patterns, and represent their thinking.

Number Talk

A **number talk,** also called a **math talk,** is a brief classroom routine that focuses on number relationships, mathematical structures, and strategies to build computational fluency. During a number talk, you present students with one or more computation problems to solve mentally. Then you encourage them to explain and justify their strategy while you record their ideas for the rest of the class to see. These explanations help the students work toward accurate, efficient, and flexible strategies (Parrish, 2011). You may conduct a number talk by following these important steps.

1. Present the number problem to your students. You might display subitizing cards, manipulatives, written math equations, and word problems.

2. Give students time to think about the solution. Encourage your students to think quietly. Some teachers encourage students to signal when they are ready to share a strategy.

3. Elicit students' strategies. Record the students' strategies as they explain their thinking. You may also want to record the students' names next to each strategy.

4. Encourage students to ask clarifying questions. You can also ask students to determine efficient and flexible strategies.

5. Repeat with a new problem if there is time.

Example: Valyn

Valyn (Ms. Wright) conducts number talks at least twice a week with her students. One day, she displays the following prompt and waits for the students to think of at least one strategy:

$$1\frac{3}{4} + \frac{1}{6} =$$

Students begin holding up one finger to show that they have at least one strategy. Some students show two or three fingers, indicating that they have two or three strategies. Valyn calls on Hailey to share a strategy.

Hailey: Well, I immediately thought of a clock. So, I changed $1\frac{3}{4}$ into $1\frac{45}{60}$ and $\frac{1}{6}$ into $\frac{10}{60}$ so I could easily add the fractions. Now, it is easy to add and I get 1 and $\frac{55}{60}$. I can simplify $\frac{55}{60}$ to $\frac{11}{12}$ so the answer is 1 and $\frac{11}{12}$.

Ms. Wright: What a great idea to use the clock, Hailey! I could visualize the clock as you explained your idea. Did anyone else convert the denominators into 60? Sheila, do you have a strategy to share?

Sheila: Well, I saw the common denominator as 12 and then changed $\frac{3}{4}$ into $\frac{9}{12}$ and $\frac{1}{6}$ into $\frac{2}{12}$. Adding it up together made it 1 and $\frac{11}{12}$.

Ms. Wright: Sheila, you quickly saw the common denominator, which is helpful when we want to add them mentally. Does anyone have any other ideas?

Manuel: Yes, I like to use estimation. I knew it was going to be really close to 2 because I changed the mixed number into an improper fraction and got $\frac{7}{4}$. If it were $\frac{8}{4}$, it would be 2. So, then, I just used 24 as my common denominator because it is easy for me to see and do it mentally. So, then $1\frac{3}{4} = 1\frac{18}{24}$ and $\frac{1}{6} = \frac{4}{24}$. Then, when I add it up, it equals $1\frac{22}{24}$ or $1\frac{11}{12}$.

Ms. Wright: How come you estimated first?

Manuel: I always estimate first because sometimes when I do mental math, I might make a mistake. If I estimate first, I know if my answer makes sense.

Valyn is pleased with the number talk. She notices that many students are flexibly changing the denominator. She is also excited about Hailey's solution. She had hoped that a student might introduce the idea of flexibly changing the denominator to make it easier to add the fractions. Even though changing the denominator to 12 was most efficient, this has been a great opportunity for students to think about alternative strategies.

 What do you notice about the number routine lesson launches? How might these kinds of number routine lesson launches be integrated into your lesson planning? Note your responses below.

_____

_____

_____

_____

WHAT DO YOU ANTICIPATE STUDENTS WILL DO?

As you plan your lesson launch, it is critical to anticipate how your students will respond to the launch you have designed. Consider the information in Chapter 1. As you plan instructional activities for your class, anticipate how individual students will react to particular activities. This can help you respond in a way that moves your students' learning forward. If you anticipate and include some typical student responses in your lesson plan, you can also plan for your next instructional move.

 How do you anticipate your students' responses to your instructional activities? Note your response below.

_____

_____

_____

_____

Standards

LI and SC

Purpose

Tasks

Materials

Student Thinking

Lesson Structures

Form. Assess.

Lesson Launch

Lesson Facilitation

Closure

Building Unit Coherence

While your lesson launches should be connected to the content you are teaching, you can support unit coherence by varying your lesson launches to reflect different Standards for Mathematical Practice and mathematical habits of mind. You can also use the lesson launch to anchor the current lesson within the unit. You can connect the lesson you are currently teaching to prior learning and forecast what you will be teaching next. Students can then eagerly engage in the launch knowing fully the place this lesson has within the unit.

The launch is also a great point to showcase rigorous tasks. The way you choose to launch the lesson should invite students with varying abilities to enter into the task with confidence.

Example: Bea

Eighth-grade teacher Bea regularly chooses the See, Think, and Wonder and Notice and Wonder lesson launches because they invite her English Language Learners to talk and share ideas with partners. She ensures that they have multiple opportunities to talk to their partners. She believes that this supports them in making connections from one lesson to another.

Notes

Sixth-Grade Snapshot

Launch the Lesson

Josh addressed Jeff, "You know how we try to do really enticing, exciting, over-the-top launches sometimes? Well, I don't think this lesson needs that kind of introduction. We really just need to connect it to the prior knowledge we develop the day before when we use Algebra Tiles for translating expressions."

"You are right, Josh," Jeff agreed. "The whole point of this procedural lesson is to get the students to connect the abstract procedure to the concepts we develop with the tiles. We are on the same page."

Launch:

Refer back to the previously taught lesson. Yesterday we used Algebra Tiles to help us model expressions. Let's see what we remember as you work with your partner to model the following:

Sam went to the fair. He bought a book of tickets for $4.00. Then he bought drinks that cost $2.00 each for his friends. What expression represents the problem?

Have students share how they modeled the word problem using Algebra Tiles. Select one student to draw a picture of his or her tiles on the document camera.

See the complete lesson plan in Appendix A on page 188.

Think about how you launched a recent lesson. Record your thoughts below.

_____

_____

_____

_____

_____

_____

_____

_____

_____

_____

_____

_____

_____

_____

_____

_____

_____

_____

Seventh-Grade Snapshot

Launch the Lesson

Kyle suggested, "I think we give them a few minutes to think about the math they might encounter when running a pet-sitting business!" Alix responded, "Oh yes, I like when they think of their own ideas. It is so important for them to be able to think about this before we tell them!" Bryan agreed, "If we tell them, they lose interest. If they think of it on their own, then they are so much more engaged!" The team decided that they could ask students to generate a list of the possible ways they would or could use math. Hopefully, they could then connect the students' ideas to the task.

Launch:

Ask the students to brainstorm all the things they might need to know to pet sit. Record the students' ideas.

Pose questions such as:

- What kinds of situations might come up while pet sitting where math might be helpful?
- What kinds of math might you need to know?
- How might the math we have been learning in the expressions and equations unit help us solve problems?

See the complete lesson plan in Appendix A on page 192.

Think about how you launched a recent lesson. Record your thoughts below.

_____
_____
_____
_____
_____
_____
_____
_____
_____
_____
_____
_____
_____
_____
_____
_____
_____
_____
_____

Eighth-Grade Snapshot

Launch the Lesson

Standards

LI and SC

Purpose

Tasks

Materials

Student Thinking

Lesson Structures

Form. Assess.

Lesson Launch

Lesson Facilitation

Closure

Serena loves preparing lesson launches. They give her the chance to invite students to be excited about what comes next. The hardest part is always coming up with an idea that middle schoolers can get excited about. While Serena was thinking about this, an announcement came over the school's PA system reminding students to buy their yearbooks before it is too late. "That's it!" Serena shouted out loud. Based on her essential question about a graph, a picture is worth a thousand words. "What a goldmine of middle school pictures old middle school yearbooks will have!" she thought, and thus her launch was begun.

Launch:

Introduce the phrase, "A picture is worth a thousand words." Ask students questions to facilitate a brief discussion. Questions may include the following:

- Have you ever seen a poster with no words? How do you know what it means?

- Holding up one face at a time, "What do you think this person is trying to tell you?"

- Can you think of any pictures you have looked at that had no words yet you knew exactly what it meant?

Lead the discussion in a mathematical direction by introducing the idea that graphs are like pictures that are worth a thousand words. In this lesson, we are going to look at many graphs and see what they tell us.

See the complete lesson plan in Appendix A on page 203.

How can you use the Notice and Wonder technique as a lesson launch?

_____

_____

_____

_____

_____

_____

_____

_____

_____

_____

_____

_____

_____

_____

_____

_____

Now it is your turn! Develop a lesson launch and anticipate how your students will respond.

Launch:

Download the full Lesson-Planning Template from resources.corwin.com/mathlessonplanning/6-8
Remember that you can use the online version of the lesson plan template to begin compiling each section into the full template as your lesson plan grows.

152 The Mathematics Lesson-Planning Handbook, Grades 6–8

PLANNING TO
FACILITATE THE LESSON

I think there is always a fine line between being well planned and recognizing when it is important, even crucial, to veer from the plan. When my students are working together on an investigation or problem, I attend to what my students are doing, saying, and representing. Some of my very best lessons have been when I have acknowledged and highlighted students' mathematical noticings and questions to make meaningful mathematical connections. I most often recognize these moments when students are engaged in discourse with each other but also when they ask really powerful and interesting questions.

Recently, I was teaching a lesson where students were investigating patterns. I asked them to represent a visual pattern of 5x + 3 in multiple ways. In my mind, I was thinking about using 5 as the starting point in the equation. I wanted them to see the slope and y-intercept in all of the representations. As the students were working, they began finding equations that looked very different from what other students had found. At first, there was a buzz in the room as students began questioning one another. I observed this taking place and waited to see what they would say and do. Finally, a student asked, "Should our answers be the same?" and "Are our solutions supposed to be the same or different?" and "Is it possible for them to be different?" The students thought that all the equations were different because they saw the pattern in a different way. At that moment, I had a very important choice. I could ask funneling questions to take them directly to my end goal, or I could allow them to explore their questions further. I stopped and said, "You know, that is a very good question!"

Being present, attentive, and responsive to my students' questions prompted a pretty magical discussion about equivalent expressions. I decided long ago that I would not take away my students' "aha" moments. If I am truly going to promote student discourse and facilitate healthy, productive struggle, then I must allow students to investigate their mathematical questions. My role is to validate those questions and support these mathematical discoveries. After all, who wants to turn down an opportunity to witness middle school students exclaim in wonder about how cool mathematics is?

Jennifer Outzs
Middle School Teacher
Maryland

Capturing those moments when students are engaged productively in mathematical thinking, reasoning, and communication is so exciting to see. Sometimes they just happen, but most likely they happen when all of your hard work in planning comes together. Planning to facilitate a lesson incorporates the selection of effective instructional activities and strategically planning how you will support and facilitate student learning during the instructional activities. Good tasks, problems, games, and activities are only just that—good— until you mindfully use care and purpose to design a teaching and learning environment that supports your students' learning through discourse and appropriate and productive struggle. This chapter will discuss the following questions:

- What is mathematical communication?

- How do you facilitate meaningful mathematical discourse?

- How do you plan for and pose purposeful questions?

- How do you facilitate productive struggle?

WHAT IS MATHEMATICAL COMMUNICATION?

Communication is an essential part of mathematics and mathematical education. *Principles to Actions: Ensuring Mathematical Success for All* (National Council of Teachers of Mathematics [NCTM], 2014b) notes that "effective teaching of mathematics facilitates discourse among students to build shared understanding of mathematical ideas by analyzing and comparing student approaches and arguments" (p. 29). Students need multiple opportunities to exchange ideas, explain and defend their reasoning, use mathematical vocabulary, and consider one another's ideas (NCTM, 1991, 2000, 2014a). There are several facets to good mathematical communication, including the following:

- *Precise use of vocabulary.* Teachers must use precise mathematical vocabulary consistently and facilitate students' use of mathematical language to promote mathematical understanding. This means that all students learn and use the correct mathematics vocabulary, even when first learning new mathematical concepts.

  Some teachers may want to focus on key words or simplify the language by using simple terms, but that can ultimately confuse students. For example, teaching students that they should always add when they see *in all* in a word problem will lead students to believe that this will always work, when in reality, it will work only in particular situations and cannot be transferred to all word problems.

- *Verbal discussion or **mathematical discourse.*** Mathematical discourse occurs when students talk about the mathematics they are learning with each other and the teacher. During this discussion, they demonstrate their understanding and reveal their reasoning. Teachers should plan for and facilitate multiple opportunities for discourse throughout the lesson to provide students many different ways to engage in conversation about the mathematics they are learning. Often, the most powerful mathematical conversations occur between students as they reason with each other to make sense of their learning.

- *Writing.* Writing in the mathematics classroom allows students to record their thinking so they can remember how they thought through a problem or how they solved it. Writing helps students focus on and build precise mathematical language, whereas words "disappear" once spoken. For students who feel shy when talking aloud, writing gives them the opportunity to explain their thinking.

  If some of your students have difficulty with writing, give them sentence starters such as, "I think the answer is ____ because____" or allow them to use representations and diagrams in their written explanations. These approaches will help them fully participate. In addition, you can show students examples of writing to help them improve their discourse skills. To do this, you can use student work on chart paper or under a document camera to show examples of what you mean by phrases like "Use representations to explain your solution."

> **What are some strategies you use to facilitate discourse? List a few below.**
> _____
> _____
> _____
> _____
> _____

HOW DO YOU FACILITATE MEANINGFUL MATHEMATICAL DISCOURSE?

Providing for and teaching mathematical communication requires explicit attention to planning lessons (Walshaw & Anthony, 2008). Building a classroom community that supports discourse requires some shifts in the traditional student and teacher roles. In particular, the students assume greater responsibility for their learning and the teacher no longer serves as the primary source of mathematical authority. Instead, the teacher consistently encourages student engagement and strategically uses questioning to position students as mathematical leaders in the classroom. *Principles to Actions* (NCTM, 2014b) notes the critical roles by considering what teachers and students are *doing* in classrooms where rich mathematical discourse is occurring.

For example, teachers are designing learning activities that prompt students to use multiple representations, describe their solutions, and explain their reasoning. Teachers also strategically facilitate conversations among students about the mathematics they are learning. When teachers are promoting mathematical discourse, a peek inside these classrooms shows students presenting their ideas to other students while other students are listening and asking questions.

You can promote effective discourse by monitoring and responding to the students as they work. You can ask particular questions that will support students to explain their thinking and reasoning. Here are some sample questions you may wish to ask:

- Was this the first strategy you tried? Why did you give up on the first strategy?

- How did you decide what to do?

- Did you try something that did not work? How did you figure out it was not going to work?

- How does what you are doing make sense to you?

The questions help students reflect on their work but also give you more information to determine which of the student strategies you want to select for the class discussion. In this way, you can plan a purposeful discussion on the strategy or strategies to focus on in the lesson. Once you make the decision about which student work you will present to the class (one, some, all), you also decide the order in which they will be presented. This purposeful planning of the discussion allows concepts to unfold in a coherent manner that you predetermine to match the learning intention (Smith & Stein, 2011). Once the students are presenting their work, you facilitate the discussion through questions that connect the strategies and concepts studied. Here are some additional sample questions:

- Is there anything in Graham's strategy that is like something we have done before?

- What mathematical vocabulary did he use that we have learned?

- Is there something in this solution that reminds you of anything we did yesterday in class?

- How is Graham's solution like or different from Smita's solution?

You should also encourage the students to ask questions of one another, thus promoting student-to-student interaction and engagement in constructing viable arguments and critiquing the reasoning of others (National Governors Association Center for Best Practices & Council of Chief State School Officers, 2010). You can encourage classroom discourse by establishing an environment and expectation for students to engage in some type of discourse every day (Rasmussen, Yackel, & King, 2003; Wood, Williams, & McNeal, 2006; Yackel & Cobb, 1996).

Many teachers of middle school students find it helpful to **unpack** what it means to be in a mathematics **learning community**. You can do this by holding classroom discussions about what math talk looks like in your classroom. You may also find it helpful to explicitly teach students how to share their ideas, actively listen, and give appropriate responses to peers (Wagganer, 2015).

Here are some additional suggestions:

- Encourage student-to-student discourse by asking students to address each other's questions: "Antonia, can you answer Jamal's question?" Or "Jamal, did you understand Antonia's solution? You can ask him a question to help him explain what he meant."

- Use a Think Aloud technique to model your own thinking and reasoning through a problem that focuses on mathematical thinking that you want your students to develop (Trocki, Taylor, Starling, Sztajn, & Heck, 2015).

- Model how to ask questions and instruct students to ask questions of each other. You can show students that it is okay to be confused and to ask for an explanation. Model a question you would like to students to ask: "Class, I am confused about this problem. Can someone help me?" Or "Jamal, why don't you ask Antonia a question about the solution?"

- Ask follow-up questions when students respond with a right or wrong answer that will lead them back to the conceptual understanding. For example, you might ask, "Can you start at the beginning and explain your thinking?"

Standards

LI and SC

Purpose

Tasks

Materials

Student Thinking

Lesson Structures

Form. Assess.

Lesson Launch

Lesson Facilitation

Closure

- Use sentence stems (Wagganer, 2015) to jumpstart student thinking and student-to-student discourse. This is helpful for all students, but especially for English Language Learners. Here are some sentence stems you might try with your students:
  - I agree with _____ because …
  - This is what I think …
  - I have a different perspective because …
  - I made a connection with what _____ said because …
  - When I thought about that question, I remembered …
  - I chose this method because …
- Use language frames to scaffold math talk (Hattie et al., 2016) and enhance student conversations while collaborating. Some language frames for mathematics include the following:
  - Another way to solve this would be …
  - In order to solve this problem, I need to know …
  - We think this answer is reasonable because …
  - If I change _____, my answer would be different because …
  - I can check my answer by …

Like most communication, mathematics discourse is messy. Middle school students, in particular, may struggle to find the right words to explain their thinking and reasoning because they worry about how their peers may react. Your patience and willingness to let students participate in lots of discourse is the key to building a rich discourse community.

> **Which discourse strategies resonate most with you? Why? Note your ideas below.**
> _____
> _____
> _____
> _____
> _____

HOW DO YOU PLAN FOR AND POSE PURPOSEFUL QUESTIONS?

Questioning is at the heart of effective mathematical discourse. The NCTM's (2014b) *Principles to Actions: Ensuring Mathematical Success for All* states, "Effective teaching of mathematics uses purposeful questions to assess and advance students' reasoning and sense making about important mathematical ideas and relationships" (p. 35). When you plan questions to ask during a lesson, you also increase access and engagement for all students because you are mindful about whom you will be calling on.

The roles of both the teacher and the students are important as teachers pose purposeful questions that advance students' mathematical understanding (NCTM, 2014b). As a teacher, you must be intentional in your planning, consider what you are doing as you ask questions, and consider what your students are doing in response to your questions. Plan and ask higher-level questions that prompt your students to provide explanations, justifications, and reasoning about the mathematics they are learning. Also, be sure to provide plenty of wait time for students to ponder, reflect, and make sense of the question. When you take these actions, your students provide deeper responses and justify their thinking with evidence. They also ask you questions to clarify and build new understanding (NCTM, 2014b).

The questions a teacher asks are the key to orchestrating positive and productive classroom discourse. As you formulate questions to challenge students to think deeply, draw conclusions, and extend the student inquiry in the lesson (Van de Walle et al., 2013), consider the purpose and type of question. *Principles to Actions: Ensuring*

Mathematical Success for All (NCTM, 2014b) organized question types into four distinct categories: gathering information, probing thinking, making the mathematics visible, and encouraging reflection and justification. NCTM's (2017) publication, *Taking Action: Implementing Effective Teaching Practices*, introduced a fifth category: engaging with the reasoning of others. The question types can also be connected to the Standards for Mathematical Practice (National Governors Association Center for Best Practices & Council of Chief State School Officers, 2010). Let's briefly look at each type of question in more detail.

Gathering Information

Teachers ask these types of questions to elicit procedural information by asking "What is" questions. Some examples appear in Figure 12.1. When students answer probing questions, they provide factual information or steps. You can also use this type of question to elicit students' precise use of mathematics vocabulary. Typically, these kinds of questions elicit right or wrong answers.

Figure 12.1

Teachers	Students
What is the value of 6^5?	7,776
What is the value of pi?	3.14
What is the formula for finding the area of the trapezoid?	The formula for the trapezoid is $A = \frac{a+b}{2} \times h$.

Probing Thinking

Teachers ask these kinds of questions to encourage students to explain their thinking and demonstrate their reasoning. Figure 12.2 gives some examples.

Figure 12.2

Teachers	Students
Why did you decide to decompose the parallelogram to find the area?	I noticed if I broke off the triangle, I could slide it to the other side to make a rectangle.
Can you tell me about how you solved this problem? Last year 325 people attended the Family Fun night, but this year only 275 people attended. What is the percent decrease?	First I subtracted 325 − 275 = 50, which is the decrease. Then I divided 50 by 325 which equaled about 15%.

Standards

LI and SC

Purpose

Tasks

Materials

Student Thinking

Lesson Structures

Form. Assess.

Lesson Launch

Lesson Facilitation

Closure

Teachers ask these kinds of questions to help the students build connections between mathematical ideas, see patterns, and understand the underlying structure of mathematical ideas. Figure 12.3 gives some examples.

Figure 12.3

Teachers	Students
How did using a pattern help you find the negative exponents?	I notice that each row starting with 4^0 is multiplied by a power of 4. So then I realized that the negative exponents are dividing by a power of 4. So cool!

4^{-3}	
4^{-2}	
4^{-1}	
4^0	1
4^1	4
4^2	16
4^3	64

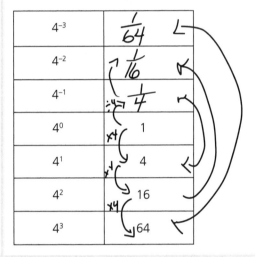

Teachers	Students
Is the mean or the median a better representation of data? When should you choose one or the other?	It depends on the data! If the data are close together with a smaller range, then the mean usually works fine. If there is a big outlier of some kind, then it is better to use the median. I like to find both to see how the data points change the mean and median!

Encouraging Reflection and Justification

Teachers ask these kinds of questions when they want to encourage students to develop mathematical arguments and justify their solutions with thorough explanations. Figure 12.4 includes some examples.

Figure 12.4

Teachers	Students
When you multiply a negative number times a positive number, does it matter the order of the numbers?	No. For example, –2 * 4 and –4 * 2 equal –8. On the number line, there are 4 groups of –2 or there are 2 groups of –4, but both equal –8. 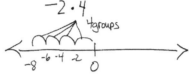 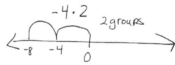
How many ways can you represent a function?	I can represent a function in a table, words, and an expression. For example, I earn $5 hour for pet sitting. Every time I pet sit, I also earn a $2 tip. I can show the function in a table. <table><tr><td>**Hours**</td><td>**Payment**</td></tr><tr><td>1</td><td>$7</td></tr><tr><td>2</td><td>$12</td></tr><tr><td>3</td><td>$17</td></tr></table> I can also show the function in an expression: 5b + 2 =
When might you use ratios in your daily life?	My family works in a soup kitchen once a month. One of my jobs is to take regular recipes and increase them to feed large groups of people. One day I was working on it and realized it was ratios!

Teachers ask these kinds of questions when they want to encourage students to explain their own thinking, construct a viable argument, and listen to the reasoning of their peers. They also ask these types of questions to encourage students to ask questions to each other. Figure 12.5 shows some examples.

Figure 12.5

Teachers	Students
I am noticing that you and Teddy solved the problem in different ways. Explain Teddy's solution, and tell why you think Teddy solved it that way. Bart had $2\frac{1}{2}$ feet of rope. He needs to cut the rope in $\frac{1}{2}$-foot sections. How many sections can he get? $2\frac{1}{2} \div 5 = 10$	Teddy solved the problem by making a number line to represent the rope. He basically subtracted $\frac{1}{2}$ sections until he didn't have any rope left.
Do you agree or disagree with Teddy's idea? Why or why not?	I agree that Teddy's solution works, but I was just thinking about using the procedure for division of fractions, but I wasn't sure I could explain why you flip the numerator and denominator and multiply!

Without strategic planning, teachers tend to ask most questions at the lowest cognitive level (fact, recall, or knowledge) and wait less than one second before calling on a student after asking a question (Walsh & Sattes, 2005). Instead, you should strive to ask higher-level questions that require students to explain and elaborate on their ideas, make the mathematics visible, and encourage justification. For example, consider the questions that Pilar Ramos, a sixth-grade teacher, asks in the following scenario.

Mrs. Ramos: What happens when you multiply a whole number and fraction?

Mariela: Well, you get a product? Something bigger—like in whole numbers.

Mrs. Ramos: Hmmmm. Can you show me the representation for 4×2 and $4 \times \frac{1}{2}$ and tell me how they are alike and different (Figure 12.6)?

Mariela: Well, first I drew four people times two cookies. My question is: If four people get two cookies each, how many cookies do I need? Then my second question is, "If four people get $\frac{1}{2}$ cookie each, how many cookies do I need?"

Figure 12.6

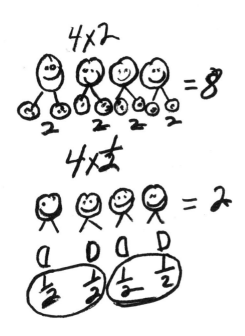

So, I noticed something different than when we multiply whole numbers, but I can't figure out why it is happening.

Mrs. Ramos: Mariela, tell us more about your thinking.

Mariela: Yes, if I multiply 4 times one half, I end up with 2! The answer is smaller than when I multiplied times 2!

Mrs. Ramos: Do you think this happens all the time when we multiply whole numbers times fractions or just some of the time?

Tori: I think it is all of the time! I think that is because the one half is smaller than a whole, so the answer is always going to be smaller. I think there is a pattern!

Mrs. Ramos: Hmmmm… . What an interesting idea! Can anyone else offer an idea or a representation? Let's turn and talk to our partners. In a few minutes, I am going to ask you to be ready to add to the ideas you heard and tell whether you agree or disagree with Mariela and Tori's ideas and why.

The first question, "What happens when you multiply a whole number and fraction?" is at the gathering information level. The teacher continues to raise the level of the students' thinking by encouraging a conversation about multiplication of whole numbers times fractions; this occurs when she asks Mariela follow-up questions and then engages the whole class in the discussion.

Have you ever asked a question, called on a student who gave the correct answer, and watched all hands disappear quickly? Good questions prompt students to provide more than answers. Note how Pilar was able to move the discussion forward instead of closing it down. When you pose purposeful questions, you promote student understanding because you ask students to make connections by building upon what they know.

Teachers tend to use two kinds of main questioning techniques: funneling (Herbel-Eisenmann & Breyfogle, 2005) and focusing (Herbel-Eisenmann, 2010; NCTM, 2014b).

- *Funneling questions* lead students in a particular direction to provide evidence of student learning; for this reason, they can squash students' thinking because the teacher is asking questions with a particular answer in mind. These kinds of questions often provide only a superficial assessment of what students know.

- *Focusing questions*, on the other hand, encourage students to think on their own and provide explanations and justifications. While the teacher has an end point in mind, the students' reasoning is most important.

Consider the questions in Figure 12.7 and note how a funneling question can be opened up to become a focusing question. Anticipate the different kinds of responses each type of question will elicit.

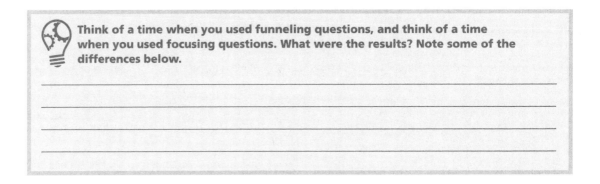

Figure 12.7

Funneling	Focusing
What is the slope?	Use your example to explain why slope is described as rise over run.
Does this graph show a function?	Convince me that this graph is or is not a graph of a function.

As you plan to facilitate your lesson, it is important to consider how you will plan for and implement purposeful and rich questions that support rich student thinking.

> **Think of a time when you used funneling questions, and think of a time when you used focusing questions. What were the results? Note some of the differences below.**
>
> _____
>
> _____
>
> _____
>
> _____

HOW DO YOU FACILITATE PRODUCTIVE STRUGGLE?

By consistently providing students with high-quality, engaging mathematics instruction, you will also invite them to productively struggle because they will be actively involved in making sense of the mathematics they are learning (NCTM, 2014b). Your students will be better able to apply their learning to new situations if you routinely ensure that they participate in mathematics learning that stretches their thinking and promotes opportunities to make and analyze their mistakes (Boaler, 2015) and that prompts them to engage in higher-level thinking (Kapur, 2010).

As you construct lessons to engage students in productive struggle, you must keep the needs of your own learners in mind. While it is tempting to rescue students by giving them answers or by overscaffolding lessons, this does not, in the long run, support their learning. On the other hand, you also do not want to send your students into an unproductive spiral of struggle. Simply telling students to try harder does not promote productive struggle when students feel that they are, in fact, trying very hard.

Creating this "sweet spot" of productive struggle for your students can be challenging, which is why it is critical to consider how you will create an environment that promotes productive struggle during the planning process. You can do this by following these steps:

1. Be explicit about what struggle looks like and feels like so students understand that it will help them.

2. Discuss perseverance with students, and actively recognize when students demonstrate it.

3. Provide plenty of time for students to struggle with tasks and move through the struggle so they know what it feels like on the other side of the struggle.

4. Plan for how you will respond when students are struggling by asking scaffolding questions.

5. Celebrate and use confusion and mistakes (yours and theirs) as an opportunity for furthering and deepening understanding.

6. Create opportunities for students to ask questions, help each other, and share how they moved through a struggle.

7. Reflect on how you respond to student confusion and struggle and plan strategic moves to use in the classroom.

> Example: Kaleem
>
> Kaleem, a sixth-grade teacher, doesn't like to watch her students struggle, even a tiny bit, but she knows that she needs to make this a class focus for the year. She recently watched Jo Boaler's (2017) video, *Brains Grow and Change,* and she wants to be able to translate that information to her sixth graders. She knows that many of them worry about getting all the answers correct.
>
> She decides to begin the school year by making a bulletin board with the title, *Mistakes Grow Your Brain,* and a picture of a giant brain. She tells them that "mistakes grow your brain" and that she wants to make sure that they know that she values those mistakes as part of learning. At the end of the class, she provides time for the students to reflect on their learning. She also provides time for the students to unpack their mistakes during discussions by having the students answer this prompt: "I used to think _____, but now I know _____ because _____." Students can post particularly interesting mistakes on the bulletin board.
>
> At the end of the week, she has students share their "Favorite Mistake" of the week.
>
> Kaleem is surprised by the positive impact of this effort on her classroom environment as students become relaxed and thoughtful about their mistakes. One of the students, Brianna, tells her, "At first I thought my mistakes were bad and I should hide them away. But then I found out that we all make mistakes. They aren't bad at all."

How might you integrate conversations about productive struggle in your own classroom? Write a few notes here.

_____
_____
_____
_____
_____
_____

HOW DO YOU MAKE SURE YOU ENGAGE STUDENTS IN THE PROCESS STANDARDS AS YOU FACILITATE THE LESSON?

The examples throughout this chapter show many ways that you can engage students in communicating mathematically, developing problem-solving behaviors, demonstrating reasoning, making connections between and among mathematical ideas, and using representations to explain and justify thinking. You can ensure that you are encouraging students to demonstrate the process standards by planning for one or two process standards for each lesson. As you plan to facilitate your lesson, consider the questions you will ask and the task you design or select that will elicit particular student mathematical behaviors. For example, Phyllis wants her seventh graders to notice and use mathematical structures and designs a word problem sorting task. She gives students eight word problems and tells them they must not solve the problems. She explains that she wants them to read the word problems and then group word problems that are alike together and explain how they are alike. Phyllis's students quickly notice that particular word problems represent inequalities.

Standards

LI and SC

Purpose

Tasks

Materials

Student Thinking

Lesson Structures

Form. Assess.

Lesson Launch

Lesson Facilitation

Closure

How can you make sure to incorporate questioning that will support students in engaging in the process standards?

_____

_____

_____

_____

_____

Building Unit Coherence

Similar to the launch, the lesson facilitation shapes coherence because you are constantly connecting prior learning to new learning. You ask questions and invite robust discourse that stimulates mathematical learning. You can do this by asking students to record their ideas and explain their thinking to peers. You can post their ideas and refer to them throughout the unit. Each new lesson offers opportunities for you to call upon students' ideas and work samples to support new mathematical concepts. With this combination of teaching moves, you create coherence because students begin to connect and link their ideas from one day to the next. Every day, you may also wish to ask the students, "Why are we learning this?" This question can help them understand that the mathematics they are learning is connected to their lives and to the new mathematics they will learn.

Notes

Sixth-Grade Snapshot

Facilitate the Lesson

Sixth-grade teachers Josh and Jeff anticipate that some students will quickly understand how to translate word problems into expressions and not need to use the Algebra Tiles for very long. They plan to monitor the students closely to meet individual student learning needs. As Josh and Jeff are observing and monitoring student understanding, they decide to plan some focusing questions to determine what the students know and what they need help with.

- What did we do yesterday with the Algebra Tiles?
- How does drawing the tiles help us the same as actually using the tiles?
- Tell me what you are thinking when you use the tiles to represent x.
- Can you explain _____'s thinking?

Facilitate:

Refer to the drawing of the tiles on the document camera. Discuss with students if the drawing is as useful as using the tiles. Encourage students to work on the Set A worksheet problems by drawing the tiles and, if possible, not using the real tiles. Walk around as students solve the problems. For students who seem to be proficient with the pictures, collect their tiles and challenge them to visualize the tiles to solve Set B's (see Figure A.2) problem abstractly. Not all students will be able to solve problems abstractly at this point. Select students you have observed having difficulty moving away from the tiles and work with them in a small group. The teacher will listen to how the students describe their thinking. The teacher uses his or her thinking to help move them away from using the tiles and drawing pictures. The teacher may also work with students who are having difficulty moving from the pictorial level to the abstract level by also pulling them into a small group.

See the complete lesson plan in Appendix A on page 188.

What do you notice about the opportunities for student discourse? Record your response below.

_____

_____

_____

_____

_____

_____

_____

_____

_____

_____

_____

_____

The seventh-grade team has been focusing on discourse for the past year. The students know that they are expected to share their ideas, ask questions, and provide feedback to one another. Bryan wondered, "I have been experimenting with a pair-to-pair share technique. First, the pairs work together and then each pair meets with another pair to share their ideas. After that, they can revise their solution." Kia exclaimed, "Oh, I like that because they are getting more opportunities for discourse! I wonder if we could have the group of four then decide on one of the solutions to record on the chart paper?" Alix chimed in, "Yes! This recording will focus them on a productive discussion and critique each other's reasoning!"

Facilitate:

Say, "You thought of some great situations where you might need to use knowledge about expressions and equations. In this lesson, we are going to get an opportunity to see how we transfer what we have learned to a new situation."

Arrange the students in pairs and introduce the context for the problem:

Congratulations! You have just been hired for your first pet-sitting job! You have agreed to take care of Teddy the Toy Poodle for four days. You never imagined a 10-pound toy poodle would cause so many problems! You must solve every problem before Teddy's owners get back from vacation. However, Teddy's owners are very intense about Teddy's care. Each day they will text you to make sure you know what you are doing. They have also asked you to keep a journal for them to read when they get back. You must be able to answer their questions or they will find a new pet sitter!

Explain to the students that they will have an opportunity to work in pairs to problem solve, but each will be responsible for recording their ideas in the pet-sitting journal. Depending on the amount of time you have for instruction, this lesson might take two days. Distribute the Teddy's Pet-Sitting Problem-Solving Journals, larger poster paper, and markers. As the groups begin solving, ask questions such as the following:

- How can you represent this problem?
- What will you do first?
- What equation might represent this problem?
- Is there another equation that might also work?
- Would drawing a picture help? Why or why not?

After the pairs have finished the first problem, hand them a slip of paper with the text from the owner (see Figure A.4). Encourage the students to solve the new problem and discuss the reasonableness of the solution.

Once the pair completes their work, arrange the students in a pair-to-pair share. (A pair-to-pair share is when two pairs form a group of four.) This is a good opportunity to strategically match pairs to share alternative ideas, solutions, and strategies. Have the pairs share their solutions and then decide on which solution to represent on the large chart paper for DAY ONE.

Repeat the same process for the next three problems (days).

1. The students will complete each problem (days) in pairs.
2. The students will receive a "text message" from the teacher at the completion of the problem. Students will then add the additional solution.
3. Pairs will be in groups to conduct a pair-to-pair share (group of four) to decide which of the solutions to represent on the large chart paper.

See the complete lesson plan in Appendix A on page 192.

What are some of the questions you use to encourage discourse in your classroom? Write them below.

Standards

LI and SC

Purpose

Tasks

Materials

Student Thinking

Lesson Structures

Form. Assess.

Lesson Launch

Lesson Facilitation

Closure

Serena wanted maximum student participation in this lesson. She wanted everyone to have the opportunity to explore the graphs and come to their own conclusions about similarities. She decided to let them work in pairs so she had to create/find nine problem situations to graph because she knew she needed at least three examples to establish a pattern and she had three patterns for the students to find. She found the problems online at various sites that were recommended to her by her online community.

She knew that having students create their own graphs and display them would be an additional motivation for the students since all of the work they would be seeing was created by their peers. She would walk around the students as they worked, asking questions and keeping everyone on track. She also was very purposeful in selecting the questions that would lead the discussions about the similarities.

Facilitate:

Divide students into pairs and randomly assign one situation A–I to each pair (alternatively, decide in advance which situation is appropriate for which pair of students). After making material available and answering questions, allow students to work. Walk around the classroom and be available to answer questions. Support pairs by asking questions such as, "Do you think there is a relationship? Does one of your variables depend on the other?"

Instruct students to hang the graphs around the room. Be sure to mix up scatterplots and linear and nonlinear graphs.

Ask pairs to sort the graphs in any way that makes sense to them. If any pair needs assistance, suggest three groupings.

Lead a discussion beginning with the scatterplots, asking students the following:

- Why is there no line to this graph?
- What do the three situations that these graphs represent have in common?
- Were you able to write an equation to model this situation?

Lead a discussion around the linear graphs:

- What is the same about all of these graphs?
- What do you think that means compared to the previous group we examined?
- How were the situations the same?
- Could you write equations for these graphs?

Lead a discussion around the nonlinear graphs:

- Is there a relationship here?
- How is this relationship different from the linear graphs? The scatterplots?
- How are the situations that led to these graphs similar to one another? How are they different from the linear stories?

Standards

LI and SC

Purpose

Tasks

Materials

Student Thinking

Lesson Structures

Form. Assess.

Lesson Launch

Lesson Facilitation

Closure

Anticipating student responses:

Most pairs will sort the graphs by lines, scattered points, and curves. Some may try to sort them further by sorting the nonlinear graphs into smaller groups. Students will notice that they could predict the answers in the linear graphs. For the discussion questions, students may feel uncomfortable about the scatterplot since there is no relationship. However, when they revisit the situations, they will conclude that none of the scenarios really made sense and that there were no relationships within them.

See the complete lesson plan in Appendix A on page 203.

How can you facilitate effective student collaboration? Record your response below.

_____

_____

_____

_____

_____

_____

_____

_____

_____

_____

_____

_____

_____

_____

_____

_____

_____

_____

_____

_____

_____

_____

_____

Chapter 12 ▪ Planning to Facilitate the Lesson **169**

Now it is your turn! What will you do to facilitate your lesson?

Facilitate:

online resources

Download the full Lesson-Planning Template from resources.corwin.com/mathlessonplanning/6-8
Remember that you can use the online version of the lesson plan template to begin compiling each section into the full template as your lesson plan grows.

170 The Mathematics Lesson-Planning Handbook, Grades 6–8

CHAPTER 13

PLANNING TO CLOSE THE LESSON

I am a bell-to-bell teacher and always want to use every minute possible for instructional time. It is really hard to not run out of time when my students are so excited about what they are learning. I often set a timer as I know closing a lesson is a critical component of good lesson planning and instruction. It is very important for my students to summarize, review, and reflect upon what has been taught during the lesson.

Mary Buck
Mathematics Coach
Montana

Almost every day, I tend to run out of time. I am getting better, but last week my class reminded me it was time to stop. My goal for this year is to improve closure at the end of our math class. I'm trying new things like exit slips and math journals. When I read what students write, I find out what they did not understand and that helps me prepare for the lesson the next day. I definitely want to know what else besides exit slips and journals can be used as closure activities.

Kathleen Londeree
Mathematics Specialist
Virginia

If you have ever looked at the classroom clock and realized you lack time for closure and have also run overtime, you are not alone. Mary and Kathleen have been using closure for many years and still work hard to fit it in to the end of a math period. Planning for closure is the first step in using it in your classroom. This chapter will discuss closure and several different formats while answering the following questions:

- Why do you need closure in a lesson?
- What are some different closure activities?
- What is an extended closure?

WHY DO YOU NEED CLOSURE IN A LESSON?

Closure is widely accepted as an important feature of lesson planning (Ganske, 2017), yet it is often neglected as a teaching practice because it gets sacrificed for critical instructional time. Middle school teachers on a 55- to 60-minute schedule need to be especially cognizant of planning for and implementing closure. By making time for this essential lesson feature, you can help students solidify learning.

While the word *closure* indicates an ending, it is more like a pause in the learning so students can reflect on or demonstrate what they learned, and teachers can collect feedback to determine next steps for learning.

Closure has two purposes—one for the teacher and one for the students. For the teacher, closure helps determine what students have learned, and it gives direction as to where to go next: reteach, correct misconceptions, or move on. Through closure activities, you collect formative assessment information to inform instructional decision making and provide valuable feedback to students (Wiliam & Thompson, 2008). For the students, closure is a cognitive activity that helps them focus on what they learned and whether the learning made sense and had meaning (Sousa, 2014) by connecting to the learning intentions and success criteria (Hattie et al., 2016).

During closure, you help students circle back to clarify the learning intentions and success criteria to focus students on the intended learning for the lesson. Closure provides the opportunity to reorganize the information from a lesson in a meaningful way by asking them to summarize, review, and demonstrate understanding of the big ideas from the lesson. Students may reflect on what occurred in the lesson, make sense of it, and link ideas to prior knowledge. An effective closure helps students increase retention and internalize what they have learned (Pollock, 2007). Closure activities that require students to think, respond, write, and discuss concepts improve learning (Cavanaugh, Heward, & Donelson, 1996).

To ensure that closure is effective and benefits both you and your students, you need to devote enough time to it because it is a reflective process that every learner must experience to make sense of the lesson. It can seldom be done in one hurried minute before the end of class. You must also be mindful of the format you use, because many closure formats require students to work in pairs or small groups. In these situations, you need to ensure every student has a chance to make meaning from the lesson.

You must also attend to the students' responses. It is not enough to just collect their work as with an exit slip. When you collect any reflection/closure response in writing, use a two-pile protocol. You sort the students' responses into two piles. The first pile is for student responses that show an understanding of the lesson. Pile two is for student responses that indicate additional instruction is needed. You can then decide where you go next with your lesson, how you organize grouping, and other lesson options based on the protocol. For example, if a pile indicates that more than half of the students need more help, then you may choose to reteach the entire lesson using a different representation. If a pile reveals that only a few students need more help, you can plan to use a lesson format to reach these individuals and correct their misconceptions or misunderstandings. Note that closure activities should not be graded.

WHAT ARE SOME DIFFERENT CLOSURE ACTIVITIES?

There are too many different lesson closure activities to name all of them here. However, the chart in Figure 13.1 provides a sampling that you can use in Grades 6 to 8.

Figure 13.1

Name and Description	Sample Prompts
Exit slips: Students respond in writing to a prompt and hand in these responses.	Write about one idea you learned in class today and one idea you still need help with.

Figure 13.1 (*Continued*)

Name and Description	Sample Prompts
Journal entries: Students respond to a prompt using numbers, symbols, graphs, equations, or words in their journals. This activity takes more time as the prompt requires a deeper explanation than one required on an exit slip.	Given the equation $3x + 7 = 2x + (3 + 4) + x$, Jerry tried to solve the equation but ended up with the statement $x = x$. He thought he made a mistake. Explain to Jerry what his answer is telling him.
Selfie: Students engage in self-reflection that allows them to assess their own learning. This can be as simple as a checklist for students to complete.	Check the statement that tells how you feel about today's lesson: _____ I got it! _____ I kinda got it. _____ I need more help. _____ I am lost!
3-2-1: Students have the opportunity to express thoughts about specific learning from the lesson.	Write three things you learned today about integers. Write two different examples of when you use integers. Write one thing you want me to know about your learning and integers.
Text message: This approach allows students to share what they learned with a specific audience. Use a template of a cellphone screen for students to write their message.	Provide the template with a prompt such as the following: Create a text to your parents about what you learned in math today about properties of operations.
Be the teacher: Students play the role of teacher by writing a math quiz. *Note that this closure activity is more appropriate for a block schedule because it takes more time to complete.	Create a five-question quiz on the material from today's lesson.
Exit task: A short task that allows students to demonstrate learning from the lesson.	Evaluate the following expression when $c = 10$: $5c - 9$

(Continued)

Standards

LI and SC

Purpose

Tasks

Materials

Student Thinking

Lesson Structures

Form. Assess.

Lesson Launch

Lesson Facilitation

Closure

Figure 13.1 (*Continued*)

Name and Description	Sample Prompts
The 3 Whats: On a prepared sheet, ask students to reflect on specific questions. Teachers can tailor the "whats."	*What?* (What did I learn today about proportional?) *So what?* (Why do I need proportional reasoning?) *Now what?* (Where can I use proportional reasoning outside of school?)
Pair/share: Students each tell their partner the answer to a specific question about the lesson. Then each of the pairs shares with the class. The teacher can take notes for the two-pile protocol.	Tell your partner the most important thing you learned today about the Pythagorean Theorem.
S-T-O-P: Students summarize the lesson orally or in writing by finishing sentence starters.	We **S**tarted the lesson _____. Our **T**opic was _____. **O**pportunities to do the math included _____. The **P**urpose of the lesson was _____.
Uh, huh! Uh, uh! and Hmmmm: Students tell about something in the lesson that they understood and may have said "Uh, huh!" to themselves, something they did not get or agree with and said "Uh, uh," and something they are still not sure about or thinking "Hmmmm."	**Uh, huh!** _____ **Uh, uh!** _____ **Hmmmm** _____
Walk-Away: Students use words, pictures, or symbols to show what they will *walk away* with from the lesson.	What will you walk away with from the lesson?

WHAT IS AN EXTENDED CLOSURE?

Some lessons may call for a more in-depth closure than the ones previously listed. This is called an **extended closure**.

When you plan a rich problem-based task that invites students to engage deeply, you will want to provide plenty of time for students to make sense of each other's work, connect representations, construct viable arguments, and link new learning to the learning intentions. During the lesson facilitation, you monitor the students as they work to represent their solutions and ask probing questions along the way. Just as you provide ample time for your students to work on the rich task, you will also want to make sure you leave plenty of time for your closure. During this time, you will want to strategically connect the students' solutions to the learning intention. Many teachers conduct a gallery walk for this purpose. A gallery walk in mathematics is similar to a gallery walk in an art exhibit. Students examine work by other students by walking around the room in groups and viewing work posted by their peers. This is a nonthreatening way for students to give and receive feedback, as well as check for understanding. They examine the work with specific questions in mind such as, "How is this example different from/the same as my work? What do I like about this students' thinking? Is this a technique I would like to try? What would have improved the work? Are there any misconceptions evident in the work?" This is an engaging way for students to examine multiple ways of thinking.

Teachers need to allot enough time for students to examine each piece of work. On a block schedule, a gallery walk can fit into the day's lesson. On a 55- to 60-minute schedule, the gallery walk may need to take place the following day.

Some teachers provide students with sticky dots so that as they go through the gallery walk, they can focus on particular questions such as placing a green dot on a poster that closely matches their thinking.

The value of a gallery walk is that it promotes thinking about and reflecting on student work. It engages students in group conversations and gives them an opportunity to refine their thinking while reflecting on peer work. Melissa used a gallery walk with the following lesson.

> Example: Melissa
>
> Melissa's learning intention was to have students engage in a problem-solving task, apply multiple solutions, and be able to communicate their solutions to others. Melissa gave the following to her students.
>
> > A boy and a girl weigh 98 pounds together. The boy and the dog weigh 68 pounds together. The girl and the dog weigh 70 pounds together. What is the total weight of the boy, the dog, and the girl?
> >
> > Solve this problem with your group and display your solution strategy on the poster paper provided. When you are finished, hang up your work for a gallery walk.
>
> As students worked to solve the problem, Melissa walked around and noticed students using many different strategies, including algebraic equations. After they displayed their work, students moved around the room to examine each other's work. Some student comments heard were, "We did it just like that!" "We never thought to use an equation," "I like the way Felicia's group solved it with pictures and subtraction. I never would have done it that way!" After the students had time to examine the work and jot down their thoughts on paper, Melissa closes the lesson by collecting the student reflections. She initiates a class discussion:
>
> **Melissa**: What do you think about the variety of different strategies used by your classmates?
>
> **Jose**: I was surprised by the different ways. I thought there was only one way and that was the way I did it!
>
> **Juan**: I didn't think of using algebra but it makes sense.
>
> **Kimi**: I don't get it. On the algebra poster, there are so many variables. I don't see how they work.
>
> **Kevin**: Kimi, the d is for the dog's weight, the g is the girl's weight, and the b is the boy's weight.
>
> The discussion continued with Melissa facilitating the student reflections. As class ends, she decides to adjust tomorrow's lesson and begin with Kimi's questions about the algebraic solution. Melissa was pleased to see that the students are beginning to recognize that you can use more than one solution strategy to solve a problem.

Standards

LI and SC

Purpose

Tasks

Materials

Student Thinking

Lesson Structures

Form. Assess.

Lesson Launch

Lesson Facilitation

Closure

You may have seen other ideas for closure. Compile a list of more closure activities that are appropriate for your students. Be sure each meets the purpose for the teacher and the student. Record the ones you would like to try first.

_____

_____

_____

_____

Building Unit Coherence

Closure provides a perfect opportunity for you to build coherence among your lessons. You can connect student reflection on the day's lesson to previous lessons to help your students make sense of the big idea/essential question that is the thread throughout the unit. For example, asking students to team up with a partner to answer the question, "How is the problem we looked at today different from or the same as the problem we looked at yesterday?" is an effective and simple way to tie lessons together and build the big ideas across the unit.

Notes

_____

_____

_____

_____

_____

_____

_____

_____

_____

_____

_____

_____

Sixth-Grade Snapshot

Close the Lesson

Josh and Jeff decide to have their students use the S-T-O-P closure activity at the end of the math period. They believe that this record will provide them with valuable information about how their students would summarize the main parts of the lesson. In S-T-O-P, students complete four sentence starters to summarize how the lesson began, the topic of the lesson, the opportunities they engaged in during the lesson, and what they perceived as the purpose of the lesson.

Closure:

Use the STOP closure. Students summarize the lesson in writing by finishing the sentence starters.

We **S**tarted the lesson _____ .

Our **T**opic was _____ .

Opportunities to do the work included _____ .

The **P**urpose of the lesson was _____ .

See the complete lesson plan in Appendix A on page 188.

How does the closure activity in this lesson satisfy the purpose of closure for the teacher and student? Note your ideas below.

_____

_____

_____

_____

_____

_____

_____

_____

_____

_____

_____

_____

_____

_____

_____

_____

_____

_____

_____

_____

The seventh-grade team pondered how to close their transfer lesson. Alix suggested, "Do you think we should have them conduct a gallery walk so they can see the different solutions?" "Yes!" Bryan, Kia, and Kyle agreed. "Then, we can have some students share particular solutions that we want to highlight," suggested Kia. "Yes, then we can have them complete a final reflection in their journals about the importance of transferring math to the real world," offered Bryan. "This is a wonderful idea, Bryan!" said Alix.

Closure:

Conduct an extended closure by asking students to participate in a gallery walk. Then, select student groups to share particular representations for each of the problems. Encourage students to ask questions during the presentations. Ask questions such as the following:

- Explain how your equation represents the problem.

- Is there only one equation that will represent this problem?

- What kinds of drawings helped you solve?

Finally, ask individual students to complete the closure prompt on the back page of their journal.

Think about all the problems you solved for the pet-sitting business. Describe when you could solve the same kind of problem in a different situation in your life.

See the complete lesson plan in Appendix A on page 192.

How does the closure activity in this lesson satisfy the purpose of closure for the teacher and student? Note your ideas below.

Close the Lesson

Serena was having trouble deciding on closure. This was an area she has always had trouble with. She would either run out of time or, since she did not plan closure, did not know what to do.

Recently, Serena joined the twitter feed for NCTM. She decided to see if they had any suggestions for her, so she tweeted, "Can anyone help an eighth-grade teacher who always runs out of time or ideas for lesson closures?"

Within five minutes, Serena was hearing from teachers all around the country about closure. She was not only excited about planning closure for this lesson but also ecstatic that she found such a community!

Closure:

Use the 3 What's:
What did I learn today about graphs?

Why do I need to know the difference between different shapes of data on a graph?

Now that I know, how can this information help me?

See the complete lesson plan in Appendix A on page 203.

How does the closure activity in this lesson satisfy the purpose of closure for the teacher and student? Note your ideas below.

_____

_____

_____

_____

_____

_____

_____

_____

_____

_____

_____

_____

_____

_____

_____

_____

_____

_____

_____

Standards | LI and SC | Purpose | Tasks | Materials | Student Thinking | Lesson Structures | Form. Assess. | Lesson Launch | Lesson Facilitation | Closure

Under Construction

Now it is your turn! Add an appropriate closure activity to your lesson plan that is under construction.

Closure:

online resources

Download the full Lesson-Planning Template from resources.corwin.com/mathlessonplanning/6-8
Remember that you can use the online version of the lesson plan template to begin compiling each section into the full template as your lesson plan grows.

180   The Mathematics Lesson-Planning Handbook, Grades 6–8

CHAPTER 14

SURVEYING YOUR RESULTS

Lesson Reflection

Honestly, I don't take enough time to reflect. I know that I should, but it seems like I am so busy that I barely have time to process all the decisions that I am making throughout the day. I know, though, that when I do reflect, I feel more in control of my teaching. Lately, I have been chatting with a friend I graduated with who is teaching at another school in the same school district. Luckily, we are both teaching seventh graders. We also face the same things—we are the newest members to the math team, and we like to use a lot of problem-based tasks. We met one day after school to share our lessons and tasks and then we actually wrote a couple together. We decided to meet once a month to share ideas. In between our meetings, we touch base about how it is going. I got into the habit of writing a couple notes down so I could remember what to share with him about how the lesson went. It has really helped me be more aware of the parts of the lesson that are working.

During one of our conversations, we realized that we needed to spend more time developing the launch part of the lesson. The students were so much more independent during the problem-solving process if they had time to talk about the problem and unpack the context. A couple of times, I went too far on this and gave away too much of the information. Reflecting about the lesson really helped me figure out what I was doing. If I don't reflect, I tend to just want to throw out the whole lesson instead of figuring out exactly what is going well and what needs to be improved.

Gina Tompkins
Teacher
California

No doubt your day is filled with endless decisions and lots of rushing from one thing to the next. Teaching middle school students does not allow much space for thinking about the day. However, teaching is an emotional and often physical challenge that requires deep processing. This chapter will consider the following questions:

- Why is it important to reflect upon lessons?

- What kind of reflection cycle supports teacher growth?

WHY IS IT IMPORTANT TO REFLECT UPON LESSONS?

Teachers can use reflection as way to focus on what works, recognize challenges, and move forward in productive ways. Your reflection should be centered on a healthy curiosity about student learning that helps you better understand and learn about your teaching practice (Danielson, 2008; Smyth, 1992). You can reflect as you are teaching, which is called **reflecting in action** (Schön, 1983), to monitor and adjust to the ebb and flow of your learners' needs. You can also reflect after you have taught, which is called **reflecting on action** (Schön, 1983), by thinking about your students and instruction after a lesson ends.

You are probably already asked to reflect as a formal part of your professional practice. Many teacher evaluation systems require some sort of reflection about teaching. These reflection prompts formalize what good teachers already do every day and focus on established criteria.

Perhaps the most powerful reflection occurs when teachers pose their own questions about their teaching because those questions help them make meaningful connections between their teaching decisions and student learning. In an analysis of John Dewey's (1933, 1944) writing on the importance of reflection, Carol Rodgers (2002) extracted four essential criteria that define effective reflection.

1. *Reflection is a meaning-making process.* Your reflection should support your ability to make connections. As it moves beyond ruminating, hashing over, or contemplating the day's events, your reflection should support a deeper understanding of your teaching choices and your students' response to those choices.

2. *Reflection is a rigorous, disciplined way of thinking, with its roots in scientific inquiry.* Your reflection should always begin with a question that probes and pushes your thinking. Inquiry nudges teachers to tell their teaching stories in new ways. Consider these questions:

   - What do I believe about how students learn? How is this reflected in my instructional planning?
   - What kinds of questions did I ask during this lesson? How was student learning affected?
   - How does planning my questioning affect my lesson facilitation?
   - What does student-centered teaching mean to me?
   - How do I know my students are learning?
   - What data did I collect today that were most powerful?

3. *Reflection needs to happen in a community, in interaction with others.* Personal reflection is important and necessary. However, reflection that happens in a community of teachers is also powerful as other teachers provide unique perspectives, ask questions, and offer insight that can reveal new ways of thinking about teaching.

4. *Reflection requires attitudes that value your personal and professional growth as well as the personal and professional growth of other teachers and leaders.* Reflection is cathartic and powerful. Without it, learning and change are not likely to happen. Making time to reflect is essential to maintaining your professional health, and this approach will support you in making good decisions about teaching and learning (Constantino & De Lorenzo, 2001; Day, 1999; Harris, Bruster, Peterson, & Shutt, 2010).

> **Describe your reflective practice. When, how, and with whom do you reflect? Write your response here.**
> _____
> _____
> _____
> _____
> _____

WHAT KIND OF REFLECTION CYCLE SUPPORTS TEACHER GROWTH?

When you take time to mindfully unpack your professional teaching practice, you can gain insight into improving your future practice. If you focus on successes before challenges, you can gain new understandings about the factors that promote success and shape new teaching decisions. Consider the reflection cycle in Figure 14.1.

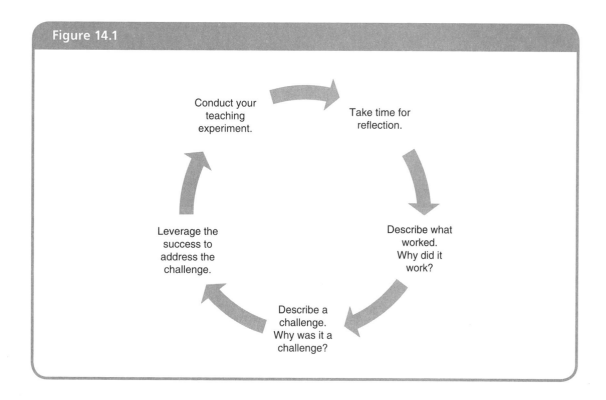

Figure 14.1

Conduct your teaching experiment.

Take time for reflection.

Describe what worked. Why did it work?

Describe a challenge. Why was it a challenge?

Leverage the success to address the challenge.

Let's look at each component of the reflecting cycle in more detail.

Take Time for Reflection

Unless you set a designated time for reflection, it can be difficult to move beyond musings about the day. Teachers are very hard on themselves and tend to focus on those most difficult moments or the problems of the day. Making time for reflection, using a specific cycle, can help you work through successes and challenges and strategically design next instructional steps. Think about how to schedule time to reflect alone and with trusted colleagues. Some teachers plan regular reflection time during professional learning meetings.

Describe What Worked

Reflect on what worked during the lesson, and describe what you and the students were doing that contributed to the success. When you ask yourself these questions, you heighten your awareness and positive potential for change (Cooperrider & Whitney, 2005). By focusing on what has worked and dissecting those elements that contributed to success, you can identify what aspects to repeat (Hammond, 1998).

Some teachers like to chart these ideas in two columns to help them discover connections (see example in Figure 14.2). This process is a key component for moving forward. Often, your inspiration about tackling challenges will come from your understanding of why a particular teaching practice was successful.

Figure 14.2

What Worked	Why
Numberless word problem	• Students were relaxed. • Students were curious. • Students immediately started putting numbers into the word problem to make sense of the problem. • Students were not encumbered with a right or wrong answer. • Students were allowed to collaborate and work together.

Describe the Challenge

By describing a challenge that you experienced in the lesson, you can begin to imagine how you can leverage your success to tackle your challenge. This could be something that is significant to this particular lesson, or it could be something that you have noticed as a pattern in your daily lessons. As the example in Figure 14.3 shows, it can be helpful to unpack the challenge by considering potential reasons why it exists.

Figure 14.3

Challenge	Why
Supporting students' productive struggle	• I am worried about pushing students too hard, and I think they know this. • I need to be better prepared with scaffolding questions. • I need to make sure that I am providing an environment that helps the students feel safe. • Some students are exhibiting learned helplessness. • Students are worried about being right and/or getting wrong answers.

Leverage the Success to Address the Challenge

By examining the elements of the success alongside the challenge, you can often uncover contributing elements of the success that you can leverage to help you with the challenge. For example, if you note your success with a numberless word problem but also your challenge with supporting productive struggle with some of your students, the details might prompt you to recognize that the numberless word problem was so successful because the students knew that there was not a correct answer. Based on this reflection, you might decide to use more open-ended problems with multiple solutions. This approach would also help you focus your students more on the process of solving, rather than on the answers.

Conduct Your Teaching Experiment

You conduct teaching experiments all the time! A teaching experiment occurs when you pose a question, try out an idea, reflect, and adjust based on the results (Tschannen-Moran & Tschannen-Moran, 2010). Teachers who share challenges often enjoy collaborating on teaching experiments and celebrating the results.

The first step in conducting your teaching experiment is to think about how to design your experiment. Consider the following questions:

- What would you like to pay more attention to in your mathematics classroom?
- What changes do you think your students would really appreciate?
- What changes would increase achievement?
- What things can you imagine doing differently?
- How might your mathematics teaching be different a few months from now?
- What changes would you like to experiment with in your mathematics teaching?

The next step is to describe your experiment and make a design plan for implementation. Consider the timeline, materials, and resources you will need to conduct your teaching experiment.

- Will you need to talk with other teachers, gain permission from your principal, or read new information to conduct your teaching experiment?
- What activities will you implement?
- What kinds of evidence will you collect?

Finally, you will need to reflect on your experiment.

- How will you know if your teaching experiment is successful?
- How will you revise your experiment?
- How will you integrate your experiment into your daily practice?
- How will you share the results of your experiment with your colleagues and leadership?

> **How can you use your reflection to design a teaching experiment through lesson planning? Record your responses here.**
>
> _____
>
> _____
>
> _____
>
> _____
>
> _____

Epilogue

You began this lesson-planning process by thinking about and examining your students' needs and considering the important ideas of coherence, rigor, and purpose. By now, we hope you have come to see the many important facets of building purposeful and cohesive mathematics lessons and maybe even fully engaged in the lesson-planning process, using the sections of this book as your guide, and filling in the lesson-planning template! Likewise, we hope you and your students are reaping the benefits of thorough planning or at the very least getting a taste of the success yet to come. Whether you have designed a lesson fully from scratch, adapted a lesson, or even just read a few sections of this book, you have likely thought about the lesson-planning process with a new perspective that has deepened your knowledge about your own choices and decisions. The teachers we work with tell us that when they study and engage in the lesson-planning process, they

- become more confident and intentional in their teaching;

- are able to listen and respond to their students more authentically and react to their students' understandings with clarity and purpose;

- find greater meaning in the lessons because they have made sense of large and small teaching decisions, including task selection or adaptation; lesson purpose; lesson format; and lesson launch, facilitation, and closure; and

- report a renewed confidence and find they are energized and excited by the lesson-planning-and-implementation cycle.

As you have hopefully experienced, lesson planning builds cohesion for both students and yourself (Jensen, 2001). Thorough lessons, strategically planned, support students' ability to build connections among and between mathematical ideas (Panasuk, Stone, & Todd, 2002). This is, after all, our goal. Teachers and students see and understand how today's learning connects to yesterday's, last week's, and even last year's learning *and* forecasts future learning.

You may have also noticed that the lesson-planning process can help you clarify your own understanding of the mathematics content, standard, and potential student misconceptions. This is perhaps one of the most powerful teacher benefits of lesson planning—a benefit that will extend beyond any one lesson you teach. The teachers we work with report that they experience new insight about the mathematics they are teaching, which, in turn, helps them to strategically facilitate their students' learning.

As you continue this journey, we recommend that you do the following:

Start slowly. Select a few pieces of the lesson-planning process to focus on, and then build from there. Start with what is most comfortable for you, and then extend or add new pieces to your planning repertoire. Before you know it, you will be able to spend your time on the parts of the lesson that need your attention the most.

Find planning partners. Search for other teachers to plan with regularly. They don't necessarily have to be in your school or grade level. Online platforms support co-creation and sharing across the country. Simply having an opportunity to share your planning decisions with others can be immensely rewarding and satisfying. Make sure you share your successes as well as your challenges.

Determine how you will organize and store your lessons. Many teachers store the lessons for each grade level by using online formats. This organization will support you in the future and reduce planning time in subsequent years. Storing lessons will also help you track revisions as you respond to the particular needs of your students. Don't forget to record reflections or thoughts about the lesson!

Communicate with leaders. As you know, planning lessons takes time and perseverance. Invite school and district leaders to participate in your planning sessions. Engage them in your process as you plan, implement, and reflect on your teaching successes and challenges.

Celebrate and showcase your success. So much of teaching is privately shared between students and teachers. Publicly sharing your lessons with teammates and school leaders can inspire others to plan and innovate powerful lessons. Organize opportunities for colleagues to share successful lessons that affected student learning.

Always remember that you are the architect of your classroom. You have the fortune to design and implement lessons that help children learn mathematics. You get to establish the learning environment you want to foster, and you have not only the opportunity but also the responsibility to build the best foundation and best structure for your learners as possible. We wish you every success.

Appendix A

Complete Lesson Plans

Big Idea(s):

Arithmetic concepts extend to understanding of algebraic expressions and equations.

Essential Question(s):

What are some everyday situations that can be expressed as algebraic expressions and equations?

Content Standard(s):

Write, read, and evaluate expressions in which letters stand for numbers.

Mathematical Practice or Process Standards:

Reason abstractly and quantitatively.

Attend to precision.

Look for and make use of structure.

Learning Intention(s):
Mathematical Learning Intentions

We are learning to:

- Write expressions that record operations with numbers and letters standing for numbers. For example, "subtract y from 5" as 5 - y.

Language Learning Intentions

We are learning to:

- Use the terms algebraic expression, sum, term, product, factor, quantity, quotient, coefficient, constant, like terms, equivalent expressions, and variables appropriately

Social Learning Intentions

We are learning to:

- Listen to the ideas of others
- Respectfully disagree with the mathematical arguments of others

Success Criteria
(written in student voice):

I know that I am successful when I can:

- Read and write expressions with letters standing for numbers
- Evaluate expressions for specific values
- Apply the order of operations to algebraic expressions
- Use the terms algebraic expression, sum, term, product, factor, quantity, quotient, coefficient, constant, like terms, equivalent expressions, and variables appropriately in writing and speaking
- Listen to the ideas of others
- Respectfully disagree with the mathematical arguments of others

Purpose:

☐ Conceptual Understanding   ☑ Procedural Fluency   ☐ Transfer

Task:

Each small group of students will solve the problems on the worksheet entitled, Soccer Kicks! (see Figure A.1). Students may rely upon the use of Algebra Tiles early in the lesson but should move to the pictorial and abstract stage by the end of the lesson.

Materials (representations, manipulatives, other):

Algebra Tiles

Paper/pencil

Soccer Kicks! Problems Set A and Set B (see Figures A.1 and A.2)

Misconceptions or Common Errors:

- Students incorrectly translate statements such as "6 less than y" as "6 - y."
- Students incorrectly use the distributive property and may only distribute the first term.
- Students forget that if a coefficient is not written, the coefficient is 1.

Format:

☐ Four-Part Lesson   ☐ Game Format   ☑ Small-Group Instruction
☐ Pairs   ☐ Other_____

Formative Assessment:

Observe students as they work on problems. Look to determine if students are drawing pictures of the manipulatives or writing the expressions abstractly. Note that a few students may still need to use Algebra Tiles.

Launch:

Refer back to the previously taught lesson. Yesterday we used Algebra Tiles to help us model expressions. Let's see what we remember as you work with your partner to model the following:

Sam went to the fair. He bought a book of tickets for $4.00. Then he bought drinks that cost $2.00 each for his friends. What expression represents the problem?

Have students share how they modeled the word problem using Algebra Tiles. Select one student to draw a picture of his or her tiles on the document camera.

Facilitate:

Refer to the drawing of the tiles on the document camera. Discuss with students if the drawing is as useful as using the tiles. Encourage students to work on the Set A worksheet problems by drawing the tiles and, if possible, not using the real tiles. Walk around as students solve the problems. For students who seem to be proficient with the pictures, collect their tiles and challenge them to visualize the tiles to solve Set B's (see Figure A.2) problem abstractly. Not all students will be able to solve problems abstractly at this point. Select students you have observed having difficulty moving away from the tiles and work with them in a small group. The teacher will listen to how the students describe their thinking. The teacher uses his or her thinking to help move them away from using the tiles and drawing pictures. The teacher may also work with students who are having difficulty moving from the pictorial level to the abstract level by also pulling them into a small group.

(Continued)

Closure:

Use the STOP closure. Students summarize the lesson in writing by finishing the sentence starters.

We **S**tarted the lesson _____ .

Our **T**opic was _____ .

Opportunities to do the work included _____ .

The **P**urpose of the lesson was _____ .

Figure A.1

Soccer Kicks! Set A

1. Mrs. Bland took her two children to the soccer game. For each child, she bought one drink for $2.50 and 3 candy bars. Write an expression to represent how much money Mrs. Bland spent.

2. Soccer uniforms cost $21.00 each. In addition to the uniform, each soccer player must purchase his or her own socks. Socks cost $5.25 a pair. Write an expression to represent the total cost of a uniform and socks.

3. The soccer team needs to raise money to participate in a spring tournament. They can sell bags of popcorn for $1.25 each and drinks for $2 each. Write an expression to represent the amount of money the soccer team can raise.

4. Lake Middle School had many games cancelled last year due to inclement weather. When compared to River Middle School, River Middle School played 6 more games than Lake. Write an expression for how many games River Middle School played.

5. Beckham lives near the soccer field. He is able to walk home from games. Last week Beckham played 5 games but he got a ride home for the last 3 miles for the last game. Write an expression for how many miles Beckham walked home from all of his games last week.

Image source: Undefined undefined/iStock.com

Soccer Kicks! Set B

1. The soccer team works out at Jim's Gym. The following chart shows monthly membership costs at the gym. Write an expression to represent the cost of gym membership for any number of months.

Number of Months	Cost in Dollars
3	60
5	100
9	180

2. Mom drives the car pool to the soccer games. She travels 6 less miles on Tuesday's practice than for Monday. Write an expression to represent how many miles she travels on Tuesday.

3. To determine gas mileage for the soccer car pool, Mom wants to figure out the miles per gallon of gas her car gets. She finds the quotient of the miles she drives and the amount she spends on gas.

4. This year Molly scored 3 times as many goals as Lucas. Write an expression showing this relationship.

5. Overall, Lake Middle School has 10 less than 4 times the number of goals this season than River Middle School. Write an expression for Lake Middle School's goals. Then, write an expression for River Middle School's goals.

Image source: Undefined undefined/iStock.com

Big Idea(s):

Students use prior understanding of the four operations with rational numbers and apply the operations in measurement contexts to solve real-world problems.

Essential Question(s):

Can an expression or equation be written to represent a real-life mathematical problem?

Content Standard(s):

Solve multistep real-life and mathematical problems posed with positive and negative rational numbers in any form (whole numbers, fractions, and decimals), using tools strategically. Apply properties of operations to calculate with numbers in any form, convert between forms as appropriate, and assess the reasonableness of answers using mental computation and estimation strategies.

Mathematical Practice or Process Standards:

Model with mathematics.

Look for and make use of structure.

Critique the reasoning of others.

Learning Intention(s):
Mathematical Learning Intentions

We are learning to:
- Represent equivalent forms of numbers
- Write an equation to represent a real-world problem
- Apply properties of operations

Language Learning Intentions

We are learning to:
- Use the terms relationship and equation
- Explain how an equation represents a real-world problem

Social Learning Intentions

We are learning to:
- Listen to the ideas of others
- Respectfully disagree with the mathematical arguments of others

Success Criteria (written in student voice):

I know that I am successful when I can:
- Write an equation, table, and graph for a linear relationship
- Recognize a linear, nonlinear, and no relationship from a graph
- Use the terms relationship and equation
- Explain how an equation represents a real-world problem
- Listen to the ideas of others
- Respectfully disagree with the mathematical arguments of others

Purpose:

☐ Conceptual Understanding   ☐ Procedural Fluency   ☑ Transfer

Task:

Taking Care of Teddy

Congratulations! You have just been hired for your first pet-sitting job! You have agreed to take care of Teddy the Toy Poodle for four days. You never imagined a 10-pound toy poodle would cause so many problems! You must solve every problem before Teddy's owners get back from vacation. However, Teddy's owners are very intense about Teddy's care. Each day they will text you to make sure you know what you are doing. They have also asked you to keep a journal for them to read when they get back. You must be able to answer their questions or they will find a new pet sitter!

Day One: Teddy Gets a Haircut

Today, Teddy has an appointment with the groomer to get his fur trimmed. Teddy's owners left $50 for you to pay the groomer. The cost of the grooming is $35.50. You have been instructed by the owners to leave a 15% tip on the cost of the grooming. You also want to buy a chew toy for $5.99. The tax rate in Teddy's state is 7.5%. Do you have enough money to get the chew toy? Write an equation to represent this situation. Then explain how the equation matches the story.

Teddy's owner texts to check on how you are doing. You tell her all about the grooming and chew toy. She texts:

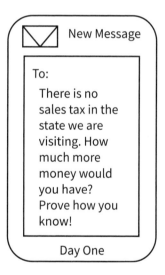

New Message

To:

There is no sales tax in the state we are visiting. How much more money would you have? Prove how you know!

Day One

Day Two: Keeping Teddy Out of the Living Room

Every time you leave Teddy, he chews up something in the living room. Yesterday, it was a pillow in the living room. Today, he knocked over a picture frame. You notice a dog gate in a box and decide to put up a gate to block Teddy from getting into the living room. You need to make sure the gate is centered correctly in the middle of the doorway. The doorway is $34\frac{3}{4}$ inches wide. The gate is $22\frac{1}{2}$ inches. How long will the bars that attach to the gate need to be? Write an equation to represent this situation. Then explain how the equation matches the story.

(Continued)

Teddy's owner texts to check on how you are doing. You tell her all about the gate!

Day Three: Teddy's Special Food

Teddy needs special food to stay healthy. You must mix his food in just the right way or Teddy will have terrible tummy troubles.

Directions: Get the 3-gallon container of DOGGY dry dog mix, which has 20% chicken, which is Teddy's favorite ingredient. Then, add the bag of PUPPY dry mix that has 30% chicken. You should now have a 10-gallon container mixed with DOGGY and PUPPY dry mix. Write an equation to describe the relationships between the different dog mixes. Then explain how the equation matches the story. What percent of the final dog food mixture is chicken?

Teddy's owner texts to check on how you are doing.

Day Four: Teddy Goes to the Dog Park

You promised Teddy's owners you would take Teddy to the dog park, but you have been warned that Teddy cannot walk more than three miles or his little joints will ache. The owners want Teddy to walk as close to three miles as possible. When you get to the dog park, there are four paths.

- Path A: 0.24 mile
- Path B: $\frac{1}{2}$ mile
- Path C: 0.6 mile
- Path D: 500 yards

Select the paths or combination of paths that will allow you to walk Teddy as close to 3 miles as possible.

Write an equation to represent this situation. Then explain how the equation matches the story.

Teddy's owner texts to check on how you are doing. You tell her all about dog walk. She texts:

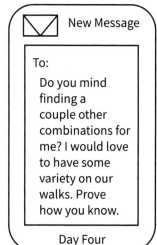

New Message

To:

Do you mind finding a couple other combinations for me? I would love to have some variety on our walks. Prove how you know.

Day Four

Materials (representations, manipulatives, other):

Teddy's Pet-Sitting Problem-Solving Journal (see Figure A.3)

Larger chart paper sectioned into four parts

DAY ONE	DAY TWO
DAY THREE	DAY FOUR

(Continued)

Misconceptions or Common Errors:

* Students may struggle with multistep problems. You may scaffold the problems by focusing on the first part of the problem.

* Encourage the students to use number lines, such as in the dog park problem. Students can also use drawings to solve.

* Students may struggle to convert measurements. Provide measurement conversions as needed.

* Students may struggle to represent the situation using an equation.

* Students may find the tax on individual items and/or compute tax incorrectly.

* Students might be challenged by the Day Three problem because they will have to buy more to increase the percentage of chicken.

An additional blank text frame is added to the resources for the teacher to add an additional question as an extension for a group that ends early.

Format:

☑ Four-Part Lesson   ☐ Game Format   ☐ Small-Group Instruction
☐ Pairs   ☐ Other_____

Formative Assessment:

Interview:

* How do you know your equation matches the problem?

* Is there another way to represent the problem?

Launch:

Ask the students to brainstorm all the things they might need to know to pet sit. Record the students' ideas.

Pose questions such as:

* What kinds of situations might come up while pet sitting where math might be helpful?

* What kinds of math might you need to know?

* How might the math we have been learning in the expressions and equations unit help us solve problems?

Facilitate:

Say, "You thought of some great situations where you might need to use knowledge about expressions and equations. In this lesson, we are going to get an opportunity to see how we transfer what we have learned to a new situation."

Arrange the students in pairs and introduce the context for the problem:

Congratulations! You have just been hired for your first pet-sitting job! You have agreed to take care of Teddy the Toy Poodle for four days. You never imagined a 10-pound toy poodle would cause so many problems! You must solve every problem before Teddy's owners get back from vacation. However, Teddy's owners are very intense about Teddy's care. Each day they will text you to make sure you know what you are doing. They have also asked you to keep a journal for them to read when they get back. You must be able to answer their questions or they will find a new pet sitter!

Explain to the students that they will have an opportunity to work in pairs to problem solve, but each will be responsible for recording their ideas in the pet-sitting journal. Depending on the amount of time you have for instruction, this lesson might take two days. Distribute the Teddy's Pet-Sitting Problem-Solving Journals, larger poster paper, and markers. As the groups begin solving, ask questions such as the following:

- How can you represent this problem?
- What will you do first?
- What equation might represent this problem?
- Is there another equation that might also work?
- Would drawing a picture help? Why or why not?

After the pairs have finished the first problem, hand them a slip of paper with the text from the owner (see Figure A.4). Encourage the students to solve the new problem and discuss the reasonableness of the solution.

Once the pair completes their work, arrange the students in a pair-to-pair share. (A pair-to-pair share is when two pairs form a group of four.) This is a good opportunity to strategically match pairs to share alternative ideas, solutions, and strategies. Have the pairs share their solutions and then decide on which solution to represent on the large chart paper for DAY ONE.

Repeat the same process for the next three problems (days).

1. The students will complete each problem (days) in pairs.

2. The students will receive a "text message" from the teacher at the completion of the problem. Students will then add the additional solution.

3. Pairs will be in groups to conduct a pair-to-pair share (group of four) to decide which of the solutions to represent on the large chart paper.

(Continued)

Closure:

Conduct an extended closure by asking students to participate in a gallery walk. Then, select student groups to share particular representations for each of the problems. Encourage students to ask questions during the presentations. Ask questions such as the following:

* Explain how your equation represents the problem.
* Is there only one equation that will represent this problem?
* What kinds of drawings helped you solve?

Finally, ask individual students to complete the closure prompt on the back page of their journal.

Think about all the problems you solved for the pet-sitting business. Describe when you could solve the same kind of problem in a different situation in your life.

Teddy's Pet-Sitting Problem-Solving Journal

Taking Care of Teddy

Congratulations! You have just been hired for your first pet-sitting job! You have agreed to take care of Teddy the Toy Poodle for four days. You never imagined a 10-pound toy poodle would cause so many problems! You must solve every problem before Teddy's owners get back from vacation. However, Teddy's owners are very intense about Teddy's care. Each day they will text you to make sure you know what you are doing. They have also asked you to keep a journal for them to read when they get back. You must be able to answer their questions or they will find a new pet sitter!

Image source: daikokuebisu/iStock.com

Think about all the problems you solved for the pet-sitting business. Describe when you could solve the same kind of problem in a different situation in your life.

- "\n\n\n"

Day Two: Keeping Teddy Out of the Living Room

Every time you leave Teddy, he chews up something in the living room. Yesterday, it was a pillow in the living room. Today, he knocked over a picture frame. You notice a dog gate in a box and decide to put up a gate to block Teddy from getting into the living room. You need to make sure the gate is centered correctly in the middle of the doorway. The doorway is $34\frac{3}{4}$ inches wide. The gate is $22\frac{1}{2}$ inches. How long will the bars that attach to the gate need to be? Write an equation to represent this situation. Then explain how the equation matches the story.

Day One: Teddy Gets a Haircut

Today, Teddy has an appointment with the groomer to get his fur trimmed. Teddy's owners left $50 for you to pay the groomer. The cost of the grooming is $35.50. You have been instructed by the owners to leave a 15% tip on the cost of the grooming. You also want to buy a chew toy for $5.99. The tax rate in Teddy's state is 7.5%. Do you have enough money to get the chew toy? Write an equation to represent this situation. Then explain how the equation matches the story.

Day Three: Teddy's Special Food

Teddy needs special food to stay healthy. You must mix his food in just the right way or Teddy will have terrible tummy troubles.

Directions: Get the 3-gallon container of DOGGY dry dog mix, which has 20% chicken, which is Teddy's favorite ingredient. Then, add the bag of PUPPY dry mix that has 30% chicken. You should now have a 10-gallon container mixed with DOGGY and PUPPY dry mix. Write an equation to describe the relationships between the different dog mixes. Then explain how the equation matches the story. What percent of the final dog food mixture is chicken?

Day Four: Teddy Goes to the Dog Park

You promised Teddy's owners you would take Teddy to the dog park, but you have been warned that Teddy cannot walk more than three miles or his little joints will ache. The owners want Teddy to walk as close to three miles as possible. When you get to the dog park, there are four paths.

- Path A: 0.24 mile
- Path B: $\frac{1}{2}$ mile
- Path C: 0.6 mile
- Path D: 500 yards

Select the paths or combination of paths that will allow you to walk Teddy as close to 3 miles as possible.

Write an equation to represent this situation. Then explain how the equation matches the story.

New Message

To: There is no sales tax in the state we are visiting. How much more money would you have? Prove how you know!

Day One

New Message

To: Please send me a drawing of the gate and make sure you label the measurements correctly!

Day Two

New Message

To: Did you mix the dog food so there is at least 40% chicken? Prove how you know.

Day Three

New Message

To: Do you mind finding a couple other combinations for me? I would love to have some variety on our walks. Prove how you know.

Day Four

New Message

To:

Day Five

Download the complete seventh-grade lesson plan and handouts from resources.corwin.com/mathlessonplanning/6–8

online resources

Big Idea(s):

Functions can be represented verbally, graphically, symbolically, physically, and in a table.

Essential Question(s):

What do different shapes of graphed data tell us?

Content Standard(s):

Understand the connections between proportional relationships, lines, and linear equations.

Mathematical Practice or Process Standards:

Model with mathematics.

Look for and make use of structure.

Learning Intention(s):
Mathematical Learning Intentions

We are learning to:

- Write an equation, table, and graph for a linear relationship
- Recognize a linear, nonlinear, and no relationship from a graph

Language Learning Intentions

We are learning to:

- Use the terms relationship, linear equation, and nonlinear relationship appropriately

Social Learning Intentions

We are learning to:

- Listen to the ideas of others
- Respectfully disagree with the mathematical arguments of others

Success Criteria
(written in student voice):

I know that I am successful when I can:

- Write an equation, table, and graph for a linear relationship
- Look at a graph and tell if there is a linear, nonlinear, or no relationship
- Use the terms relationship, linear equation, and nonlinear relationship appropriately when I communicate with others in writing or speaking
- Listen to the ideas of others
- Respectfully disagree with the mathematical arguments of others

Purpose:

☑ Conceptual Understanding ☐ Procedural Fluency ☐ Transfer

Task:

Each pair of students graphs data from one of nine different situations (see situations in Figure A.5). Three situations are linear relationships, three are nonlinear, and three have no relationship. Pairs post the graphs of their situations. In pairs, students sort the graphs based on the shape of the data. After sorting, there is a class discussion about what the shape of the data means.

(Continued)

Materials (representations, manipulatives, other):

An assortment of pictures of faces that demonstrate emotions such as a baby crying, a woman smiling, a boy angry, etc.; chart-size graph paper; markers; inch or centimeter cubes; pennies; stopwatch; rugs worksheet; a soup can (or any can); and prepared exit slips (see Figure A.6).

Misconceptions or Common Errors:

*   Students may try to connect the points on the scatterplot where there is no relationship.
*   Some students confuse the x and y axes.

Format:

☐ Four-Part Lesson   ☐ Game Format   ☐ Small-Group Instruction
☑ Pairs   ☐ Other_____

Formative Assessment:

Hinge question (after the sorting): How do each of these graphs reflect the information in the story?

Launch:

Introduce the phrase, "A picture is worth a thousand words." Ask students questions to facilitate a brief discussion. Questions may include the following:

*   Have you ever seen a poster with no words? How do you know what it means?
*   Holding up one face at a time, "What do you think this person is trying to tell you?"
*   Can you think of any pictures you have looked at that had no words yet you knew exactly what it meant?

Lead the discussion in a mathematical direction by introducing the idea that graphs are like pictures that are worth a thousand words. In this lesson, we are going to look at many graphs and see what they tell us.

Facilitate:

Divide students into pairs and randomly assign one situation A-I to each pair (alternatively, decide in advance which situation is appropriate for which pair of students). After making material available and answering questions, allow students to work. Walk around the classroom and be available to answer questions. Support pairs by asking questions such as, "Do you think there is a relationship? Does one of your variables depend on the other?"

Instruct students to hang the graphs around the room. Be sure to mix up scatterplots and linear and nonlinear graphs.

Ask pairs to sort the graphs in any way that makes sense to them. If any pair needs assistance, suggest three groupings.

Lead a discussion beginning with the scatterplots, asking students the following:

- Why is there no line to this graph?
- What do the three situations that these graphs represent have in common?
- Were you able to write an equation to model this situation?

Lead a discussion around the linear graphs:

- What is the same about all of these graphs?
- What do you think that means compared to the previous group we examined?
- How were the situations the same?
- Could you write equations for these graphs?

Lead a discussion around the nonlinear graphs:

- Is there a relationship here?
- How is this relationship different from the linear graphs? The scatterplots?
- How are the situations that led to these graphs similar to one another? How are they different from the linear stories?

Anticipating student responses:

Most pairs will sort the graphs by lines, scattered points, and curves. Some may try to sort them further by sorting the nonlinear graphs into smaller groups. Students will notice that they could predict the answers in the linear graphs. For the discussion questions, students may feel uncomfortable about the scatterplot since there is no relationship. However, when they revisit the situations, they will conclude that none of the scenarios really made sense and that there were no relationships within them.

Closure:

Use the 3 What's: What did I learn today about graphs?

Why do I need to know the difference between different shapes of data on a graph?

Now that I know, how can this information help me?

A

A PE teacher believed that the shorter a person's hair was cut, the more jumping jacks that person could do in a minute. Do you agree?

Test the hypothesis by performing the experiment with eight classmates who have different hair lengths. Record the data on a chart and then graph the data on large chart paper with markers. Label your graph with a title.

What does the graph tell you? Can you write an equation to model the relationship?

Image source: bubaone/iStockcom

B

Marvin goes for a job at Floors-R-Us. During his interview, the manager asks him if he knows the relationship between area and perimeter of a rug. Marvin says he does. The bigger the area, the bigger the perimeter.

Was Marvin correct? Use the set of rectangular rugs on the worksheet to determine if there is a relationship between perimeter and area. Put your data in a chart and then graph the results on large chart paper using markers. Label the graph.

What does the graph tell you? Is there a relationship?

Image source: albertc111/iStock.com

C

Grayson works at Shoes-for-Less. Shanique comes in for a pair of shoes. Grayson measures her thumb to tell her what size she needs. Grayson says, "You can tell a person's shoe size by the length of his or her thumb." Shanique says, "That is ridiculous!" "No, really," argued Grayson. "It is a scientific fact!"

Is it a fact that your thumb length can predict your shoe size? Do an experiment with eight of your classmates collecting data on their thumb length and shoe size. Enter the data in a table and graph on the large chart paper with a marker. Title the graph.

Is Grayson telling the truth? How do the data back up your answer?

Image source: ONYXprj/iStock.com

D

You were asked to create a double-sided staircase for a friend. You decide to make a scale model first using cubes. The staircase should look like this:

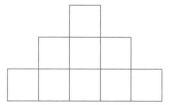

Your friend never said how tall the staircase should be. Create eight staircases, each one layer of cubes taller. Put the results on a table comparing the number of cubes needed to the heights. Graph on large chart paper. Is there a relationship between the number of cubes and the height of the staircase? Can you write an equation to model these data?

E

You have a penny. You toss it once and your outcome possibilities are H and T. When you toss it twice, your possible outcomes are HH, TT, HT, TH. You want to continue tossing the coin up to eight times. On a table, keep track of the number of tosses and the number of possibilities. For example, on the first toss, there were two possible outcomes.

Graph the data from the table. Do you see a relationship? Can you write an equation?

Image source: MisterVector/iStock.com

(Continued)

F

In the futuristic movie *Cloning,* the main character has an eight-day cloning catastrophe! On the first day, he cloned himself. On the second day, he cloned himself again and his clone from the day before. This continued for eight days before his clones got him into so much trouble, he had to end the cloning.

Keep a table comparing the day and the number of clones. Graph these data on chart paper. Is there a pattern? Is there an equation that can model this situation?

Image source: Yevhenii Dubinko/iStock.com

G

Rolling can be fun. Let's take a soup can for a roll. Mark a beginning spot on the can. Then roll the can on the floor once starting and stopping on your mark. Measure how far the can rolled. Do it again; this time, let the can roll around all the way twice. Measure distance traveled again. Repeat this for three, four, five, six, seven, and eight rolls. Record the data on a table comparing the number of times the can rolled and the distance it traveled. Graph these data on chart paper.

Is there a pattern? Can you predict the distance the can will travel on nine rolls? Explain. Can you write an equation to model the roll and distance?

Image source: solargaria/iStock.com

H

Rocky rents rollerblades. He charges a fee of $25 to everyone for renting the blades and then $20 per hour for each hour they keep them. To make things easy for customers, Rocky wants to post a graph with the prices a customer must pay for one hour, two hours, and up to eight hours to rent the roller blades. Create a table comparing the number of hours a person rents rollerblades to how much he or she will pay for up to eight hours. Graph these data on chart paper. Add a title to the graph.

Write an equation for Rocky's pricing. Is there a pattern?

Image source: Vect0r0vich/iStock.com

I

Tebo's T-Shirts is opening in your neighborhood. You can design your own logo on a T-shirt and Tebo will make them for you. Tebo charges $12 to put your design on a T-shirt and $8 per T-shirt you order. You are not sure how many T-shirts you need. It is somewhere between one and eight, so you ask Tebo to give you the prices for one, two, three, and so forth up to eight T-shirts. To make it easy, Tebo gives you a graph.

Create the graph Tebo gives to his customers. First, create a table that shows the number of T-shirts and the price charged, including the logo fee. Graph that data on chart paper.

Write an equation to show the relationship between the number of T-shirts and the cost.

Image source: NYstudio/iStock.com

Exit Slip

"A picture is worth a thousand words." How do you think this applies to the graphs we studied today? Explain for each type discussed in class.

_____

_____

_____

_____

_____

_____

 Download the complete eighth-grade lesson plan and handouts from
resources.corwin.com/mathlessonplanning/6-8

Appendix B

Lesson-Planning Template

Big Idea(s):

Essential Question(s):

Content Standard(s):

Mathematical Practice or Process Standards:

Learning Intention(s) (mathematical/language/social):

Success Criteria (written in student voice):

Purpose:

☐ Conceptual Understanding ☐ Procedural Fluency ☐ Transfer

Task:

Materials (representations, manipulatives, other):

Misconceptions or Common Errors:

Format:

☐ Four-Part Lesson   ☐ Game Format   ☐ Small-Group Instruction

☐ Pairs   ☐ Other_____

Formative Assessment:

Launch:

Facilitate:

Closure:

Appendix C

Further Reading/Resources

Online

Mathematics Content, Standards, and Virtual Manipulatives

http://www.achievethecore.org

A nonprofit organization dedicated to helping teachers and school leaders implement high-quality, college- and career-ready standards. The site includes planning materials, professional development resources, assessment information, and implementation support.

http://illustrativemathematics.org

A variety of videos, tasks, and suggestions for professional development accessible to all teachers.

http://ime.math.arizona.edu/progressions

The series of progressions documents written by leading researchers in the field summarizing the standards progressions for specific mathematical content domains.

http://nlvm.usu.edu

The National Library of Virtual Manipulatives offers a library of uniquely interactive, web-based virtual manipulatives or concept tutorials for mathematics instruction.

Sources for Problems, Tasks, and Lesson Protocols

https://bstockus.wordpress.com/numberless-word-problem

Numberless word problems designed to provide scaffolding that allows students the opportunity to develop a better understanding of the underlying structure of word problems.

https://gfletchy.com

3-Act Lessons and Mathematical Progressions videos for Grades K–7.

http://www.pz.harvard.edu/projects/visible-thinking

Harvard Zero Project describes thinking routines that can be applied to K–12 mathematics classrooms.

http://illuminations.nctm.org

A collection of high-quality tasks, lessons, and activities that align with the Common Core standards and include the standards for mathematical practice.

http://mathforum.org

The Math Forum at NCTM provides a plethora of online resources, including Problem of the Week and the Notice and Wonder protocol.

http://mathpickle.com

A free online resource of original mathematical puzzles, games, and unsolved problems for K–12 teachers. It is supported by the American Institute of Mathematics.

http://nrich.maths.org

Free enrichment materials, curriculum maps, and professional development for mathematics teachers.

http://www.openmiddle.com

A crowd-sourced collection of challenging problems for Grades K–12. Open middle problems all begin with the same initial problem and end with the same answer, but they include multiple paths for problem solving and require a higher depth of knowledge than most problems that assess procedural and conceptual understanding.

http://robertkaplinsky.com/lessons

A collection of free real-world, problem-based lessons for Grades K–12.

http://www.stevewyborney.com

A collection of ideas and activities for K–8 teachers.

Books

Fennell, F., Kobett, B. M., & Wray, J. A. (2017). *The formative 5: Everyday assessment techniques for every math classroom.* Thousand Oaks, CA: Corwin.

Harbin Miles, R., & Williams, L. (2018). *Your mathematics standards companion: What they mean and how to teach them.* Thousand Oaks, CA: Corwin.

Hattie, J., Fisher, D., Frey, N., Gojak, L. M., Moore, S. D., & Mellman, W. (2016). *Visible learning for mathematics, grades K–12: What works best to optimize student learning.* Thousand Oaks, CA: Corwin.

Hull, T., Harbin Miles, R., & Balka, D. S. (2014). *Realizing rigor in the mathematics classroom.* Thousand Oaks, CA: Corwin.

Knudsen, J., Stevens, H. S., Lara-Meloy, T., Kim, H., & Shechtman, N. (2018). *Mathematical argumentation in the middle school: The what, why, and how.* Thousand Oaks, CA: Corwin.

National Council of Teachers of Mathematics. (2014). *Principles to actions: Ensuring mathematical success for all.* Reston, VA: NCTM.

National Council of Teachers of Mathematics. (2017). *Taking action: Implementing effective mathematics teaching practices in grades 6–8.* Reston, VA: NCTM.

O'Connell, S., & SanGiovanni, J. (2013). *Putting the practices into action: Implementing the Common Core standards for mathematical practice, K–8.* Portsmouth, NH: Heinemann.

Ray-Reik, M. (2013). *Powerful problem solving: Activities for sense making with the mathematical practices.* Portsmouth, NH: Heinemann.

SanGiovanni, J., & Novak, J. (2018). *Mine the gap for mathematical understanding: Common holes and misconceptions and what to do about them.* Thousand Oaks, CA: Corwin.

Schrock, C., Norris, K., Pugalee, D., Seitz, R., & Hollingshead, F. (2013). *NCSM great tasks for mathematics 6–8.* Reston, VA: NCTM.

Smith, M. S., & Stein, M. K. (2010). *Five practices for orchestrating productive mathematics discussions.* Reston, VA: NCTM.

Smith, M. S., & Stein, M. K. (2018). *Five practices for orchestrating productive mathematics discussions* (2nd ed.). Reston, VA: National Council of Teachers of Mathematics and Corwin.

Smith, N. N. (2017). *Every math learner: A doable approach to teaching with learning differences in mind, grades 6–12.* Thousand Oaks, CA: Corwin.

Van de Walle, J. A., Karp, K. S., & Bay Williams, J. M. (2015). *Elementary and middle school mathematics: Teaching developmentally* (9th ed.). Upper Saddle River, NJ: Pearson Education.

Appendix D

Glossary

absolute value. Distance a number is from zero on the number line.

academic language. The vocabulary used in schools, textbooks, and other school resources.

access to high-quality mathematics instruction. Phrase refers to the National Council of Teachers of Mathematics (NCTM) position statement on equal opportunity to a quality K–12 education for all students. Related to the NCTM position on equitable learning opportunities.

agency. The power to act. Students exercise agency in mathematics when they initiate discussions and actively engage in high-level thinking tasks. When students exercise agency, they reason, critique the reasoning of others, and engage in productive struggle.

algorithm. In mathematics, it is a series of steps or procedures that, when followed accurately, will produce a correct answer.

allocated time. Total amount of time for teacher instruction and student learning.

big ideas. Statements that encompass main concepts in mathematics that cross grade levels, such as place value.

classroom discourse. Conversation that occurs in a classroom. Can be teacher to student(s), student(s) to teacher, or student(s) to student(s).

close-ended questions. Questions with only one correct answer.

closure. The final activity in a lesson with two purposes (1) helps the teacher determine what students have learned and gives direction to next steps and (2) provides students the opportunity to reorganize and summarize the information from a lesson in a meaningful way.

coherence. Logical sequencing of mathematical ideas. Can be vertical, as in across the grades (e.g., 6–8), or can be horizontal, as in across a grade level (e.g., sixth-grade lessons from September through December).

common errors. Mistakes made by students that occur frequently; usually these mistakes are anticipated by the teacher due to their frequency.

conceptual understanding. Comprehension of mathematical concepts, operations, and relationships.

content standards. See *standards.*

discourse. See *classroom discourse.*

distributed practice. See *spaced practice.*

district-wide curriculum. A K–12 document outlining the curriculum for a school system.

drill. Repetitive exercises on a specific math skill or procedure.

English Language Learner (ELL). A person whose first language is not English but who is learning to speak English.

essential question. A question that unifies all of the lessons on a given topic to bring the coherence and purpose to a unit. Essential questions are purposefully linked to the big idea to frame student inquiry, promote critical thinking, and assist in learning transfer.

exit task. A task given at the end of a lesson or group of lessons that provides a sampling of student performance. An exit task is more in depth than an *exit slip.*

exit ticket/exit slip. A form of lesson closure where students answer a question about or reflect on the main idea of the lesson on a slip of paper. Teachers collect these slips of paper.

extended closure. An in-depth form of closure usually taking more time than closure.

formative assessment. Also called *formative evaluation.* The ongoing collection of information about student learning as it is happening and the process of responding to that information by adapting instruction to improve learning.

formative evaluation. See *formative assessment.*

habits of mind. Ways of thinking about mathematics as mathematicians do (e.g., always choosing solution methods, asking questions, and having productive attitudes). These habits help us understand mathematics and solve problems, and they are linked to process standards. Habits of mind include (but are not limited to) perseverance in problem solving, comparing, finding patterns, and asking "what if …" questions.

high-cognitive-demand task. Characteristic of a problem or task that requires using higher-order thinking skills as defined by Bloom's Taxonomy. Also see *higher-order thinking skills.*

higher-order thinking skills. The more complex thinking skills as defined by Bloom's Taxonomy. Examples include predicting, creating, synthesizing, and analyzing.

hinge questions. A classroom-based assessment technique where the teacher delivers a question at a pivotal point in a lesson. Student responses to the question determine the path the teacher takes on the next part of the lesson.

horizontal coherence. See *coherence.*

identity. How individuals know and see themselves such as student, teacher, good at sports, and how others know and see us such as short, smart, shy. Defined broadly, it is a concept that brings together all the interrelated elements that teachers and students bring to the classroom, including beliefs, attitudes, and emotions.

Individualized Education Plan (IEP). A road map for a particular student's learning. Usually written for students in a special education program, it includes goals and accommodations needed for the child to be successful.

instructional decisions. Decisions made that affect classroom teaching and learning.

interleaving. The practice of cycling back to a previous skill, concept, or big idea to help children build their understanding of that topic.

interview. A classroom-based assessment technique where the teacher has a brief talk with a student to collect more information on the student's thinking.

learning community. A group of teachers (usually at the same grade level)—and sometimes other professionals—who work together to plan lessons, discuss student concerns, and support one another's teaching.

learning intention. Statement of what a student is expected to learn from a lesson. Also known as the lesson goal. There are three types: mathematical, social, and language goals.

learning progressions. Specific sequence of mathematical knowledge and skills that students are expected to learn as they progress from kindergarten through high school and beyond.

lesson format. The manner in which students are organized for a lesson. Whole-group lessons and small-group lessons are two examples.

lesson launch. How the teacher introduces a lesson.

manipulative. Any concrete material that can be used by students to further their mathematical understanding. Examples include counters, blocks, coins, and fraction circles. Also a type of mathematical models.

math anxiety. A feeling of stress, fear, or worry about one's ability to do mathematics, which may interfere with one's mathematical performance.

math talk. See *number talk.*

mathematical discourse. See *classroom discourse.*

metacognitive. Adjective for *metacognition,* the process of thinking about one's thinking. One type of metacognition includes knowing about using certain strategies for problem solving.

misconception. An incorrect understanding or belief about a mathematical topic or concept.

multiple entry points. The many different methods one can use to attack a problem. Methods can range from simple approaches to more complex approaches.

number routine. A mathematics activity that takes place on a regular basis (e.g., daily, every Friday, etc.).

number sense routine. A number routine that focuses on building students' reasoning about numbers.

number talk. Also known as *math talk.* A number routine that focuses on building student number sense through scaffolded problem-solving experiences where students verbalize and justify their solutions to one another and the teacher.

numberless word problem. A word problem with the numbers blocked out, encouraging students to make sense of the problem before they work with the numbers.

observation. A classroom-based formative assessment technique where the teacher informally watches students and documents what is seen in order to inform instruction.

open-ended. Description for mathematical problems, questions, or tasks that have more than one acceptable answer and multiple solution strategies.

pacing guide. Grade-level document for district-wide implementation that determines the order of the standards to be taught and the amount of time to be spent on each topic. The level of specificity of these documents varies.

practice. Brief, engaging, and purposeful exercises, tasks, or experiences on the same idea spread out over time.

precise use of vocabulary. Using exact mathematical language as a strategy to build a shared understanding of important mathematical terms. Some common mathematics terms have nonmathematical meanings. Precise use of vocabulary refers to using the mathematical definition.

prior knowledge. Mathematical knowledge students know before they begin a topic or task.

problem solving. The process of finding a solution to a situation for which no immediate answer is available. What may be a problem for one student may not be a problem for another.

procedural fluency. The ability to carry out procedures/algorithms flexibly, accurately, efficiently, and appropriately.

process standards. See *standards.*

productive struggle. Students wrestle with ideas to make sense of mathematics; this phrase describes the effort involved in solving a problem when an immediate solution is not available.

reflecting in action. See *reflection.*

reflecting on action. See *reflection.*

reflection. The process of thinking about one's learning. For teachers, there is *reflecting in action,* which occurs during teaching so that the teacher can monitor and adjust instruction as it occurs. *Reflecting on action* occurs when the teacher looks back on a lesson and the students after instruction takes place.

representations. Any concrete, pictorial, or symbolic model that can stand for a mathematical idea.

resources. For a primary mathematics teacher, anything that can be used to assist in the design and implementation of lessons (e.g., textbooks, curriculum guides, manipulatives, and supplemental materials).

rigor. Results from active participation in rich mathematical problem-solving tasks. The two types of rigor are **content** and **instructional.** **Content rigor** results from a deep connection among the concepts and the breadth of supporting skills that students are expected to master. **Instructional rigor** is the continuous interaction between the instruction and students' reasoning about concepts, skills, and challenging tasks.

scaffold. Name for a variety of teaching strategies that support student learning; techniques that help students bridge from what they know to something new.

Show Me. A classroom-based assessment technique where the teacher asks students to demonstrate what they have learned. Students may use any materials such as manipulatives or drawings.

spaced practice. Also called **distributed practice.** A learning strategy where practice is broken up into a number of short sessions over a period of time.

standards. Concise, written descriptions of what students are expected to know and be able to do at a specific grade level, age, or stage of development. In mathematics, there are *content standards* (what students are expected to know) and *process standards* (how students are expected to do the mathematics). Process standards are closely linked to mathematical habits of mind. The *Standards for Mathematical Practice* define the processes for the Common Core State Standards for Mathematics (CCSS-M).

Standards for Mathematical Practice. See *standards.*

subitizing. The ability to immediately identify a quantity without counting.

success criteria. Defines what learning looks like when achieved.

summative assessment. Testing used to determine students' achievement levels at specific points in time, such as at the end of teaching units, semesters, and grade level.

task. A mathematical problem. Rich tasks or worthwhile tasks are problems with several characteristics, such as accessibility, authenticity, and being active with a focus on significant mathematics for the grade level.

team teaching. An organizational structure where a group of teachers shares the responsibility for instruction for a particular group of students.

textbook. In mathematics, textbooks are one of the many types of resources teachers use; contents follow a logical teaching order and usually match the curriculum being taught.

transfer. One of the three main types of math lessons that prompt students to demonstrate their ability to use content knowledge and skill in a problem situation.

unintended consequences. Unforeseen outcomes from a purposeful action.

unit plan. Several coherent lessons on a given topic that flow logically from one another.

unpack. Using one's knowledge to extract the main ideas and knowledge embedded in the standard; to break down a standard into its main ideas.

vertical coherence. See *coherence.*

virtual manipulative. Interactive technology that allows students to interact with manipulatives presented on a screen such as on a computer or handheld device.

whole group. A type of classroom grouping where the entire class is instructed as one large group. This contrasts with small groups, where the whole class is divided into small groups of students for instruction.

References

Aguirre, J. M., Mayfield-Ingram, K., & Martin, D. B. (2013). *The impact of identity in K–8 mathematics learning and teaching: Rethinking equity-based practices.* Reston, VA: NCTM.

Association for Middle Level Education. (2010). *This we believe: Keys to educating young adolescents.* Westerville, OH: Author.

Annenberg Learner Foundation. (2003). *Teaching math, Grades 3–5.* Retrieved from https://learner.org/courses/teachingmath/grades3_5/session_05/index.html

Banse, H. W., Palacios, N. A. G., Merritt, E. G., & Rimm-Kaufman, S. (2016). 5 strategies for scaffolding math discourse with ELLs. *Teaching Children Mathematics, 23*(2), 100–108.

Barousa, M. (2017). *Which one doesn't belong?* Retrieved from http://wodb.ca

Boaler, J. (1997). *Experiencing school mathematics: Teaching styles, sex, and setting.* Buckingham, UK: Open University Press.

Boaler, J. (2012, July). Timed tests and the development of math anxiety. *Education Week.* Retrieved from www.edweek.org/ew/articles/2012/07/03/36boaler.h31.html

Boaler, J. (2015). *Mathematical mindsets: Unleashing students' potential through creative math, inspiring messages and innovative teaching.* San Francisco, CA: Jossey-Bass.

Boaler, J. (2017). *Brains grow and change.* Retrieved from www.youcubed.org/resources/many-ways-see-mathematics-video

Boaler, J., & Staples, M. (2008). Creating mathematical futures through an equitable teaching approach: The case of Railside School. *Teachers College Record, 110*(3), 608–645.

Bransford, J. D., Brown, A., & Cocking, R. (2000). *How people learn: Mind, brain, experience, and school.* Washington, DC: National Research Council.

Braswell, J. S., Dion, G. S., Daane, M. C., & Jin, Y. (2005). *The nation's report card: Mathematics 2003* (NCES 2005–451). U.S. Department of Education, Institute of Education Sciences, National Center for Education Statistics. Washington, DC: Government Printing Office.

Brighton, K. L. (2007). *Coming of age: The education and development of young adolescents.* Westerville, OH: National Middle School Association.

Bushart, B. (2017). *Numberless word problems.* Retrieved from https://bstockus.wordpress.com/numberless-word-problems/

Calmenson, S. (1991). *The principal's new clothes.* New York, NY: Scholastic.

Caskey, M., & Anfara, V. A., Jr. (2014, October). *Developmental characteristics of young adolescents.* Retrieved from http://www.amle.org/BrowsebyTopic/WhatsNew/WNDet.aspx?ArtMID=888&ArticleID=455

Cavanaugh, R. A., Heward, W. L., & Donelson, F. (1996). Effects of response cards during lesson closure on the academic performance of secondary students in an earth science course. *Journal of Applied Behavior Analysis, 29*(3), 403–406.

Committee on Early Childhood Mathematics National Research Council. (2009). *Mathematics learning in early childhood: Paths toward excellence and equity.* Washington, DC: National Academies Press.

Constantino, P. M., & De Lorenzo, M. N. (2001). *Developing a professional teaching portfolio: A guide for success.* Boston, MA: Allyn & Bacon.

Cooperrider, D. L., & Whitney, D. (2005). Appreciative inquiry: A positive revolution in change. In P. Holman & T. Devane (Eds.), *The change handbook* (pp. 245–263). Oakland, CA: Berrett-Koehler.

Crayton, C. (2017). *Robert Q. Berry: Think of math as a social endeavor.* Retrieved from https://ced.ncsu.edu/news/2017/08/05/robert-q-berry-think-of-math-as-a-social-endeavor/

Danielson, C. (2016). *Which one doesn't belong?* Retrieved from http://wodb.ca

Danielson, L. M. (2008). Making reflective practice more concrete through reflective decision making. *The Educational Forum, 72,* 129–137.

Day, C. (1999). Researching teaching through reflective practice. In J. J. Loughran (Ed.), *Researching teaching: Methodologies and practices for understanding pedagogy* (pp. 215–232). London, UK: Falmer.

Dewey, J. (1933). *How we think: A restatement of the relation of reflective thinking to the educative process.* New York, NY: D. C. Heath.

Dewey, J. (1944). *Democracy in education.* New York, NY: Free Press. (Original work published 1916)

Dolezal, S. E., Welsh, L. M., Pressley, M., & Vincent, M. M. (2003). How nine third-grade teachers motivate student academic engagement. *The Elementary School Journal*, 103(3), 239–267.

Eichhorn, D. H. (1966). *The middle school.* New York, NY: Center for Applied Research in Education, Inc.

Erickson, K., Drevets, W., & Schulkin, J. (2003). Glucocorticoid regulation of diverse cognitive functions in normal and pathological emotional states. *Neuroscience & Biobehavioral Reviews*, 27(3), 233–246.

Farah, M. J., Shera, D. M., Savage, J. H., Betancourt, L., Giannetta, J. M., Brodsky, N. L., Malmud, E. K., & Hurt, H. (2006). Childhood poverty: Specific associations with neurocognitive development. *Brain Research*, 1110(1), 166–174.

Fennell, F. (2006), December. Go ahead! Teach to the test! *NCTM News Bulletin.* Retrieved from www.nctm.org/News-and-Calendar/Messages-from-the-President/Archive/Skip-Fennell/Go-Ahead,-Teach-to-the-Test!/

Fennell, F., Kobett, B. M., & Wray, J. A. (2017). *The formative 5: Everyday assessment techniques for every math classroom.* Thousand Oaks, CA: Corwin.

Fletcher, G. (2017). *3-acts lessons.* Retrieved from https://gfletchy.com/3-act-lessons/

Ganske, K. (2017). Lesson closure: An important piece of the student learning puzzle. *The Reading Teacher*, 71(1), 95–100.

Gelman, R., & Lucariello, J. (2002). Role of learning in cognitive development. In H. Pashler (Series Ed.) & C. R. Gallistel (Vol. Ed.), *Stevens' handbook of experimental psychology: Vol. 3. Learning, motivation, and emotion* (3rd ed., pp. 395–443). New York, NY: John Wiley.

The Great School Partnership. (2013). *The glossary of education reform.* Retrieved from http://www.edglossary.org/teaming

Grootenboer, P. (2000). Appraisal for quality learning. *Waikato Journal of Education*, 6(1), 121–132.

Hackmann, D. G., Petzko, U. N., Valentine, J. W., Clark, D. C., Nori, J. R., & Lucas, S. E. (2002). Beyond interdisciplinary teaming: Finding and implications of the NASSP National Middle Level Study. *NASSP Bulletin*, 86(632), 33–47.

Hammond, S. (1998). *The thin book of appreciative inquiry.* Plano, TX: Thin Book Publishing.

Hanover Research. (2015). *Best practices in middle school design.* Retrieved from https://www.boyertownasd.org/cms/lib07/PA01916192/Centricity/Domain/4/Best%20Practices%20in%20Middle%20School%20Design%20-%20Boyertown%20Area%20School%20District%20-%20Hanover%20Research.pdf

Harris, A. S., Bruster, B., Peterson, B., & Shutt, T. (2010). *Examining and facilitating reflection to improve professional practice.* Lanham, MD: Rowman & Littlefield.

Harvard Center for the Developing Child. (2007). *The impact of poverty on early development.* Retrieved from http://46y5eh11f hgw3ve3ytpwxt9r.wpengine.netdna-cdn.com/wp-content/uploads/2015/05/inbrief-adversity-1.pdf

Hattie, J. (2009). *Visible learning: A synthesis of over 800 meta-analyses relating to achievement.* New York, NY: Routledge.

Hattie, J., Fisher, D., Frey, N., Gojak, L. M., Moore, S. D., & Mellman, W. (2016). *Visible learning for mathematics, Grades K–12: What works best to optimize student learning.* Thousand Oaks, CA: Corwin.

Hattie, J., & Yates, G. C. (2013). *Visible learning and the science of how we learn.* New York, NY: Routledge.

Herbel-Eisenmann, B. (2010). Beyond tacit language choice to purposeful discourse practices. In L. Knott (Eds.), *The role of mathematics discourse in producing leaders of discourse* (pp. 451–485). Charlotte, NC: Information Age Publishing.

Herbel-Eisenmann, B., & Breyfogle, M. (2005). Questioning our patterns of questioning. *Mathematics Teaching in the Middle School*, 10(9), 484–489.

Hiebert, J. (1999). Relationships between research and the NCTM standards. *Journal for Research in Mathematics Education*, 30(1), 3–19.

Hiebert, J., & Morris, A. (2012). Teaching, rather than teachers, as a path toward improving classroom instruction. *Journal of Teacher Education*, 63(2), 92–102.

Hogan, M. P. (2008). The tale of two Noras: How a Yup'ik middle schooler was differently constructed as a math learner. *Diaspora, Indigenous, and Minority Education, 2*(2), 90–114.

Hull, T., Harbin Miles, R., & Balka, D. S. (2014). *Realizing rigor in the mathematics classroom.* Thousand Oaks, CA: Corwin.

Illustrative Mathematics. (2017). *Content standards.* Retrieved from www.illustrativemathematics.org/content-standards

Inside Mathematics. (2017). *Problem of the month.* Retrieved from www.insidemathematics.org/problems-of-the-month/download-problems-of-the-month

Institute of Educational Sciences (IES). (2009). *Assisting students struggling with mathematics: Response to intervention (RtI) for elementary and middle schools.* Retrieved from https://ies.ed.gov/ncee/wwc/PracticeGuide/2

Isaacs, A. C., & Carroll, W. M. (1999). Strategies for basic-facts instruction. *Teaching Children Mathematics, 5*(9), 508–515.

Jensen, L. (2001). Planning lessons. In M. Celce-Murcia (Ed.), *Teaching English as a second or foreign language* (pp. 403–408). Boston, MA: Heinle & Heinle.

Kaplinsky, R. (2017). *Lessons.* Retrieved from http://robertkaplinsky.com/lessons/

Kapur, M. (2010). Productive failure in mathematical problem solving. *Instructional Science, 38*(6), 523–550.

Karp, K. S., Bush, S. B., & Dougherty, B. J. (2014). 13 rules that expire. *Teaching Children Mathematics, 21*(1), 18–25.

Kazemi, E., & Hintz, A. (2014). *Intentional talk: How to structure and lead productive mathematical discussions.* Portland, ME: Stenhouse.

Kellough, R., & Kellough, N. (2008). *Teaching young adolescents: A guide to methods and resources for middle school teaching* (5th ed.). New York, NY: Pearson.

Lager, C. A. (2006). Types of mathematics-language reading interactions that unnecessarily hinder algebra learning and assessment. *Reading Psychology, 27*(2–3), 165–204.

Lappan, L., & Briars, D. (1995). How should mathematics be taught? In I. M. Carl (Ed.), *75 Years of progress: Prospects for school mathematics* (pp. 131–156). Reston, VA: NCTM.

Larson, J. (2002). Packaging process: Consequences of commodified pedagogy on students' participation in literacy events. *Journal of Early Childhood Literacy, 2*(1), 65–95.

Leinwand, S. (2009). *Accessible mathematics: 10 instructional shifts that raise student achievement.* Portsmouth, NH: Heinemann.

Leinwand, S. (2014), July. *Math misconceptions.* Paper presented at the Summer Utah Academy, Salt Lake, UT.

Lucariello, J. (2012). *How my students think: Diagnosing student thinking.* Retrieved from www.apa.org/education/k12/student-thinking.aspx

Lupien, S. J., King, S., Meaney, M. J., & McEwen, B. S. (2001). Can poverty get under your skin? Basal cortisol levels and cognitive function in children from low and high socioeconomic status. *Development and Psychopathology, 13*(3), 653–676.

Markworth, K., McCool, J., & Kosiak, J. (2015). *Problem solving in all seasons.* Reston, VA: NCTM.

Math Forum. (2015). *Beginning to problem solve with "I notice, I wonder."* Retrieved from http://mathforum.org/pow/noticewonder/intro.pdf

Math Forum. (2017). *Primary problems of the week.* Retrieved from http://mathforum.org/library/problems/primary.html

Math Learning Center. (2017). *Free math apps.* Retrieved from www.mathlearningcenter.org/resources/apps

Math Pickle. (2017). *Puzzles, games and mini-competitions organized by grade.* Retrieved from http://mathpickle.com/organized-by-grade/

McClure, L., Woodham, L., & Borthwick, A. (2011). Using low threshold high ceiling tasks. *NRICH.* Retrieved from https://nrich.maths.org/7701

McLeod, J., Fisher, J., & Hoover, G. (2003). *The key elements of classroom management: Managing time and space, student behavior and instructional strategies.* Alexandria, VA: Association for Supervision and Curriculum Development.

Middleton, J. A., & Jansen, A. (2011). *Motivation matters and interest counts: Fostering engagement in mathematics.* Reston, VA: NCTM.

Mohyuddin, R. G., & Khalil, U. (2016). Misconceptions of students in learning mathematics at primary level. *Bulletin of Education and Research*, 38(1), 133–162.

Morris, A., & Hiebert, J. (2017). Effects of teacher preparation courses: Do graduates use what they learned to plan mathematics lessons? *American Educational Research Journal*, 54(3), 524–567.

Moyer-Packenham, P. S., & Bolyard, J. (2016). Revisiting the definition of a virtual manipulative. In P. Moyer-Packenham (Ed.), *International perspectives on teaching and learning mathematics with virtual manipulatives* (pp. 5–16). New York, NY: Springer.

Moyer-Packenham, P. S., & Milewicz, E. (2002). Learning to question: Categories of questioning used by preservice teachers during diagnostic mathematics interviews. *Journal of Mathematics Teacher Education*, 5(4), 293–315.

Moyer-Packenham, P. S., Salkind, G., & Bolyard, J. (2008). Virtual manipulatives used by K–8 teachers for mathematics instruction: Considering mathematical, cognitive and pedagogical fidelity. *Contemporary Issues in Technology and Teacher Education*, 8(3), 202.

National Center for Children in Poverty. (2017). *Child poverty*. Retrieved from www.nccp.org/topics/childpoverty.html

National Council of Supervisors of Mathematics. (2009). Improving student achievement in mathematics by addressing the needs of English language learners. *NSCM Student Achievement Series*, 6.

National Council of Teachers of English (NCTE). (2008). *English language learners: A policy research brief produced by the National Council of Teachers of English*. Retrieved from www.ncte.org/library/NCTEFiles/Resources/PolicyResearch/ELLResearchBrief.pdf

National Council of Teachers of Mathematics. (1991). *Professional standards for teaching mathematics*. Reston, VA: Author.

National Council of Teachers of Mathematics. (2000). *Professional standards for teaching mathematics*. Reston, VA: Author.

National Council of Teachers of Mathematics (NCTM). (2014a). *Access and equity in mathematics education*. Retrieved from www.nctm.org/uploadedFiles/Standards_and_Positions/Position_Statements/Access_and_Equity.pdf

National Council of Teachers of Mathematics (NCTM). (2014b). *Principles to actions: Ensuring mathematical success for all*. Reston, VA: Author.

National Council of Teachers of Mathematics (NCTM). (2017). *Taking action: Implementing effective teaching practices*. Reston, VA: Author.

National Governors Association Center for Best Practices & Council of Chief State School Officers. (2010). *Common core state standards for mathematics*. Washington, DC: Author.

National Institute of Child Health and Human Development Early Child Care Research Network. (2005). Duration and developmental timing of poverty and children's cognitive and social development from birth through third grade. *Child Development*, 4(76), 795–810.

National Library of Virtual Manipulatives. (2017). *All topics, grades 6–8*. Retrieved from http://nlvm.usu.edu/en/nav/grade_g_3.html

National Research Council. (2001). *Adding it up: Helping children learn mathematics* (J. Kilpatrick, J. Swafford, & B. Findell, Eds.). Washington, DC: National Academies Press.

NRICH. (2017). *Primary curriculum*. Retrieved from http://nrich.maths.org/12632

Open Middle. (2017). *Open middle: Challenging problems worth solving* [kindergarten, Grade 1, Grade 2]. Retrieved from http://www.openmiddle.com

Panasuk, R., Stone, W., & Todd, J. (2002). Lesson planning strategy for effective mathematics teaching. *Education*, 122(4), 808–829.

Parrish, S. (2011). Number talks build numerical reasoning. *Teaching Children Mathematics*, 18(3), 198–206.

Piaget, J. (1964). Part I: Cognitive development in children: Piaget development and learning. *Journal of Research in Science Teaching*, 2(3), 176–186.

Piaget, J., & Inhelder, B. (1969). *The psychology of the child*. New York, NY: Basic Books.

Pollock, J. E. (2007). *Improving student learning one teacher at a time*. Alexandria, VA: Association for Supervision and Curriculum Development.

Powell, A. B. (2004). The diversity backlash and the mathematical agency of students of color. In M. J. Høines & A. B. Fuglestad (Eds.), *Proceedings of the twenty-eighth conference of the International Group for the Psychology of Mathematics Education* (Vol. 1, pp. 37–54). Bergen, Norway: Bergen University College.

Protheroe, N. (2007). What does good math instruction look like? *Principal, 87*(1), 51–54.

Raposo, J., & Stone, J. (1972). *One of these things is not like the other* [Song lyrics]. Retrieved from www.metrolyrics.com/one-of-these-things-is-not-like-the-others-lyrics-sesame-street.html

Rasmussen, C., Yackel, E., & King, K. (2003). Social and sociomathematical norms in the mathematics classroom. In R. Charles (Ed.), *Teaching mathematics through problem solving: It's about learning mathematics* (pp. 143–154). Reston, VA: National Council of Teachers of Mathematics.

Ray-Reik, M. (2013). *Powerful problem solving: Activities for sense making with the mathematical practices.* Portsmouth, NH: Heinemann.

Reimer, K., & Moyer, P. S. (2005). Third-graders learn about fractions using virtual manipulatives: A classroom study. *Journal of Computers in Mathematics and Science Teaching, 24*(1), 5–10.

Resnick, L. B. (1982). Syntax and semantics in learning to subtract. In T. Carpenter, J. Moser, & T. A. Romberg (Eds.), *Addition and subtraction: A cognitive perspective* (pp. 136–156). Hillsdale, NJ: Lawrence Erlbaum.

Resnick, L. B. (1983). A developmental theory of number understanding. In H. P. Ginsburg (Ed.), *The development of mathematical thinking* (pp. 109–151). New York, NY: Academic Press.

Resnick, L. B., & Omanson, S. F. (1987). Learning to understand arithmetic. In R. Glaser (Ed.), *Advances in instructional psychology* (Vol. 3, pp. 41–95). Hillsdale, NJ: Lawrence Erlbaum.

Ridgway, J., Swan, M., & Burkhardt, H. (2001). Assessing mathematical thinking via FLAG. In D. Holton and M. Niss (eds.), *The teaching and learning of mathematics at university level* (pp. 423–430). Dordrecht, the Netherlands: Springer.

Ritchhart, R., Church, M., & Morrison, K. (2011). *Making thinking visible: How to promote engagement, understanding, and independence for all learners.* New York, NY: John Wiley.

Rodgers, C. (2002). Defining reflection: Another look at John Dewey and reflective thinking. *Teachers College Record, 104*(4), 842–866.

Rohrer, D. (2012). Interleaving helps students distinguish among similar concepts. *Educational Psychology Review, 24,* 355–367.

SanGiovanni, J., & Novak, J. R. (2018). *Mine the gap for mathematical understanding: Common holes and misconceptions and what to do about them.* Thousand Oaks, CA: Corwin.

Scales, P. C. (2010). Characteristics of young adolescents. In Association for Middle Level Education, *This we believe: Keys to educating young adolescents* (pp. 62–63). Westerville, OH: National Middle School Association.

Scales, P. C., Blyth, D. A., Berkas, T. H., & Kielsmeier, J. C. (2000). The effects of service-learning on middle school students' social responsibility and academic success. *Journal of Early Adolescence, 20,* 332–358.

Schmidt, W. H., Wang, H. C., & McKnight, C. (2005). Curriculum coherence: An examination of US mathematics and science content standards from an international perspective. *Journal of Curriculum Studies, 37*(5), 525–559.

Schön, D. A. (1983). *The reflective practitioner: How professionals think in action.* New York, NY: Basic Books.

Schrock, C., Norris, K. Pugalee, D. Seitz, R., & Hollingshead, F. (2013). *Great tasks for mathematics, K–5.* Denver, CO: National Council of Supervisors of Mathematics.

Sealander, K. A., Johnson, G. R., Lockwood, A. B., & Medina, C. M. (2012). Concrete-semiconcrete-abstract (CSA) instruction: A decision rule for improving instructional efficacy. *Assessment for Effective Intervention, 30,* 53–65.

Smith, M. S., & Stein, M. K. (1998). Selecting and creating mathematical tasks: From research to practice. *Mathematics Teaching in the Middle School, 3*(5),344–350.

Smith, M. S., & Stein, M. K. (2011). *Five practices for orchestrating productive mathematics discussions.* Reston, VA: National Council of Teachers of Mathematics.

Smyth, J. (1992). Teachers' work and the politics of reflection. *American Educational Research Journal, 29*(2), 267–300.

Sousa, D. (2014). *How the brain learns mathematics.* Thousand Oaks, CA: Corwin.

Steen, K., Brooks, D., & Lyon, T. (2006). The impact of virtual manipulatives on first grade geometry instruction and learning. *Journal of Computers in Mathematics and Science Teaching, 25*(4), 373–391.

Stein, M. K., Engle, R. A., Smith, M. S., & Hughes, E. K. (2008). Orchestrating productive mathematical discussions: Five practices for helping teachers move beyond show and tell. *Mathematical Thinking and Learning, 10*(4), 313–340.

Stein, M. K., & Smith, M. S. (1998). Mathematical tasks as a framework for reflection: From research to practice. *Mathematics Teaching in the Middle School, 3*(4), 268–275.

Thompson, P., & Lambdin, D. (1994). Research into practice: Concrete materials and teaching for mathematical understanding. *Arithmetic Teacher, 41*(9), 556–558.

Tooke, J., Hyatt, B., Leigh, M., Snyder, B., & Borda, T. (1992). Why aren't manipulatives used in every middle school mathematics classroom? *Middle School Journal, 24*(2), 61–62.

Trocki, A., Taylor, C., Starling, T., Sztajn, P., & Heck, D. (2015). Launching a discourse-rich mathematics lesson. *Teaching Children Mathematics, 21*(5), 276–281.

Troiano, J. (2001). *Spookley the square pumpkin.* Wilton, CT: Holiday Hill Enterprises, LLC.

Tschannen-Moran, B., & Tschannen-Moran, M. (2010). *Evocative coaching: Transforming schools one conversation at a time.* Hoboken, NJ: John Wiley.

U.S. Department of Education. (2008). *Organization of U.S. education.* Retrieved from http://www.ed.gov/about/offices/list/ous/international/usnei/edlite-index.html

Van de Walle, J., Karp, K., & Bay-Williams, J. (2013). *Elementary and middle school mathematics: Teaching developmentally.* New York, NY: Pearson.

Van de Walle, J., Karp, K., & Bay-Williams, J. (2016). *Elementary and middle school mathematics: Teaching developmentally* (2nd ed.). New York, NY: Pearson.

Vogler, K. E. (2008), Summer. Asking good questions. *Educational Leadership, 65* (9). Retrieved from www.ascd.org/publications/educational-leadership/summer08/vol65/num09/Asking-Good-Questions.aspx

Vygotsky, L. S. (1964). Thought and language. *Annals of Dyslexia, 14*(1), 97–98.

Vygotsky, L. S. (1978). *Mind in society: The development of higher mental processes* (M. Cole, V. John-Steiner, S. Scribner, & E. Souberman, Eds.). Cambridge, MA: Harvard University Press.

Waddell, L. R. (2010). How do we learn? African American elementary students learning reform mathematics in urban classrooms. *Journal of Urban Mathematics Education, 3*(2), 116–154.

Wagganer, E. L. (2015). Creating math talk communities. *Teaching Children Mathematics, 22*(4), 248–254.

Walsh, J. A., & Sattes, B. D. (2005). *Quality questioning: Research-based practice to engage every learner.* Thousand Oaks, CA: Corwin.

Walshaw, M., & Anthony, G. (2008). The role of pedagogy in classroom discourse: A review of recent research into mathematics. *Review of Educational Research, 78*, 516–551.

Wenmoth, D. (2014). Ten trends 2014: Agency [Video file]. Retrieved from https://vimeo.com/85218303

Wiliam, D. (2011). *Embedded formative assessment.* Bloomington, IN: Solution Tree Press.

Wiliam, D., & Thompson, M. (2008). Integrating assessment with instruction: What will it take to make it work? In C. A. Dwyer (Ed.), *The future of assessment: Shaping teaching and learning* (pp. 53–82). Mahwah, NJ: Lawrence Erlbaum.

Wilson, L. M., & Horch, H. W. (2002). Implications of brain research for teaching young adolescents: What research says. *Middle School Journal, 34*(1), 57–61.

Wood, K. (2015). *Interdisciplinary instruction: Unit and lesson planning strategies, K–8.* Long Grove, IL: Waveland.

Wood, T., Williams, G., & McNeal, B. (2006). Children's mathematical thinking in different classroom cultures. *Journal for Research in Mathematics Education, 37*, 222–255.

Yackel, E., & Cobb, P. (1996). Sociomathematical norms, argumentation, and autonomy in mathematics. *Journal for Research in Mathematics Education, 27*, 458–477.

Young, C. B., Wu, S. S., & Menon, V. (2012). The neurodevelopmental basis of math anxiety. *Psychological Science, 23*(5), 492–501.

Index

language learning intentions and, 41, 42 (figure),
 44, 47, 48, 49
Lesson-Planning Template for, 50
mathematics learning intentions and, 40–41,
 40–42 (figures), 45, 47, 48, 49
prior knowledge, role of, 41
purposes of, 40
scaffolded learning and, 40
seventh-grade math instruction and, 48, 54, 54 (figure)
sixth-grade math instruction and, 47, 52, 52–53 (figure)
social learning intentions and, 42–43, 42–43 (figures),
 44, 47, 48, 49
standards and, 40, 40 (figure), 42 (figure)
student-centered nature of, 40, 40 (figure)
success criteria, connection to, 45
unit coherence and, 46
See also Success criteria
Learning profile, 10–11, 11 (figure)
Learning progressions, 29
Leigh, M., 89
Leinwand, S., 98
Lesson facilitation, 153
 eighth-grade math instruction and, 168–169
 engaging with others' reasoning questions and, 160–161,
  160–161 (figures)
 focusing questions and, 161, 162 (figure)
 follow-up questions and, 155
 funneling questions and, 161, 162 (figure)
 higher-order thinking skills and, 160–161, 161 (figure)
 information gathering questions and, 157,
  157 (figure), 161
 language frames, scaffolded math talk and, 156
 learning communities, understanding within, 155
 Lesson-Planning Template for, 170
 making the math visible questions and, 158, 158 (figure)
 mathematical communication and, 154
 mathematical discourse and, 154, 155–156
 mathematics vocabulary, precise use of, 31, 41, 154
 meaningful/effective discourse, facilitation
  of, 154–156
 probing thinking questions and, 157, 157 (figure)
 process standards, student engagement and, 163
 productive struggle and, 162–163
 purposeful questions, planning/posing of, 156–162
 questioning practice and, 155
 reflection/justification questions and, 159, 159 (figure)
 sentence stems, conversation jumpstart and, 156
 seventh-grade math instruction and, 166–167
 sixth-grade math instruction and, 165
 student-to-student discourse and, 155
 Think Aloud technique and, 155
 unit coherence and, 164
 unpacking process and, 155
 writing practices and, 154
 See also Closure; Formative assessment; Lesson
  planning; Teaching practices

Lesson formats, 107, 108
 allocated time and, 108
 departmental planning time, scheduling of, 108
 eighth-grade math instruction and, 116
 format selection, questions for, 108
 four-part lesson plan and, 109–110, 109 (figure), 115
 game format and, 110, 111 (figure)
 individual needs, response to, 111, 112
 interdisciplinary instruction, planning for, 113
 Lesson-Planning Template for, 117
 mini-lessons and, 111
 pair discussion format and, 112, 116
 school schedules, planning/instruction and, 108
 seventh-grade math instruction and, 115
 sixth-grade math instruction and, 114
 small-group instruction and, 111–112,
  111–112 (figures), 114
 team teaching and, 108
 unit coherence, multiple lesson formats and, 113
 whole-group instruction and, 109, 111, 111 (figures)
 See also Lesson planning; Teaching practices
Lesson launch, 108, 136
 always/sometimes/never true lesson launch, 145
 anticipating student response and, 147
 definition of, 137
 eighth-grade math instruction and, 151
 English Language Learners and, 137
 estimation lesson launch, 143–144, 143 (figure)
 interleaving practice and, 137
 Lesson-Planning Template for, 152
 mathematical concepts lessons and, 141–142
 notice/wonder lesson launch, 139–140
 number lines lesson launch, 144, 144 (figure)
 number sense routine lessons and, 143–147
 number talk lesson launch, 146–147
 numberless word problem lesson launch, 140–141
 one of these things is not like the others lesson launch,
  141–142, 142 (figure)
 problem-solving lessons and, 137–141
 see/think/wonder lesson launch, 137–139,
  138–139 (figures)
 seventh-grade math instruction and, 150
 sixth-grade math instruction and, 149
 splats lesson launch, 145–146, 145 (figure)
 unit coherence and, 148
 warmups and, 137
 See also Closure; Formative assessment;
  Lesson facilitation; Lesson planning;
  Teaching practices
Lesson plan examples:
 eighth-grade complete lesson plan, 203–205,
  206–210 (figures)
 seventh-grade complete lesson plan, 192–198,
  199–202 (figures)
 sixth-grade complete lesson plan, 188–190,
  190–191 (figures)

About the Authors

Lois A. Williams, EdD, has worked in mathematics education (K–Algebra I) teaching, supervising, coaching, and consulting for more than 30 years. She is a former mathematics specialist for the Virginia Department of Education. Currently Lois is an adjunct professor at Mary Baldwin University and is an International Fellow with the Charles A. Dana Center. She is a recipient of a Fulbright Teacher Exchange and honored as a Virginia Middle School Teacher of the Year.

Beth McCord Kobett, EdD, is an associate professor in the School of Education at Stevenson University where she works with preservice teachers and leads professional learning efforts in mathematics education both regionally and nationally. She is also the lead consultant for the Elementary Mathematics and Specialist and Teacher Leadership Project. She is a former classroom teacher, elementary mathematics specialist, adjunct professor, and university supervisor. Beth is a current Board member of the National Council of Teachers of Mathematics (NCTM) Board of Directors, a past president of the Association of Maryland Mathematics Teacher Educators (AMMTE), and former chair of the Professional Development Services Committee of the National Council of Teachers of Mathematics (NCTM). Dr. Kobett is a recipient of the Mathematics Educator of the Year Award from the Maryland Council of Teachers of Mathematics (MCTM). She has also received Stevenson University's Excellence in Teaching Award as both an adjunct and full-time member of the Stevenson faculty.

Ruth Harbin Miles coaches rural, suburban, and inner-city school mathematics teachers. Her professional experience includes coordinating the K–12 Mathematics Teaching and Learning Program for the Olathe, Kansas, public schools for more than 25 years; teaching mathematics methods courses at Virginia's Mary Baldwin University; and serving on the Board of Directors for the National Council of Supervisors of Mathematics, the National Council of Teachers of Mathematics, and the Kansas Association of Teachers of Mathematics. Ruth is a coauthor of 37 books, including 11 Corwin publications. As an International Fellow with the Charles A. Dana Center, Ruth works with classroom teachers in Department of Defense Schools, helping them implement College and Career Ready Standards. Developing teachers' content knowledge and strategies for engaging students to achieve high standards in mathematics is Ruth's specialty.

Supporting TEACHERS
Empowering STUDENTS

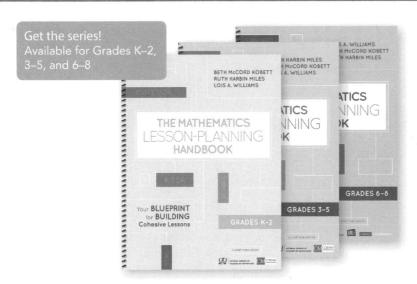

Get the series!
Available for Grades K–2,
3–5, and 6–8

BETH McCORD KOBETT, RUTH HARBIN MILES, AND LOIS A. WILLIAMS

Your blueprint to planning math lessons for maximum impact and understanding

Grades K–2
Grades 3–5
Grades 6–8

PAGE KEELEY AND CHERYL ROSE TOBEY

Everything you need to promote mathematical thinking and learning

Grades K–12

JOHN HATTIE, DOUGLAS FISHER, NANCY FREY, LINDA M. GOJAK, SARA DELANO MOORE, AND WILLIAM MELLMAN

The what, when, and how of teaching practices that evidence shows work best for student learning in mathematics

Grades K–12

FRANCIS (SKIP) FENNELL, BETH McCORD KOBETT, AND JONATHAN A. WRAY

Move the needle on math instruction with these 5 assessment techniques

Grades K–8

eCourse and PD Resource Center now available!

Corwin educator discount
★★★
20% OFF
EVERY DAY!
★★★

ALL students should have the opportunity to be successful in math!

Trusted experts in math education offer clear and practical guidance to help students move from surface to deep mathematical understanding, from procedural to conceptual learning, and from rote memorization to true comprehension. Through books, videos, consulting, and online tools, we offer a truly blended learning experience that helps you demystify math for students.

JOHN SANGIOVANNI AND JENNIFER ROSE NOVAK

See what's going on in your students' minds, plus get access to hundreds of rich tasks to use in instruction or assessment

Grades K–2
Grades 3–5
Grades 6–8

Your whole-school solution to mathematics standards
When it comes to math, standards-aligned is achievement-aligned...

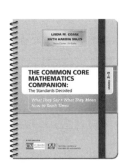

LINDA M. GOJAK AND RUTH HARBIN MILES

Grades K–2

LINDA M. GOJAK AND RUTH HARBIN MILES

Grades 3–5

RUTH HARBIN MILES AND LOIS A. WILLIAMS

Grades 6–8

FREDERICK L. DILLON, W. GARY MARTIN, BASIL M. CONWAY IV, AND MARILYN E. STRUTCHENS

High School

New series for states with state-specific mathematics standards

Grades K–2, Grades 3–5, Grades 6–8, High School

CORWIN **Mathematics**

A SAGE Publishing Company

CORWIN HAS ONE MISSION: to enhance education through intentional professional learning.

We build long-term relationships with our authors, educators, clients, and associations who partner with us to develop and continuously improve the best evidence-based practices that establish and support lifelong learning.

NATIONAL COUNCIL OF
TEACHERS OF MATHEMATICS

The National Council of Teachers of Mathematics supports and advocates for the highest-quality mathematics teaching and learning for each and every student.

The Association for Middle Level Education is dedicated to improving the educational experiences of all students ages 10 to 15 by providing vision, knowledge, and resources to educators and leaders.